LANGUAGE LESSONS:
Stories for Teaching and Learning English

Ruth Spack
BENTLEY COLLEGE

Vivian Zamel
UNIVERSITY OF
MASSACHUSETTS, BOSTON

EDITORS

Ann Arbor
THE UNIVERSITY OF MICHIGAN PRESS

ISBN-13: 978-0-472-03115-3

Contents

Acknowledgments

We would like to thank our respective institutions, Bentley College and the University of Massachusetts Boston. Without their generous grant support, this book project could not have gone forward. We also want to acknowledge Chadwick Allen, who brought Patricia Grace's work to our attention, as well as the students who graciously granted permission for us to reprint their writing.

We appreciate the combined efforts of the people who played a critical role in the production of this book. Christina Chan's help in the preparation of the manuscript saved us valuable time. The reviewers' enthusiastic and thoughtful feedback confirmed our belief in the need for and value of this book. The staff at the University of Michigan Press did a wonderful job of bringing this project to fruition. We are especially grateful to our editor, Kelly Sippell, who responded to our idea for this collection instantaneously and with encouraging, insightful, and heartfelt comments. Throughout the process of composing and editing, she guided us with exemplary professionalism.

Grateful acknowledgement is given to the following authors, publishers, and individuals for permission to reprint previously published materials.

Bilingual Press for "Nothing in Our Hands but Age" by Raquel Puig Zaldívar from *Hispanics in the United States: An Anthology of Creative Literature* (1980), edited by G. Keller and F. Jímenez. Reprinted by permission of Bilingual Press/Editorial Bilingüe, Arizona State University, Tempe, AZ.

Book Distributors of New Zealand Ltd. for "Kura" by Patricia Grace from *Baby No-Eyes*. Copyright © 1998. Reprinted by permission of Book Distributors New Zealand, a trading division of Pearson New Zealand Ltd.

Lindsley Cameron for "Private Lesson," which originally appeared in *The New Yorker*. Copyright © Lindsley Cameron 1988.

Farrar, Straus and Giroux, LLC, for "The German Refugee" by Bernard Malamud from *Idiots First*. Copyright © 1963 by Bernard Malamud. Copyright renewed 1991 by Ann Malamud. Reprinted by permission of Farrar, Straus and Giroux, LLC.

International Creative Management, Inc., for "What Do You Know About Friends?" by Lily Brett from *Things Could Be Worse.* Reprinted by permission of International Creative Management, Inc. Copyright © 1990 by Lily Brett.

Goose Lane Editions for "English Lessons" by Shauna Singh Baldwin from *English Lessons and Other Stories.* Reprinted by permission of Goose Lane Editions. Copyright © 1996.

Maria M. Hara for "Fourth Grade Ukus" from *Bananaheart.* Copyright © 1990. Reprinted by permission of Marie M. Hara.

Andrew Lam for "Show and Tell" by Andrew Lam from *Crab Orchard Review,* 1998. Reprinted by permission of Andrew Lam.

The Library of Congress for photographs on pages 12 and 100.

Nicholasa Mohr for "The English Lesson" from *In Nueva New York.* Reprinted by permission of Nicholasa Mohr. Copyright © 1986, 1988.

Han Nguyen for photographs on pages 60 and 164.

W. W. Norton & Company, Inc., for "The Unforgetting" by Lan Samantha Chang from *Hunger.* Copyright © 1998 by Lan Samantha Chang. Used by permission of W. W. Norton & Company, Inc.

Harold Ober Associates Incorporated for "Chike's School Days" by Chinua Achebe from *Girls at War and Other Stories,* copyright © 1972, 1973 by Chinua Achebe. Used by permission of Doubleday, a division of Random House, Inc. Reprinted by permission of Harold Ober Associates Incorporated.

The Rosten Family LLC for "The Rather Baffling Case of H*Y*M*A*N K*A*P*L*A*N" by Leonard Ross from *The Education of Hyman Kaplan,* copyright 1937 by Harcourt, Inc. and renewed 1965 by Leo C. Rosten. Reprinted by permission of The Rosten Family LLC.

Seven Stories Press for "Prisoner with a Dictionary" by Linh Dinh from *Blood and Soap*. Reprinted by permission of Seven Stories Press. Copyright © 2004.

Syracuse University Press for "Albert and Esene" by Frances Khirallah Noble from *The Situe Stories*. Reprinted by permission of Syracuse University Press. Copyright © 2000 by Frances Khirallah Noble.

University of New Mexico Press for "Inside Out" by Francisco Jiménez from *The Circuit Stories from the Life of a Migrant Child*, © 1997. Reprinted by permission of University of New Mexico Press.

University of Pittsburgh Press for "English as a Second Language" by Lucy Honig from *The Truly Needy and Other Stories*, © 1999 by University of Pittsburgh Press. Reprinted by permission of the University of Pittsburgh Press.

Rudy Wiebe for "Speaking Saskatchewan" from *More than Words Can Say*. Reprinted by permission of Rudy Wiebe. Copyright © 1990.

Zitkala-Ša for "The School Days of an Indian Girl." Originally published in the *Atlantic Monthly* in 1900.

Every effort has been made to contact the copyright holders for permission to reprint borrowed material. We regret any oversights that may have occurred and will rectify them in future printings of this book.

The Role of Stories
in Educational Settings

As classrooms in English-medium countries become more linguistically diverse and as the influence of English expands globally, it is essential for both teachers and students to gain a deeper understanding of the process of acquiring English and the multiple factors that shape that process. Reference books and textbooks that are designed to promote this understanding can enable teachers and learners to reflect on their experiences in meaningful ways, but these texts typically approach the subject from a theoretical or practical perspective. What is often missing in these materials is the *human story* of language teaching and learning. *Language Lessons: Stories for Teaching and Learning English* captures this human dimension through fictional works that reveal the inner thoughts and lives of language teachers and learners in a poignant and evocative way, allowing readers to engage emotionally as they reflect on the issues involved in acquiring a new language.

THE STORIES IN THIS COLLECTION

Language Lessons is a groundbreaking fiction anthology that focuses on the role language plays in the lives of those who are negotiating new cultures or identities. This collection adds an aesthetic component to our understanding of the issues involved in language teaching and learning. The writers of these narratives share a vibrant imagination, a striking gift for storytelling, a mastery of nuanced language, and a compassionate ear. The stories' imaginative elements—gripping plots, symbolic settings, idiosyncratic characters, dramatic dialogues, interior monologues, shifting time frames, overlapping perspectives, and enigmatic imagery—are crafted to captivate readers and shape readers' meaning-making. The narratives are further characterized by serendipitous circumstances, unexpected relationships, and surprising outcomes. These literary features—and the raw truths the stories reveal—draw readers in, inviting them to reflect on their own assumptions, experiences, and emotional responses. At the same time, ironically, the very fact that the stories are imaginary, that the writers have created fictional worlds, establishes a distance that enables a more measured analysis as readers examine the characters' behaviors and motivations in the context of the circumstances surrounding their lives.

The authors of the stories in *Language Lessons* are acclaimed writers who have had first-hand experiences moving back and forth between languages and cultures and, in most cases, have learned or taught English as an additional language. Their stories introduce us to learners of English whose public and private lives are shaped by political and social realities that, in turn, shape their language-learning experiences. We see the devastating effects of enforced English-only education on Native American children in the United States; the identity-transforming impact of colonialism on young English language learners in Nigeria, New Zealand, and Hawaii; the frightening prospect of school for children of Mennonite immigrants in Canada and of Mexican migrants in the United States; the lingering consequences of oppressive regimes or war on refugees and exiles from Germany, Poland, Cuba, and Vietnam; the disruptive impact of economic instability on immigrants from China, Sicily, and the Dominican Republic; the haunting influence of murder and rape on women who have fled Guatemala and India; the isolating effects of the lack of language and literacy on individuals from Puerto Rico and the Middle East; and the unique challenges faced by learners who choose to study English as a foreign language in their home countries.

Virtually all of the main characters in *Language Lessons* have a dire need to learn English in order to escape oppression, succeed in school, find a job, advance a career, or gain entry into their new social world. As the stories reveal, their language learning processes are rarely smooth and often traumatic. In story after story, we witness how illusions and dreams are shattered by real and imagined barriers, how moments of accomplishment are undermined by incidents that bring shame and tragedy. And yet we also see how fear or loss can be offset by opportunity and achievement, how frustration and embarrassment can give way to humor and joy.

In a number of the stories, we enter classroom scenes in which we observe how teachers respond to learners' language use, or to their silence, and we learn how classroom participants are affected in both painful and amusing ways by such interactions. As readers, we often know or understand something that the teachers and learners in these scenarios do not know or understand. This vantage point allows us to see how the characters' outward behaviors may contradict or be in conflict with their internal thoughts and feelings. In revealing such discrepancies and incongruities, the stories capture the complicated, multilayered context of language teaching and learning.

Many of the stories in *Language Lessons* provide insight not only into the classroom experience but also into the home experience. We come to understand how language affects the family, for example, when a child strives to learn language to fulfill familial expectations, when a husband uses language to limit his wife's opportunities, when aging spouses struggle together to master a new tongue. These stories represent the complex realities of students' worlds and thus serve to underline the inextricable link between home life and language acquisition.

Several stories also show the role language plays in the public sphere, for example, when characters are confronted with the challenge of using their English to attain a goal, demonstrate their achievements, or even just tell a story. As we learn of the harsh realities many characters face, we see why their goals are so difficult to achieve and why their stories are rarely told or heard.

Language Lessons spans a broad range of time periods, a feature that allows readers to understand how language learning issues have played out over time and how these issues, though arising out of particular historical circumstances, continue to resonate. The collection also represents multiple geographic, cultural, and linguistic backgrounds: The characters in the stories have lived in nineteen countries and speak at least sixteen languages in addition to English. Reflecting on these varied experiences, readers can come to understand how similarities and differences across languages and cultures may influence pedagogical choices and approaches as well as the learning process itself. Across and within the stories, too, we learn how age and gender, linguistic and geographical background, social and economic positioning, legal or illegal status, and racial and religious identity play a role in students' educational lives, influencing whether, when, how, and to what extent they acquire a new language and adopt new ways of behaving and knowing. These wide-ranging experiences and perspectives highlight the multiple and overlapping factors that shape learners' language acquisition and adaptation to new world views.

ORGANIZATION OF THE BOOK

Language Lessons has four parts. The first two parts center on the experiences of children: *Colonial Encounters,* Part I, focuses on students who learn English in a colonized setting in the United States, Nigeria, New Zealand, and Hawaii, while *Childhood Transformations,* Part II, focuses on students who learn English in mainstream classrooms in Canada and the United States. The final two parts center on the experiences of adults: *Adult Education,* Part III, features students who study English in night school and college in the United States and Australia, while *Private Lessons,* Part IV, features students who learn English privately in the United States, Japan, and an unnamed country.

Each part begins with an overview of its theme. The headnote that precedes each story includes information about the author and provides clues to the context in which the story is set. Each story is followed by a series of questions that suggest possibilities for reflecting on and analyzing the story in depth, with particular attention to issues related to language teaching and learning. The Questions for Reflection and Analysis across the Stories (pages 214–16) suggest possibilities for making connections across the four parts of the book. Throughout the book, our questions are intended to be suggestive, not exhaustive. We encourage readers to generate their own questions.

Although we have divided the stories in *Language Lessons* into four parts, each of which highlights a particular theme, we do not mean for these divisions to be rigid or constricting. There are multiple ways to read the stories, generating a number of thematic possibilities. For example, stories about children can be paired with stories about adults, stories about learning in colonized settings with stories about learning in the context of immigration, or stories that focus on classroom learning with stories that take place in private settings. Each new pairing can give rise to new understandings.

USING THE BOOK IN EDUCATIONAL SETTINGS

Language Lessons can be used in a variety of educational contexts. For example, the collection can be used in graduate and undergraduate courses in TESOL, Literacy Studies, or Language Arts, and in workshops and programs that prepare teachers or tutors to work with multilingual learners.

In our own graduate and undergraduate courses designed for prospective and practicing English language teachers and tutors, we aim to engage students in the process of reflecting on their pedagogical assumptions, expectations, and practices and on the ways these factors inform and shape one another. In these courses we assign historical, theoretical, and research-based readings that address critical issues related to language and literacy acquisition. We also assign memoirs in which the authors describe their own journeys through language. But perhaps the most compelling readings we assign are the short stories in *Language Lessons*. Through literary portrayals of learners' and teachers' inner lives in and out of school, the stories generate a deeper appreciation of the complexity of language-learning issues. The juxtaposition of these different types of texts allows students in our courses to consider the relationship between the principles derived from theory and research, on the one hand, and the unpredictable and irreducible nature of language learning and teaching, on the other. In our experience, the stories breathe life into the subject matter of the course but not only because they illuminate, complicate, or even challenge the theoretical texts. These stories resonate for readers because they render, not just explain, the multifaceted processes of teaching and learning.

As we do in all of the courses we teach, we ask students to capture their responses to the assigned reading in writing, which serves as a generative source for thinking, speculating, and reflecting. Writing in response to reading provides readers with the opportunity to formulate and extend their own analyses and interpretations. Writing about fiction, which entails close readings of texts, has an added benefit for teachers and tutors in that it leads them to observe scenes with an attention to detail and level of analysis that they can apply to their own teaching or tutoring experiences. For example, through her comparison of a fictional and a real classroom, one tutor reflected on the failings of an adult English language class to which she was assigned. She wrote:

> "The English Lesson" by Nicholasa Mohr has a passage that I felt reflected part of my tutoring experience this week:
>
> "Mrs. Hamma selected each student who was to speak from a different part of the room, rather than in the more conventional orderly fashion of row by row, or front to back, or even alphabetical order. . . . Mrs. Hamma enjoyed catching the uncertain looks on the faces of her students. A feeling of control over the situation gave her a pleasing thrill." (p. 120)
>
> In class on Monday, the substitute teacher was randomly calling on the students to answer or ask different questions. I felt that because this was a very different setting and because they were not used to being screamed at during their lesson, none of them wanted to participate. The teacher was correcting them on every single part of their pronunciation and seemed to be confusing them more. A few of the students will put an *e* in front of the words they speak in Spanish so that their sentence would read: "I espeak Espanish." Obviously, this is not correct, but I did not feel that they needed to be called out every time they pronounced something incorrectly. Similar to Mrs. Hamma's class, the students would almost slouch down and look away when the teacher was looking around the room to call on someone. They did not feel comfortable speaking with her.

Such close readings of classroom scenes can lead teachers and tutors to develop productive teaching philosophies, as is evident in this response to the final scene in Lucy Honig's "English as a Second Language," in which a character struggles to tell a story to her classmates in English:

> The teacher's role in this scene helps the students teach themselves. She is just there for support. The students seem to know words of the new language, they just need to practice what they have learned. The teacher only intercedes when none of the students know the proper way and look

for her help. This allows the students to correct each other and learn from each other and teach each other about their cultural differences as well. This is seen when the student says "heat" when she meant "hit"; the students knew that her sentence did not make sense but they could not figure out exactly what she meant. The teacher came in the conversation and corrected them. The teacher was a listener, a watcher, and therefore a teacher because the students seemed to be learning a great deal from each other.

The short stories in *Language Lessons* allow readers to get inside the heads of English language learners in ways that are not otherwise possible, engendering new understandings and insights. In Honig's "English as a Second Language," we learn what a refugee from Guatemala is thinking when the mayor repeatedly interrupts her while she is telling a story at an award ceremony for adult English language learners. A close reading of this scene led one student to theorize about second language acquisition, as the following excerpt from her written response demonstrates:

It is important to focus on the positive aspects of students' learning, not just to correct their mistakes. Students should not feel ashamed when they make mistakes, but learn from them instead. As Maria made a mistake [at the award ceremony] in Honig's story, she "realized she had not used the past tense and felt a deep, horrible stab of shame for herself, shame for her teacher. She was a disgrace!" (p. 139). Maria should not have focused so much on her mistake as on the fact that she was able to get her main ideas across in English. It is of course easier to say this than to practice it, but if students are made comfortable while learning and learn from their mistakes, they should not be as embarrassed when making errors.

In addition to generating their own theories and principles about language teaching and learning, students in our courses regularly make connections between the stories and the scholarly and pedagogical readings we assign, for example, by using the theories or principles they have studied to explain a character's behavior, as the following excerpt from a student's informal response shows:

> I enjoyed Nicholasa Mohr's "The English Lesson," although Mrs. Hamma's character really bothered me. I felt like she was very condescending toward her students. This relates back to the articles we read by Henry Widdowson[1] and Stephanie Vandrick,[2] and it reminds me of the idea of the "ownership of English." Vandrick points out that when teachers feel they are doing something positive for ESL students by endowing them with the English language and with knowledge of Western academe and culture—something that the teachers have possession of—a superior attitude can cloud their work, and make it extremely difficult for them to actually help their students. However, I do not feel that one can own a language. It belongs to all who speak it. In the story, Mrs. Hamma feels as though she is the great holder of knowledge, and she is doing such a good deed by bestowing this knowledge upon her students. As described in the story, I believe even the students in the ESL class feel this. Also, her constant referrals to the "American" way of life were a frustrating thing to read. Mrs. Hamma keeps making references to democracy, and the way it is done in America, and I feel as though it is exceptionally demeaning to the students.

When students in our courses are themselves still in the process of acquiring English as an additional language, they can identify with many of the scenarios depicted and, based on their own experiences, empathize with the characters' struggles and successes and critically evaluate academic or social situations that may undercut or promote language acquisition. And precisely because these stories are carefully crafted works of fiction, when students attend to the authors' use of language and stylistic choices, their own acquisition of language is enhanced. The words on the page become the students' words as well. The following excerpt from a student's text, for example, reveals the impact that reading Bernard Malamud's "The German Refugee" had on this student's

---

[1]Widdowson, H. (2002). The ownership of English. In V. Zamel & R. Spack (Eds.), *Enriching ESOL pedagogy: Readings with activities for engagement, reflection, and inquiry* (pp. 381–392). Mahwah, NJ: Erlbaum.

[2]Vandrick, S. (2002). ESL and the colonial legacy: A teacher faces her "missionary kid" past. In V. Zamel & R. Spack (Eds.), *Enriching ESOL pedagogy* (pp. 411–436).

understanding of his own process of acquiring language and literacy. The excerpt further demonstrates how Malamud's very use of language not only captures the student's experiences but also infuses his efforts to use English to express himself:

> Some lines from Bernard Malamud's "The German Refugee," especially impressed me. Malamud, referring to some foreigners who have just arrived to the United States, writes:
>
> "To many of these people, articulate as they were, the great loss was the loss of language—that they could not say what was in them to say. *You have some subtle thought and it comes out like a piece of broken bottle.* They could, of course, manage to communicate but just to communicate was frustrating." [p. 169, emphasis added by student]
>
> These lines wonderfully express what I have felt many times during these two last semesters. In the last months I have had to write many pages, I have had to put my ideas on paper, in a language that is not my native one. It was sometimes exasperating to realize that I had no words to express a good idea—well, it also may happen when one writes in her/his own language. Some others, it was frustrating to find out that my ideas appeared expressed with much less richness or elegance than when I write in Spanish. Many "subtle thoughts" have come out like pieces of "broken bottle" in my writings of this semester, and it was frustrating. But all my work for this seminar and the other courses has helped me to mend the broken bottle. I think I write English much better than when I came to the United States. I feel myself more comfortable writing in that language than at the beginning of the semester. Finally, I have realized that I will be able to improve even more these skills if I continue reading and writing English in the future.

In all of our courses—graduate and undergraduate alike—we use students' written work as a means through which to promote further engagement and collaboration in the classroom. Not only do we read and respond to students' texts, but students often read and write responses to each other's writing. This ongoing written interchange reinforces their efforts, makes it possible for them to consider their own interpretations in light of other readers' analyses, and enables them to draw on their own authority to respond back. Given that the root word of *authority* is *author,* when students exchange their writing in this way, they become authors alongside the published authors we've read. And when they share the ideas they have had the time to formulate and reflect on, class discussions are more informed, dynamic, and enriching.

SUGGESTIONS FOR WRITING IN RESPONSE TO THE STORIES

The following suggestions for writing are designed to elicit thoughtful responses to each story in *Language Lessons*.

- Reflect on what you find intriguing, surprising, or confusing in the story.
- Explore the associations and experiences you bring to the story.
- Respond to one or more of the questions that follow the story.
- Write double-entry notes by copying a short passage from a story that resonates for you, and write a reaction to that passage, revealing why you find the passage significant or meaningful.
- Explore the connections between the story and other stories in this book by responding to the questions that appear at the end of the book (pages 214–16).
- Consider how the story can shed light on other texts that you are familiar with and that deal with similar subject matter, including fiction, nonfiction, and visual media.
- Explain what you perceive to be the fiction writer's overall idea, vision, or belief. You might, for example, follow the clues the writer provides to show a character's motivation and emotional state. To that end, you can examine the character's inner thoughts as well as the character's interactions and conflicts with other characters and with the physical, social, cultural, political, economic, or spiritual environment. Then analyze these clues to discover why the characters behave the way they do and to interpret why things happen as they do.
- Write creatively in response to the stories. For example, you might write a letter from a character to an author, or vice versa, or from one character to another; construct an interior monologue for a character in a particular scene; create a dialogue between char-

acters either within a story or across stories; or extend a story by writing an additional scene.

- Compose an original short story about an English language learner or teacher. The story can be drawn from your imagination; your experiences as a language learner, teacher, or tutor; your observations of language classrooms; or your research about issues related to language learning. You may use a short story in *Language Lessons* as a model and set your own story in one or more relevant sites, for example, the classroom, the home, the community, or the workplace. Provide rich details, narration, and dialogue. Keep in mind that your goal is to bring a reader to a deeper understanding of the lived experience of your main character as a learner or teacher of English.

I.

COLONIAL ENCOUNTERS

In the context of colonialism, political and cross-cultural tensions profoundly affect how children learn language. In these four stories, the authors portray classrooms whose assumed purpose is to introduce students to a superior language and culture. We observe children as they negotiate the unfamiliar linguistic and cultural terrain. We also see how their teachers respond to them: what the teachers understand about these students and what they fail to grasp. In Zitkala-Ša's "The School Days of an Indian Girl," a Dakota child is taken to an English-only boarding school far from her home on a Western reservation. In Chinua Achebe's "Chike's School Days," a young boy learns from both Ibo and Christian culture. In Patricia Grace's "Kura," a Maori woman tells her grandchildren about her experience in an English-only school. In Marie Hara's "Fourth Grade Ukus," a speaker of Hawaii Creole English struggles to use Standard English in the classroom. Together, these stories demonstrate how indigenous cultures can become marginalized, disrupted, or destroyed when teachers and language learners encounter one another in a colonial context.

The School Days of an Indian Girl

Zitkala-Ša

(1876–1938)

Zitkala-Ša, also known as Gertrude Simmons Bonnin, was born at the Yankton Agency in Dakota Territory to a Dakota mother and French–American father. She learned English as a young child at an English-only manual labor boarding school in Indiana and later attended Earlham College and the New England Conservatory of Music. After a literary and musical career, Zitkala-Ša became an activist for Native American rights. She is the author of *Old Indian Legends* (1901) and *American Indian Stories* (1921). "The School Days of an Indian Girl" is set in the late nineteenth century.

I

THE LAND OF RED APPLES

There were eight in our party of bronzed children who were going East with the missionaries. Among us were three young braves, two tall girls, and we three little ones, Judéwin, Thowin, and I.

We had been very impatient to start on our journey to the Red Apple Country, which, we were told, lay a little beyond the great circular horizon of the Western prairie. Under a sky of rosy apples we dreamt of roaming as freely and happily as we had chased the cloud shadows on the Dakota plains. We had anticipated much pleasure from a ride on the iron horse, but the throngs of staring palefaces disturbed and troubled us.

Zitkala-Ša, "The School Days of an Indian Girl." Originally published in the *Atlantic Monthly* in 1900.

On the train, fair women, with tottering babies on each arm, stopped their haste and scrutinized the children of absent mothers. Large men, with heavy bundles in their hands, halted near by, and riveted their glassy blue eyes upon us.

I sank deep into the corner of my seat, for I resented being watched. Directly in front of me, children who were no larger than I hung themselves upon the backs of their seats, with their bold white faces toward me. Sometimes they took their forefingers out of their mouths and pointed at my moccasined feet. Their mothers, instead of reproving such rude curiosity, looked closely at me, and attracted their children's further notice to my blanket. This embarrassed me, and kept me constantly on the verge of tears.

I sat perfectly still, with my eyes downcast, daring only now and then to shoot long glances around me. Chancing to turn to the window at my side, I was quite breathless upon seeing one familiar object. It was the telegraph pole which strode by at short paces. Very near my mother's dwelling, along the edge of a road thickly bordered with wild sunflowers, some poles like these had been planted by white men. Often I had stopped, on my way down the road, to hold my ear against the pole, and, hearing its low moaning, I used to wonder what the paleface had done to hurt it. Now I sat watching for each pole that glided by to be the last one.

In this way I had forgotten my uncomfortable surroundings, when I heard one of my comrades call out my name. I saw the missionary standing very near, tossing candies and gums into our midst. This amused us all, and we tried to see who could catch the most of the sweetmeats.

Though we rode several days inside of the iron horse, I do not recall a single thing about our luncheons.

It was night when we reached the school grounds. The lights from the windows of the large buildings fell upon some of the icicled trees that stood beneath them. We were led toward an open door, where the brightness of the lights within flooded out over the heads of the excited palefaces who blocked the way. My body trembled more from fear than from the snow I trod upon.

Entering the house, I stood close against the wall. The strong glaring light in the large whitewashed room dazzled my eyes. The noisy hurrying of hard shoes upon a bare wooden floor increased the whirring in my ears. My only safety seemed to be in keeping next to the wall. As I was wondering in which direction to escape from all this confusion, two warm hands grasped me firmly, and in the same moment I was tossed high in midair. A rosy-cheeked paleface woman caught me in her arms. I was both frightened and insulted by such trifling. I stared into her eyes, wishing her to let me stand on my own feet, but she jumped me up and down with increasing enthusiasm. My mother had never made a plaything of her wee daughter. Remembering this I began to cry aloud.

They misunderstood the cause of my tears, and placed me at a white table loaded with food. There our party were united again. As I did not hush my crying, one of the older ones whispered to me, "Wait until you are alone in the night."

It was very little I could swallow besides my sobs, that evening.

"Oh, I want my mother and my brother Dawée! I want to go to my aunt!" I pleaded; but the ears of the palefaces could not hear me.

From the table we were taken along an upward incline of wooden boxes, which I learned afterward to call a stairway. At the top was a quiet hall, dimly lighted. Many narrow beds were in one straight line down the entire length of the wall. In them lay sleeping brown faces, which peeped just out of the coverings. I was tucked into bed with one of the tall girls, because she talked to me in my mother tongue and seemed to soothe me.

I had arrived in the wonderful land of rosy skies, but I was not happy, as I had thought I should be. My long travel and the bewildering sights had exhausted me. I fell asleep, heaving deep, tired sobs. My tears were left to dry themselves in streaks, because neither my aunt nor my mother was near to wipe them away.

THE CUTTING OF MY LONG HAIR

The first day in the land of apples was a bitter-cold one; for the snow still covered the ground, and the trees were bare. A large bell rang for breakfast, its loud metallic voice crashing through the belfry overhead and into our sensitive ears. The annoying clatter of shoes on bare floors gave us no peace. The constant clash of harsh noises, with an undercurrent of many voices murmuring an unknown tongue, made a bedlam within which I was securely tied. And though my spirit tore itself in struggling for its lost freedom, all was useless.

A paleface woman, with white hair, came up after us. We were placed in a line of girls who were marching into the dining room. These were Indian girls, in stiff shoes and closely clinging dresses. The small girls wore sleeved aprons and shingled hair. As I walked noiselessly in my soft moccasins, I felt like sinking to the floor, for my blanket had been stripped from my shoulders. I looked hard at the Indian girls, who seemed not to care that they were even more immodestly dressed than I, in their tightly fitting clothes. While we marched in, the boys entered at an opposite door. I watched for the three young braves who came in our party. I spied them in the rear ranks, looking as uncomfortable as I felt.

A small bell was tapped, and each of the pupils drew a chair from under the table. Supposing this act meant they were to be seated, I pulled out mine and at once slipped into it from one side. But when I turned my head, I saw that I was the only one seated, and all the rest at our table remained standing. Just as I began to rise, looking shyly around to see how chairs were to be used, a second bell was sounded. All were seated at last, and I had to crawl back into my chair again. I heard a man's voice at one end of the hall, and I looked around to see him. But all the others hung their heads over their plates. As I glanced at the long chain of tables, I caught the eyes of a paleface woman upon me. Immediately I dropped my eyes, wondering why I was so keenly watched by the strange woman. The man ceased his mutterings, and then a third bell was tapped. Every one picked up his knife and fork and began eating. I began crying instead, for by this time I was afraid to venture anything more.

But this eating by formula was not the hardest trial in that first day. Late in the morning, my friend Judéwin gave me a terrible warning. Judéwin knew a few words of English; and she had overheard the paleface woman talk about cutting our long, heavy hair. Our mothers had taught us that only unskilled warriors who were captured had their hair shingled by the enemy. Among our people, short hair was worn by mourners, and shingled hair by cowards!

We discussed our fate some moments, and when Judéwin said, "We have to submit, because they are strong," I rebelled.

"No, I will not submit! I will struggle first!" I answered.

I watched for my chance, and when no one noticed I disappeared. I crept up the stairs as quietly as I could in my squeaking shoes—my moccasins had been exchanged for shoes. Along the hall I passed, without knowing whither I was going. Turning aside to an open door, I found a large room with three white beds in it. The windows were covered with dark green curtains, which made the room very dim. Thankful that no one was there, I directed my steps toward the corner farthest from the door. On my hands and knees I crawled under the bed, and cuddled myself in the dark corner.

From my hiding place I peered out, shuddering with fear whenever I heard footsteps near by. Though in the hall loud voices were calling my name, and I knew that even Judéwin was searching for me, I did not open my mouth to answer. Then the steps were quickened and the voices became excited. The sounds came nearer and nearer. Women and girls entered the room. I held my breath, and watched them open closet doors and peep behind large trunks. Some one threw up the curtains, and the room was filled with sudden light. What caused them to stoop and look under the bed I do not know. I remember being dragged out, though I resisted by kicking and scratching wildly. In spite of myself, I was carried downstairs and tied fast in a chair.

I cried aloud, shaking my head all the while until I felt the cold blades of the scissors against my neck, and heard them gnaw off one of my thick braids. Then I lost my spirit. Since the day I was taken from my mother I had suffered extreme indignities. People had stared at me. I had been tossed about in the air like a wooden puppet. And now my long hair was shingled like a coward's! In my anguish I moaned for my mother, but no one came to comfort me. Not a soul reasoned quietly with me, as my own mother used to do; for now I was only one of many little animals driven by a herder.

THE SNOW EPISODE

A short time after our arrival we three Dakotas were playing in the snow-drifts. We were all still deaf to the English language, excepting Judéwin, who always heard such puzzling things. One morning we learned through her ears that we were forbidden to fall lengthwise in the snow, as we had been doing, to see our own impressions. However, before many hours we had forgotten the order, and were having great sport in the snow, when a shrill voice called us. Looking up, we saw an imperative hand beckoning us into the house. We shook the snow off ourselves, and started toward the woman as slowly as we dared.

Judéwin said: "Now the paleface is angry with us. She is going to pun-
ish us for falling into the snow. If she looks straight into your eyes and talks
loudly, you must wait until she stops. Then, after a tiny pause, say, 'No.' " The
rest of the way we practiced upon the little word "no."

As it happened, Thowin was summoned to judgment first. The door
shut behind her with a click.

Judéwin and I stood silently listening at the keyhole. The paleface woman
talked in very severe tones. Her words fell from her lips like crackling embers,
and her inflection ran up like the small end of a switch. I understood her
voice better than the things she was saying. I was certain we had made her
very impatient with us. Judéwin heard enough of the words to realize all too
late that she had taught us the wrong reply.

"Oh, poor Thowin!" she gasped, as she put both hands over her ears.

Just then I heard Thowin's tremulous answer, "No."

With an angry exclamation, the woman gave her a hard spanking. Then
she stopped to say something. Judéwin said it was this: "Are you going to
obey my word the next time?"

Thowin answered again with the only word at her command, "No."

This time the woman meant her blows to smart, for the poor frightened
girl shrieked at the top of her voice. In the midst of the whipping the blows
ceased abruptly, and the woman asked another question: "Are you going to
fall in the snow again?"

Thowin gave her bad passwood another trial. We heard her say feebly,
"No! No!"

With this the woman hid away her half-worn slipper, and led the child out,
stroking her black shorn head. Perhaps it occurred to her that brute force is
not the solution for such a problem. She did nothing to Judéwin nor to me. She
only returned to us our unhappy comrade, and left us alone in the room.

During the first two or three seasons, misunderstandings as ridiculous
as this one of the snow episode frequently took place, bringing unjustifiable
frights and punishments into our little lives.

Within a year I was able to express myself somewhat in broken English.
As soon as I comprehended a part of what was said and done, a mischievous
spirit of revenge possessed me. One day I was called in from my play for some
misconduct. I had disregarded a rule which seemed to me very needlessly
binding. I was sent into the kitchen to mash the turnips for dinner. It was
noon, and steaming dishes were hastily carried into the dining room. I hated

turnips, and their odor which came from the brown jar was offensive to me. With fire in my heart, I took the wooden tool that the paleface woman held out to me. I stood upon a step, and, grasping the handle with both hands, I bent in hot rage over the turnips. I worked my vengeance upon them. All were so busily occupied that no one noticed me. I saw that the turnips were in a pulp, and that further beating could not improve them; but the order was, "Mash these turnips," and mash them I would! I renewed my energy; and as I sent the masher into the bottom of the jar, I felt a satisfying sensation that the weight of my body had gone into it.

Just here a paleface woman came up to my table. As she looked into the jar, she shoved my hands roughly aside. I stood fearless and angry. She placed her red hands upon the rim of the jar. Then she gave one lift and a stride away from the table. But lo! the pulpy contents fell through the crumbled bottom to the floor! She spared me no scolding phrases that I had earned. I did not heed them. I felt triumphant in my revenge, though deep within me I was a wee bit sorry to have broken the jar.

As I sat eating my dinner, and saw that no turnips were served, I whooped in my heart for having once asserted the rebellion within me.

THE DEVIL

Among the legends the old warriors used to tell me were many stories of evil spirits. But I was taught to fear them no more than those who stalked about in material guise. I never knew there was an insolent chieftain among the bad spirits, who dared to array his forces against the Great Spirit, until I heard this white man's legend from a paleface woman.

Out of a large book she showed me a picture of the white man's devil. I looked in horror upon the strong claws that grew out of his fur-covered fingers. His feet were like his hands. Trailing at his heels was a scaly tail tipped with a serpent's open jaws. His face was a patchwork: he had bearded cheeks, like some I had seen palefaces wear; his nose was an eagle's bill, and his sharp-pointed ears were pricked up like those of a sly fox. Above them a pair of cow's horns curved upward. I trembled with awe, and my heart throbbed in my throat, as I looked at the king of evil spirits. Then I heard the paleface woman say that this terrible creature roamed loose in the world, and that little girls who disobeyed school regulations were to be tortured by him.

That night I dreamt about this evil divinity. Once again I seemed to be in my mother's cottage. An Indian woman had come to visit my mother. On opposite sides of the kitchen stove, which stood in the centre of the small house, my mother and her guest were seated in straight-backed chairs. I played with a train of empty spools hitched together on a string. It was night, and the wick burned feebly. Suddenly I heard some one turn our doorknob from without.

My mother and the woman hushed their talk, and both looked toward the door. It opened gradually. I waited behind the stove. The hinges squeaked as the door was slowly, very slowly pushed inward.

Then in rushed the devil! He was tall! He looked exactly like the picture I had seen of him in the white man's papers. He did not speak to my mother, because he did not know the Indian language, but his glittering yellow eyes were fastened upon me. He took long strides around the stove, passing behind the woman's chair. I threw down my spools, and ran to my mother. He did not fear her, but followed closely after me. Then I ran round and round the stove, crying aloud for help. But my mother and the woman seemed not to know my danger. They sat still, looking quietly upon the devil's chase after me. At last I grew dizzy. My head revolved as on a hidden pivot. My knees became numb, and doubled under my weight like a pair of knife blades without a spring. Beside my mother's chair I fell in a heap. Just as the devil stooped over me with outstretched claws my mother awoke from her quiet indifference, and lifted me on her lap. Whereupon the devil vanished, and I was awake.

On the following morning I took my revenge upon the devil. Stealing into the room where a wall of shelves was filled with books, I drew forth The Stories of the Bible. With a broken slate pencil I carried in my apron pocket, I began by scratching out his wicked eyes. A few moments later, when I was ready to leave the room, there was a ragged hole in the page where the picture of the devil had once been.

IRON ROUTINE

A loud-clamoring bell awakened us at half past six in the cold winter mornings. From happy dreams of Western rolling lands and unlassoed freedom we tumbled out upon chilly bare floors back again into a paleface day. We had short time to jump into our shoes and clothes, and wet our eyes with icy water, before a small hand bell was vigorously rung for roll call.

There were too many drowsy children and too numerous orders for the day to waste a moment in any apology to nature for giving her children such a shock in the early morning. We rushed downstairs, bounding over two high steps at a time, to land in the assembly room.

A paleface woman, with a yellow-covered roll book open on her arm and a gnawed pencil in her hand, appeared at the door. Her small, tired face was coldly lighted with a pair of large gray eyes.

She stood still in a halo of authority, while over the rim of her spectacles her eyes pried nervously about the room. Having glanced at her long list of names and called out the first one, she tossed up her chin and peered through the crystals of her spectacles to make sure of the answer "Here."

Relentlessly her pencil black-marked our daily records if we were not present to respond to our names, and no chum of ours had done it successfully for us. No matter if a dull headache or the painful cough of slow consumption had delayed the absentee, there was only time enough to mark the tardiness. It was next to impossible to leave the iron routine after the civilizing machine had once begun its day's buzzing; and as it was inbred in me to suffer in silence rather than to appeal to the ears of one whose open eyes could not see my pain, I have many times trudged in the day's harness heavy-footed, like a dumb sick brute.

Once I lost a dear classmate. I remember well how she used to mope along at my side, until one morning she could not raise her head from her pillow. At her deathbed I stood weeping, as the paleface woman sat near her moistening the dry lips. Among the folds of the bedclothes I saw the open pages of the white man's Bible. The dying Indian girl talked disconnectedly of Jesus the Christ and the paleface who was cooling her swollen hands and feet.

I grew bitter, and censured the woman for cruel neglect of our physical ills. I despised the pencils that moved automatically, and the one teaspoon which dealt out, from a large bottle, healing to a row of variously ailing Indian children. I blamed the hard-working, well-meaning, ignorant woman who was inculcating in our hearts her superstitious ideas. Though I was sullen in all my little troubles, as soon as I felt better I was ready again to smile upon the cruel woman. Within a week I was again actively testing the chains which tightly bound my individuality like a mummy for burial.

The melancholy of those black days has left so long a shadow that it darkens the path of years that have since gone by. These sad memories rise above those of smoothly grinding school days. Perhaps my Indian nature is the moaning wind which stirs them now for their present record. But, however tempestuous this is within me, it comes out as the low voice of a curiously colored seashell, which is only for those ears that are bent with compassion to hear it.

FOUR STRANGE SUMMERS

After my first three years of school, I roamed again in the Western country through four strange summers.

During this time I seemed to hang in the heart of chaos, beyond the touch or voice of human aid. My brother, being almost ten years my senior, did not quite understand my feelings. My mother had never gone inside of a schoolhouse, and so she was not capable of comforting her daughter who could read and write. Even nature seemed to have no place for me. I was neither a wee girl nor a tall one; neither a wild Indian nor a tame one. This deplorable situation was the effect of my brief course in the East, and the unsatisfactory "teenth" in a girl's years.

It was under these trying conditions that, one bright afternoon, as I sat restless and unhappy in my brother's cabin, I caught the sound of the spirited step of my brother's pony on the road which passed by our dwelling. Soon I heard the wheels of a light buckboard, and Dawée's familiar "Ho!" to his pony. He alighted upon the bare ground in front of our house. Tying his pony to one of the projecting corner logs of the low-roofed cottage, he stepped upon the wooden doorstep.

I met him there with a hurried greeting, and, as I passed by, he looked a quiet "What?" into my eyes.

When he began talking with my mother, I slipped the rope from the pony's bridle. Seizing the reins and bracing my feet against the dashboard, I wheeled around in an instant. The pony was ever ready to try his speed. Looking backward, I saw Dawée waving his hand to me. I turned with the curve in the road and disappeared. I followed the winding road which crawled upward between the bases of little hillocks. Deep water-worn ditches ran parallel on either side. A strong wind blew against my cheeks and fluttered my sleeves. The pony reached the top of the highest hill, and began an even race on the level lands. There was nothing moving within that great circular horizon of the Dakota prairies save the tall grasses, over which the wind blew and rolled off in long, shadowy waves.

Within this vast wigwam of blue and green I rode reckless and insignificant. It satisfied my small consciousness to see the white foam fly from the pony's mouth.

Suddenly, out of the earth a coyote came forth at a swinging trot that was taking the cunning thief toward the hills and the village beyond. Upon the moment's impulse, I gave him a long chase and a wholesome fright. As I turned away to go back to the village, the wolf sank down upon his haunches for rest, for it was a hot summer day; and as I drove slowly homeward, I saw his sharp nose still pointed at me, until I vanished below the margin of the hilltops.

In a little while I came in sight of my mother's house. Dawée stood in the yard, laughing at an old warrior who was pointing his forefinger, and again waving his whole hand, toward the hills. With his blanket drawn over one shoulder, he talked and motioned excitedly. Dawée turned the old man by the shoulder and pointed me out to him.

"Oh han!" (Oh yes) the warrior muttered, and went his way. He had climbed the top of his favorite barren hill to survey the surrounding prairies, when he spied my chase after the coyote. His keen eyes recognized the pony and driver. At once uneasy for my safety, he had come running to my mother's cabin to give her warning. I did not appreciate his kindly interest, for there was an unrest gnawing at my heart.

As soon as he went away, I asked Dawée about something else.

"No, my baby sister, I cannot take you with me to the party tonight," he replied. Though I was not far from fifteen, and I felt that before long I should enjoy all the privileges of my tall cousin, Dawée persisted in calling me his baby sister.

That moonlight night, I cried in my mother's presence when I heard the jolly young people pass by our cottage. They were no more young braves in blankets and eagle plumes, nor Indian maids with prettily painted cheeks. They had gone three years to school in the East, and had become civilized. The young men wore the white man's coat and trousers, with bright neckties. The girls wore tight muslin dresses, with ribbons at neck and waist. At these gatherings they talked English. I could speak English almost as well as my brother, but I was not properly dressed to be taken along. I had no hat, no ribbons, and no close-fitting gown. Since my return from school I had thrown away my shoes, and wore again the soft moccasins.

While Dawée was busily preparing to go I controlled my tears. But when I heard him bounding away on his pony, I buried my face in my arms and cried hot tears.

My mother was troubled by my unhappiness. Coming to my side, she offered me the only printed matter we had in our home. It was an Indian Bible, given her some years ago by a missionary. She tried to console me. "Here, my child, are the white man's papers. Read a little from them," she said most piously.

I took it from her hand, for her sake; but my enraged spirit felt more like burning the book, which afforded me no help, and was a perfect delusion to my mother. I did not read it, but laid it unopened on the floor, where I sat on my feet. The dim yellow light of the braided muslin burning in a small vessel of oil flickered and sizzled in the awful silent storm which followed my rejection of the Bible.

Now my wrath against the fates consumed my tears before they reached my eyes. I sat stony, with a bowed head. My mother threw a shawl over her head and shoulders, and stepped out into the night.

After an uncertain solitude, I was suddenly aroused by a loud cry piercing the night. It was my mother's voice wailing among the barren hills which held the bones of buried warriors. She called aloud for her brothers' spirits to support her in her helpless misery. My fingers grew icy cold, as I realized that my unrestrained tears had betrayed my suffering to her, and she was grieving for me.

Before she returned, though I knew she was on her way, for she had ceased her weeping, I extinguished the light, and leaned my head on the window sill.

Many schemes of running away from my surroundings hovered about in my mind. A few more moons of such a turmoil drove me away to the Eastern school. I rode on the white man's iron steed, thinking it would bring me back to my mother in a few winters, when I should be grown tall, and there would be congenial friends awaiting me.

INCURRING MY MOTHER'S DISPLEASURE

In the second journey to the East I had not come without some precautions. I had a secret interview with one of our best medicine men, and when I left his wigwam I carried securely in my sleeve a tiny bunch of magic roots. This possession assured me of friends wherever I should go. So absolutely did I believe in its charms that I wore it through all the school routine for more than a year. Then, before I lost my faith in the dead roots, I lost the little buckskin bag containing all my good luck.

At the close of this second term of three years I was the proud owner of my first diploma. The following autumn I ventured upon a college career against my mother's will.

I had written for her approval, but in her reply I found no encouragement. She called my notice to her neighbors' children, who had completed their education in three years. They had returned to their homes, and were then talking English with the frontier settlers. Her few words hinted that I had better give up my slow attempt to learn the white man's ways, and be content to roam over the prairies and find my living upon wild roots. I silenced her by deliberate disobedience.

Thus, homeless and heavy-hearted, I began anew my life among strangers.

As I hid myself in my little room in the college dormitory, away from the scornful and yet curious eyes of the students, I pined for sympathy. Often I wept in secret, wishing I had gone West, to be nourished by my mother's love, instead of remaining among a cold race whose hearts were frozen hard with prejudice.

During the fall and winter seasons I scarcely had a real friend, though by that time several of my classmates were courteous to me at a safe distance.

My mother had not yet forgiven my rudeness to her, and I had no moment for letter-writing. By daylight and lamplight, I spun with reeds and thistles, until my hands were tired from their weaving, the magic design which promised me the white man's respect.

At length, in the spring term, I entered an oratorical contest among the various classes. As the day of competition approached, it did not seem possible that the event was so near at hand, but it came. In the chapel the classes assembled together, with their invited guests. The high platform was carpeted, and gayly festooned with college colors. A bright white light illumined the room, and outlined clearly the great polished beams that arched the domed ceiling. The assembled crowds filled the air with pulsating murmurs. When the hour for speaking arrived all were hushed. But on the wall the old clock which pointed out the trying moment ticked calmly on.

One after another I saw and heard the orators. Still, I could not realize that they longed for the favorable decision of the judges as much as I did. Each contestant received a loud burst of applause, and some were cheered heartily. Too soon my turn came, and I paused a moment behind the curtains for a deep breath. After my concluding words, I heard the same applause that the others had called out.

Upon my retreating steps, I was astounded to receive from my fellow students a large bouquet of roses tied with flowing ribbons. With the lovely flowers I fled from the stage. This friendly token was a rebuke to me for the hard feelings I had borne them.

Later, the decision of the judges awarded me the first place. Then there was a mad uproar in the hall, where my classmates sang and shouted my name at the top of their lungs; and the disappointed students howled and brayed in fearfully dissonant tin trumpets. In this excitement, happy students rushed forward to offer their congratulations. And I could not conceal a smile when they wished to escort me in a procession to the students' parlor, where all were going to calm themselves. Thanking them for the kind spirit which prompted them to make such a proposition, I walked alone with the night to my own little room.

A few weeks afterward, I appeared as the college representative in another contest. This time the competition was among orators from different colleges in our state. It was held at the state capital, in one of the largest opera houses.

Here again was a strong prejudice against my people. In the evening, as the great audience filled the house, the student bodies began warring among themselves. Fortunately, I was spared witnessing any of the noisy wrangling before the contest began. The slurs against the Indian that stained the lips of our opponents were already burning like a dry fever within my breast.

But after the orations were delivered a deeper burn awaited me. There, before that vast ocean of eyes, some college rowdies threw out a large white flag, with a drawing of a most forlorn Indian girl on it. Under this they had printed in bold black letters words that ridiculed the college which was represented by a "squaw." Such worse than barbarian rudeness embittered me. While we waited for the verdict of the judges, I gleamed fiercely upon the throngs of palefaces. My teeth were hard set, as I saw the white flag still floating insolently in the air.

Then anxiously we watched the man carry toward the stage the envelope containing the final decision.

There were two prizes given, that night, and one of them was mine!

The evil spirit laughed within me when the white flag dropped out of sight, and the hands which furled it hung limp in defeat.

Leaving the crowd as quickly as possible, I was soon in my room. The rest of the night I sat in an armchair and gazed into the crackling fire. I laughed no more in triumph when thus alone. The little taste of victory did not satisfy a hunger in my heart. In my mind I saw my mother far away on the Western plains, and she was holding a charge against me.

Questions for Reflection and Analysis

1. What strikes you about the story as a whole? Is there a particular aspect of the story that elicits a memory or concern about teaching and learning?

2. Drawing from the story's details, explain the purpose of the nineteenth-century mission school from the perspective of the missionaries. Given the narrator's account of her experiences at the school, how successfully do you think the missionaries' purpose is fulfilled?

3. What do you learn about the narrator's cultural background from the descriptive images Zitkala-Ša uses to portray the narrator's situation, for example, the telegraph pole (p. 15), the school bells (pp. 15–17, 22), the shoes (pp. 16–17, 22)? What points about cultural difference might the author be making through these and other evocative images?

4. What changes do you observe in the narrator's behavior and personality as she acquires English language proficiency over time? What do these changes reveal about the relationship between her second language acquisition and her behavior?

5. How do the narrator's Native identity and background impact her academic success and her own assessment of her achievements in college? How might this insight into the realities of her life inform her teacher's understanding about what the acquisition of a new language may actually entail?

■ *Chike's School Days*

Chinua Achebe

(1930–)

Chinua Achebe was born in Nigeria to devout Christian parents 30 years before Nigeria gained independence from Great Britain. His first language was Ibo; he began to learn English at age 8. After attending University College, Ibadan, and London University, he worked for the Nigerian Broadcasting Corporation and studied at the British Broadcasting Corporation in London. He has been a professor of English at universities in Nigeria and in the United States, an editor and publisher, an activist in Nigerian politics, and a guest speaker at events in numerous countries throughout the world. An award-winning author, his many publications include *Things Fall Apart* (1958), *Anthills of the Savanna* (1987), and *Home and Exile* (2000).

Sarah's last child was a boy, and his birth brought great joy to the house of his father, Amos. The child received three names at his baptism—John, Chike, Obiajulu. The last name means "the mind at last is at rest." Anyone hearing this name knew at once that its owner was either an only child or an only son. Chike was an only son. His parents had had five daughters before him.

Like his sisters Chike was brought up "in the ways of the white man," which meant the opposite of traditional. Amos had many years before bought a tiny bell with which he summoned his family to prayers and hymn-singing first thing in the morning and last thing at night. This was one of the ways of the white man. Sarah taught her children not to eat in the neighbours' houses because "they offered their food to idols." And thus she set herself against the age-old custom which regarded children as the common responsibility of all so that, no matter what the relationship between parents, their children played together and shared their food.

One day a neighbour offered a piece of yam to Chike, who was only four years old. The boy shook his head haughtily and said, "We don't eat heathen food." The neighbour was full of rage, but she controlled herself and only muttered under her breath that even an *Osu* was full of pride nowadays, thanks to the white man.

And she was right. In the past an *Osu* could not raise his shaggy head in the presence of the free-born. He was a slave to one of the many gods of the clan. He was a thing set apart, not to be venerated but to be despised and almost spat on. He could not marry a free-born, and he could not take any of the titles of his clan. When he died, he was buried by his kind in the Bad Bush.

Now all that had changed, or had begun to change. So that an *Osu* child could even look down his nose at a free-born, and talk about heathen food! The white man had indeed accomplished many things.

Chike's father was not originally an *Osu*, but had gone and married an *Osu* woman in the name of Christianity. It was unheard of for a man to make himself *Osu* in that way, with his eyes wide open. But then Amos was nothing if not mad. The new religion had gone to his head. It was like palm-wine. Some people drank it and remained sensible. Others lost every sense in their stomach.

The only person who supported Amos in his mad marriage venture was Mr. Brown, the white missionary, who lived in a thatch-roofed, red-earth-walled parsonage and was highly respected by the people, not because of his sermons, but because of a dispensary he ran in one of his rooms. Amos had emerged from Mr. Brown's parsonage greatly fortified. A few days later he told his widowed mother, who had recently been converted to Christianity and had taken the name of Elizabeth. The shock nearly killed her. When she recovered, she went down on her knees and begged Amos not to do this thing. But he would not hear; his ears had been nailed up. At last, in desperation, Elizabeth went to consult the diviner.

This diviner was a man of great power and wisdom. As he sat on the floor of his hut beating a tortoise shell, a coating of white chalk round his eyes, he saw not only the present, but also what had been and what was to be. He was called "the man of the four eyes." As soon as old Elizabeth appeared, he cast his stringed cowries and told her what she had come to see him about. "Your son has joined the white man's religion. And you too in your old age when you should know better. And do you wonder that he is stricken with insanity? Those who gather ant-infested faggots must be prepared for the visit of lizards." He cast his cowries a number of times and wrote with a finger on a bowl of sand, and all the while his *nwifulu*, a talking calabash, chatted to itself. "Shut up!" he roared, and it immediately held its peace. The diviner then muttered a few incantations and rattled off a breathless reel of proverbs that followed one another like the cowries in his magic string.

At last he pronounced the cure. The ancestors were angry and must be appeased with a goat. Old Elizabeth performed the rites, but her son remained insane and married an *Osu* girl whose name was Sarah. Old Elizabeth renounced her new religion and returned to the faith of her people.

We have wandered from our main story. But it is important to know how Chike's father became an *Osu*, because even today when everything is upside down, such a story is very rare. But now to return to Chike who refused heathen food at the tender age of four years, or maybe five.

Two years later he went to the village school. His right hand could now reach across his head to his left ear, which proved that he was old enough to tackle the mysteries of the white man's learning. He was very happy about his new slate and pencil, and especially about his school uniform of white shirt and brown khaki shorts. But as the first day of the new term approached, his young mind dwelt on the many stories about teachers and their canes. And he remembered the song his elder sisters sang, a song that had a somewhat disquieting refrain:

Onye nkuzi ewelu itali piagbusie umuaka.

One of the ways an emphasis is laid in Ibo is by exaggeration, so that the teacher in the refrain might not actually have flogged the children to death. But there was no doubt he did flog them. And Chike thought very much about it.

Being so young, Chike was sent to what was called the "religious class" where they sang, and sometimes danced, the catechism. He loved the sound of words and he loved rhythm. During the catechism lesson the class formed a ring to dance the teacher's question. "Who was Caesar?" he might ask, and the song would burst forth with much stamping of feet.

Siza bu eze Rome
Onye nachi enu uwa dum.

It did not matter to their dancing that in the twentieth century Caesar was no longer ruler of the whole world.

And sometimes they even sang in English. Chike was very fond of "Ten Green Bottles." They had been taught the words but they only remembered the first and the last lines. The middle was hummed and hie-ed and mumbled:

> *Ten grin botr angin on dar war,*
> *Ten grin botr angin on dar war,*
> *Hm hm hm hm hm*
> *Hm, hm hm hm hm hm,*
> *An ten grin botr angin on dar war.*

In this way the first year passed. Chike was promoted to the "Infant School," where work of a more serious nature was undertaken.

We need not follow him through the Infant School. It would make a full story in itself. But it was no different from the story of other children. In the Primary School, however, his individual character began to show. He developed a strong hatred for arithmetic. But he loved stories and songs. And he liked particularly the sound of English words, even when they conveyed no meaning at all. Some of them simply filled him with elation. "Periwinkle" was such a word. He had now forgotten how he learned it or exactly what it was. He had a vague private meaning for it and it was something to do with fairyland. "Constellation" was another.

Chike's teacher was fond of long words. He was said to be a very learned man. His favourite pastime was copying out jaw-breaking words from his *Chambers' Etymological Dictionary*. Only the other day he had raised applause from his class by demolishing a boy's excuse for lateness with unanswerable erudition. He had said: "Procrastination is a lazy man's apology." The teacher's erudition showed itself in every subject he taught. His nature study lessons were memorable. Chike would always remember the lesson on the methods of seed dispersal. According to teacher, there were five methods: by man, by animals, by water, by wind, and by explosive mechanism. Even those pupils who forgot all the other methods remembered "explosive mechanism."

Chike was naturally impressed by teacher's explosive vocabulary. But the fairyland quality which words had for him was of a different kind. The first sentences in his *New Method Reader* were simple enough and yet they filled him with a vague exultation: "Once there was a wizard. He lived in Africa.

He went to China to get a lamp." Chike read it over and over again at home and then made a song of it. It was a meaningless song. "Periwinkles" got into it, and also "Damascus." But it was like a window through which he saw in the distance a strange, magical new world. And he was happy.

Questions for Reflection and Analysis

1. What strikes you about the story as a whole? Is there a particular aspect of the story that elicits a memory or concern about teaching and learning?

2. What do the different responses to Christianity at the beginning of the story reveal about Achebe's attitude toward religion and tradition in the context of colonialism?

3. What does the English language represent for Chike? What might Achebe be suggesting about the nature of this child's language learning in a colonial context?

4. What is the difference, for Chike, between the language of his nature study lessons and the language of the stories in his *New Method Reader*? What might Achebe be suggesting here about the way language is acquired?

5. How does Achebe provide a context to allow for a reader's understanding of what each italicized phrase and passage in the story means? What underlying assumption might Achebe be making about the relationship between a reader's background knowledge and the ability to understand unfamiliar language?

 # *Kura*

Patricia Grace

(1937–)

Patricia Grace was born in New Zealand of Ngati Toa, Ngati Raukawa, and Te Ati Awa descent, and she is affiliated to Ngati Porou by marriage. Grace's first language is English; she knows various registers of Maori English. Educated at St. Mary's College and Wellington Teachers' Training College, she also received a diploma in the Teaching of English as a Second Language and taught in primary and secondary schools before becoming a full-time writer. An award-winning author, her publications include *Waiariki* (1975), *Dogside Story* (2001), and *Tu* (2004). "Kura" is a story told by the character Gran Kura in Grace's novel, *Baby No-Eyes* (1998).

There was a school. Our grandfather gave land for it so that we could have our education. It was what we wanted. The school was along by the creek where Staffords live now. It was there for our parents and us, and then for our children. But after our children grew up our school was left empty because many people had left the area by then. Their land was gone, and the children's children, who were only a few, had to travel by bus to the big school in town.

Our grandfather's mother was the eldest daughter of Te Wharekapakapa and Kapiri Morehua, both people of high birth and status—so it was through her parents that our great-grandmother came to have jurisdiction over land from beyond the foothills to the sea, and from Awakehua to Awapango. I mention this not to be boastful but only to tell you that we did not come from slaves.

Our school was painted light brown with dark brown window frames and door. There was one big room with a high roof, and a low porch on one end. Joined to it at the other end was a little low-roofed shelter. The big children were taught by the headmaster in the big room with its blackboards and big windows, its polished wood floors and varnished walls, while the primer children were taught by the headmaster's wife in the little joined-on room.

When I first started school this primer room had a board floor and one little window. Inside was a blackboard on an easel. Beside it was the teacher's desk. There were six desks in a row for the older children, and a table with forms on either side where the littlest ones sat. By the time Riripeti started school I was eight and had a desk of my own. When I took Riripeti to school on her first day I took her to the table where the little ones sat. That's where I put her. I believed it was the right thing to do.

I was up early that day. I hurried all morning because I had this important work to do—to take Riripeti to school. My mother and Riripeti's father were sister and brother, which in those days made Riripeti a sister to me. She was my teina.

That morning before I went to get Riripeti my mother said, "Look after your little sister at school, help her, teach her what to do." All right I was very happy. I was proud of this work I'd been given.

When I arrived at Riripeti's place she was ready, wearing a new dress that grandmother had made for her. Her hair had been plaited and tied with ribbons made from strips of the dress material. There was a hanky in her sleeve and a bandage on her knee.

Grandmother was there with Aunty Heni and Uncle Taare to see Riripeti off to school. "Look after your teina, take her by the hand," Grandmother said to me. "Do as your tuakana says," she said to Riripeti. "Your tuakana will help you so that you'll know what to do. Listen to what she says."

Then our grandmother said to me, "We know you're a good girl. We know you'll do what you're told, we know you'll help your little sister and look after her. We don't want our children to be hurt at school. That's why you have to be very good. You have to listen, you have to obey. We know that you're clever and we know you'll learn. That's what our school is for, for you to learn, for our children to learn. You're very lucky to have a school and to be allowed to go to school. Look after your little sister."

Perhaps I was told to take Riripeti to the headmaster or the teacher before taking her into the classroom, perhaps I forgot this, being too excited to hear.

Sixty years ago I was a tiny girl, small for my age. See that leaf—like that. Thin like that, without weight. You could see through me those days, just as you can see through that leaf now, but I was not too light and leafy to have this important job. I was this important girl, this happy leaf and I loved my teina with her new clothes, her hair in pigtails, a rag hanky in her sleeve. She was a black girl, six years old.

The teacher didn't notice Riripeti marching into school with me, and was busy writing on the blackboard when I stood Riripeti by Tihi at the little children's table. I was the one who told her to stand there. I straightened her, put her feet together, put her shoulders back and went to stand by my own desk. We said our good mornings to the teacher before we all sat down.

"Who is this?" the teacher said when she saw Riripeti sitting on the form. I put my hand up because that was the right thing to do, but the teacher didn't look at my hand. "Who are you and where are your manners, coming in and sitting down as though you own the place?" she said to Riripeti, but Riripeti didn't know what the teacher was saying. "Stand up when you're spoken to," the teacher said. I wanted to whisper in our language so this teina of mine would know what to do, but I knew I wasn't allowed to speak our language so I made a little movement with my hands trying to tell her to stand. She didn't understand and sat there smiling, swinging her shoulders, swinging her eyes—to me, then back again to the teacher.

I knew Riripeti shouldn't smile so much. I knew she shouldn't fidget herself or roll her eyes. At that moment I didn't want her to be a girl so black that it would make the teacher angry.

"Get that smile off your face. Do you think this is a laughing matter?" the teacher said, taking Riripeti by the arm and standing her.

Riripeti could speak some English. Of course. We all could. But Riripeti had not heard words like the words she was now hearing. "Go and stand in the corner until you learn better manners," the teacher said, but Riripeti didn't know what she was being told to do. I wanted to call out to her but speaking wasn't allowed.

The teacher turned Riripeti and poked her in the back while she shuffled forward, but not fast enough, not fast enough, still swerving her head and eyes towards me—until she was standing in the corner at the front of the room where bad children always stood.

But how was she to know she was bad? She had said no words that would make her bad, spelled nothing wrong to be bad, given no answers to be wrong. "Face the corner," the teacher said, because Riripeti was still twisting her neck to look at me. She didn't know what she had been told to do. The teacher jolted her head round and gave her a smacking on the legs, then Riripeti stood stiff and still without moving, facing the corner.

At playtime, I ran with our cousins Kuini, Hama and Jimmy to hide in the bushes, where we put our arms round each other. No one from the little classroom played that morning. The ones not crying sat close together eating bread, turning the balls of their feet into the ground, watching their feet make dents in the dust.

After play the teacher turned Riripeti round and asked her for her name but Riripeti wouldn't say it. Instead she smiled and smiled and moved her eyes from side to side. So the teacher asked Dulcie, who was the eldest in our class, what Riripeti's name was. But then the teacher became angry with Dulcie too because she wouldn't speak the name slowly and loudly enough. The teacher gave Dulcie a piece of paper to take to Riripeti's family. Full name, date of birth, English name, it said. She turned Riripeti into the corner again, but allowed her to come out with us at lunchtime.

After school, Dulcie, who didn't live anywhere near Riripeti or me, gave the note to me to take home to my aunty and uncle. Her family was where the Beckets are now—that was their land then. I took the paper home and the next day gave it back to Dulcie to give to the teacher. It gave Riripeti's name, her date of birth and her English name, Betty.

On the way to school we taught Riripeti to say, "Yes Mrs. Wood, No Mrs. Wood, Yes please Mrs. Wood, No thank you Mrs. Wood." We thought it very funny that our teachers were called Mr. and Mrs. Wood, and once we were out of the school grounds Mr. Mrs. Rakau is what we called them. We had this silly song to make ourselves laugh: "Mr. Mrs. Rakau, patu patu *wood*." *Wood* was the loud word. It was the word to scare anyone with. We'd call it out to the kids we didn't like, call it out to the ones chasing us, or we'd jump out from a tree where we'd been hiding and call, "Mr. Mrs. Rakau, patu patu *wood*," and off we'd run.

It was no good. School turned out no good for Riripeti. How did she know her name was Betty? That second day she was in the bad corner for not answering when her name was called, and for not speaking when she was spoken to. On the way to and from school we'd tell her the right things to say, but even though she tried she still couldn't say the words the teacher wanted. She spent most of her time in the corner. Every day she was given smackings by the teacher.

Other children were smacked and caned and punished too, but not as much as Riripeti. We were much naughtier children than what she was, that's how we knew what to do. I knew my name was Kate at school. Minaroa knew her name was Dulcie. And we had ways of sending messages to each other with our faces, ways of guessing the teacher's mind, knew which lies were the right ones to tell. If the teacher gave us a lesson about the right food to have for breakfast, when questioned we would tell her that's what we had—bacon, egg, toast, class of milk. It was the right answer—bacon, egg, toast, class of milk. "*Glass, glass,* a *glass* of milk,*"* the teacher would say. After a while we could say it, making this choking *g* sound right down in our throats. But we didn't know it meant milk in a glass, didn't know what it meant. Didn't know a glass was right for milk and a cup was right for tea, because at home we had enamel plates and enamel mugs for everything. We didn't speak until we'd learned, didn't speak unless we had to because we were afraid our bad language might come out, but we became good at guessing the answers we had to give.

Riripeti was too good to guess what to say, too good to know what lies to tell, too good to know what to do. It was so difficult for me to be her tuakana. It was so difficult to take her to school every day with her footsteps getting slower and slower the nearer we came. By the gate she'd say, "Kura, Kura, he puku mamae," and she'd hold her stomach and bend over. Her face would be pale.

"Never mind, never mind," I'd say. "You got to go to school every day. We got to learn so we be clever." I'd pull her along so that I wouldn't be in trouble with our mothers. I was trying so hard to do this important work that my grandmother had given me to do.

All the way to school I'd talk to her, tell her what to say and what to do. And she did know, she did learn. She was very brave and tried to do everything I told her. She remembered to speak in English, except that the teacher didn't know it was English she was speaking because Riripeti was too afraid to make the words come out loudly. "Do I have to shake that language out of you, do I do I?" the teacher would say, shaking and shaking her. Then Riripeti would be smacked and sent to stand in the bad place. She did mimi there sometimes. Sometimes she sicked there, then cleaned it all up with a cloth and bucket. I would've helped her if I'd thought I'd be allowed. After a while it was only Riripeti who went to the bad corner. It became her corner. She smelled like an animal and spoke like an animal, had to go to the corner until she stopped being an animal. I could see that she was getting smaller and that it was only her eyes and her teeth that were growing. We didn't tell our mothers, or anyone, what was happening, but sometimes Riripeti was told off at home for her dirty wet clothes.

One morning Riripeti sat down by the track and said she couldn't go to school any more. Usually when she did that we would manage to persuade her, but that day I believed her. It was true that she couldn't go to school. Her spirit was out of her, gone roaming. Her hair was as dry as a horse's tail, rough and hard, her eyes were like flat shadows, not at all like eyes. I had seen a dying dog look like that, which made me think it might be true what the teacher said, that my teina was changing into an animal. "Go home to aunty," I said.

"No, I'll wait for you."

"Go in the trees."

So she agreed and I gave my bread to her. Down the bank she went, across the creek and into the trees where perhaps she would become an animal, a bird.

When Mrs. Wood asked where Betty was, I said she was sick, so Mrs. Wood asked the other children too where Betty was, to see if I was telling the truth. "Betty is sick Mrs. Wood," was what each of the children replied, but Mrs. Wood was not happy with this answer. She became angry because how did we all know Betty was sick when we all lived in different directions? Sometimes it was difficult to know the right words to say.

After school I called to Riripeti by the track and I heard her coming. When she came up the bank I could see that her spirit had returned to her. It was looking at me out of her eyes, pleased to see me.

So that's what Riripeti did every day after that, hid in the trees. Mrs. Wood was waiting for her to come back to school with a note and I felt afraid that we'd be found out. But the end of the year came. We had long holidays and Riripeti and I went to stay with our grandmother.

When our grandmother went to town she wore a grey suit and a cream blouse with a high collar and pintucks across the front. She had black Red Cross shoes which she polished the night before, on paper spread on the floor by the hearth. She had a black hat with a small turned-up brim.

In those days no one would take a Maori bag to town or to the shop, not even to a tangihanga, not even to land meetings. It wasn't like these days when you see these baskets everywhere—all colors, all sorts of patterns, not always pretty either. Sometimes they're ragged like the old ones we used for getting pipi, but even a Pakeha will carry a Maori bag now, paying a lot of money for one. In those days all the kete were on top of people's wardrobes with photos in them, or hanging on nails behind the bedroom doors.

Our grandmother had a good leather handbag for her money and combs and handkerchiefs. She had a deep cane basket with black and orange stripes around it for the shopping. Riripeti and I liked to carry the shopping. We were happy to go to town with our grandmother and to carry the basket between us.

We didn't go to town often because in those days we had our own store down the road with everything we needed. We all had our own killers, our own gardens and our own milking cow. So nobody went to town much, but our grandmother sometimes had business there and she'd take us with her for company. When she'd finished her business we'd go and buy whitebait, or whatever she wanted to take home, and then we'd make our way to the railway station where she'd let us buy something to eat. Not for herself. Our grandmother would never eat in town but she would let us buy a sandwich and a melting moment, which we would eat while we waited for the train.

That day grandmother took us to a shop that sold dress materials and bought remnants to make new dresses for Riripeti and me to wear to school. One of the pieces of material was brown with white spots on it, the other was plain dark blue. What a good day it was.

But on our way to the railway station Riripeti's feet began to slow down. "Come on, catch up to Grandmother," I said. Our grandmother was already going up the steps to the station. Riripeti stopped walking, "I don't want a dress," she said.

"Come on, come on," I said pulling her by the hand and talking about the sandwich and the cake. I knew she was thinking about school.

There was a woman in our village who was good at making dresses. We only had to take material to her and she would make anything we asked, but it was our grandmother who wanted to make these dresses for Riripeti and me. Riripeti didn't want to watch Grandmother make the dresses or to have her dress tried on. Didn't want to talk about the dresses. She told me she wanted to go back to her mother and father and kept urging me to ask our grandmother if she could go home, but I wouldn't. I wasn't old enough to ask our grandmother a thing like that.

Riripeti's dress was the spotted one, mine was the plain blue. When they were finished we went home to our parents. The day after that was the day school began again.

Riripeti wanted to hide down by the creek on that first day but I wouldn't let her because I didn't want to be in trouble and didn't want to have to tell lies to the teacher. "I'll tell aunty and uncle if you don't come," I said. "I'll tell grandmother." She was too good not to listen to me. That was how I made her come to school.

But when we arrived at school we found out something that made us both cry. We found that I was to go into the other classroom, the one for the older children, and that Riripeti was to stay in the little room as before.

There were plenty of children crying that day—little children, big children. I don't know what for but some of it was to do with Waana who was Dulcie's little brother, brought up by their grandfather. The grandfather had brought Waana to the steps of the classroom and was talking to him, trying to make his grandson let go of his leg. The headmaster came out and said in a loud voice, "I'd like to remind you Mr. Williams that I don't allow any of that language in my school or in these school grounds." We all got a fright because Waana's grandfather took no notice of the headmaster and kept talking to Waana. The headmaster became angry. "I'm asking you to leave these grounds at once," he said. "Off you go and take your language with you. We're not having any of that in *my* school and in front of these children."

"I go, yes, take my grandson too," the grandfather said to him in English. He lifted Waana and off he went. Waana never came to school again. His grandfather hid him from the authorities, telling them that Waana had gone to live somewhere else.

Riripeti was silly, because when it was time for me to go to the other classroom she cried and put her arms around me. I promised her my bread, I promised her my dress, but she wouldn't let go. In the end I had to wriggle myself away, had to pull her hands off me and run because I could see the teacher coming.

It was when I ran off that Riripeti called out to me but forgot to speak in English. Well, all the holidays we had been speaking in that Maori language of ours, so perhaps that's why she forgot. Mrs. Wood grabbed Riripeti by the shoulders and brought her to Mr. Wood for the cane. We all had to stand in our lines and watch this caning so we would learn how bad our language was.

Riripeti wouldn't hold her hand out, which I knew was from fear and not from being stubborn. She had her eyes shut and stood without moving while Mr. Wood gave her a caning round the legs, then Mrs. Wood got her by the arm so she wouldn't run away. I thought what an evil thing our language was to do that to my teina.

It was a bad time for all of us. Some of us learned to be good and to keep ourselves out of trouble most of the time. Others were bad—swore at the teachers, got canings, or were sent home and not allowed to return.

Riripeti came to school every day. She didn't try to go and hide any more, and even though she began vomiting each day as we came near to school, still she came. She was always good. We were known as a good family. I'm not saying that to be boastful but just to let you understand about Riripeti.

One day during the holidays our grandmother said to Riripeti, "Why are you small? Why are you thin?" And she took Riripeti to live with her, gave her wai kohua, gave her malt and Lane's emulsion and meat. Riripeti was all right too. For a while she was happy and we played together, then when it was near time to go to school again she became sick and couldn't eat. Her throat closed and wouldn't let any food go down. Her skin was moist all the time and she couldn't get out of bed.

Not long after that she died.

Killed by school.

Dead of fear.

My heart broke for my teina. Oh I cried. She was mine, she was me, she was all of us. She was the one who had died but we were the ones affected, our shame taking generations to become our anger and our madness. She was my charge, my little sister, my work that I'd been given to do, mine to look after. What an evil girl I was to let her die.

We never told our mothers and fathers what we knew. They thought Riripeti had a Maori sickness, thought some angry person had put a makutu on her—which was right perhaps, but they didn't know who. Or they thought it could've been part of the cursing of Pirinoa that was still being handed down and affecting us all.

After that I became sick too. I couldn't eat and I couldn't go to school. I went to bed and couldn't get up, just like Riripeti. I think I nearly died too. There were people coming and going, talking to me, talking amongst themselves, putting their hands on me, speaking that language over me—that evil language which killed my teina and which I never spoke again.

One day my grandmother took me out of bed, wrapped a blanket round me and sat in an armchair with me on her knee. She held me against her and rocked me. I think we stayed like that for days and nights. While she held me and rocked me she spoke to me of God's Kingdom. She told me about Riripeti's special place in God's Kingdom with the Lord, who alone was merciful, who alone was good. Riripeti was heaven's bright gold. She talked about the journey that is life, how we must walk its pathways in goodness and righteousness, how we would all be together one day in glory. We all prayed together and the Lord answered our prayers.

Soon I was able to eat. Soon I could sit in the armchair on my own with pillows round me. After a time I was able to get up. Three months after Riripeti died I returned to school with God in my heart. There were new teachers there who were different in their ways, but I only stayed at school for two more years because I was needed at home.

So we children never spoke of what had happened to Riripeti. It became our secret and our shame. It's a story that has never had words, not until today. Today the words were jolted from my stomach by Shane, where they have been sitting for sixty years. They came to my throat, gathering there until the sun went down, when they spilled out on to the verandah in front of the children's children, who may not be strong enough for them.

We keep our stories secret because we love our children, we keep our language hidden because we love our children, we disguise ourselves and hide our hearts because we love our children. We choose names because we love our children.

Shane.[1]

---

[1]Editors' note: "Shane" is the English name of a character in the novel *Baby No-Eyes* who, in the previous chapter of the book, demands that Gran Kura tell him the family secrets, including his Maori name.

Questions for Reflection and Analysis

1. What strikes you about the story as a whole? Is there a particular aspect of the story that elicits a memory or concern about teaching and learning?

2. What are the consequences of the attitudes of the school's teachers and headmaster toward the children and their language use?

3. How do Riripeti's interactions with the teacher differ from her interactions with her family during holidays? What insights can you draw from these differences about the kinds of behavior and circumstances that enable or impede her growth as a language learner?

4. Why do you think the narrator, Gran Kura, makes reference to her family's background and position? How does this information affect your understanding of the story?

5. If you are able to make sense of the Maori words in the story, why can you do so? If you are unable to understand the words, why is this the case? What does your analysis suggest about the process of understanding language?

■ *Fourth Grade Ukus*

Marie Hara

(1959–)

Marie Hara was born of mixed race in Hawaii the same year Hawaii became a state in the United States of America. She received a B.A. and M.A. from the University of Hawai'i at Manoa, where she teaches English composition, literature, and creative writing. Hara co-directed the first Talk Story Conference in 1978, which set as its goal stimulating a new Hawaiian literature, written by locals in their own language, and which took its name from a pidgin expression meaning "to shoot the breeze." An award-winning writer, Hara is the author of the short story collection *Bananaheart* (1990) and co-editor of *Intersecting Circles: The Voices of Hapa Women in Poetry and Prose* (1999). "Fourth Grade Ukus" is set in 1952.

Until the right time came for me to meet my father, I would be patient. Mama made plans all the time. She had figured out what to do. Soon after we settled into a small rental house, we walked over to Lincoln School, a gracious stone building with many trees. None of the students there had to do any manual labor. They used the newest books. They were always featured in newspaper articles and photos that she pointed out to me. Mama had heard that the best Lincoln graduates were sometimes accepted into the private high schools, which was how they "got ahead."

Once in the office I saw that all the teachers were *haole*, and it was a good thing I wore the socks and new shoes Mama had adjusted. I sat with each foot in her lap and great impatience to get accepted. Several teachers watched me watching the other kids playing on the immaculate playground equipment. This part was called The Observation. Once outdoors I took my time taking off my shoes and socks to keep them good for the next wearing. I kept munching softly on a strand of hair that hung comfortably near my mouth. Mama sat on a bench away from the other chatting mothers. She had one bare foot out of her slipper and rested it on top of the other foot still in its slipper. They, too, were new and hurt her. She looked tired. She was still waiting to hear about a better job than being a cook in a dormitory. I could see thoughts which made her cranky cross her face.

By the time we were back in the office for the part called The Interview, which was really a test to see if I could speak perfect Standard English, I knew something was funny. I could smell it.

The woman tester was young and Japanese and smiley. I relaxed, thinking for sure I wouldn't have to act "put on" with her. But she kept after me to say the printed words on the picture cards that she, now unsmiling, held before my eyes.

"Da bolacano," I repeated politely at the cone shaped mountain where a spiral of smoke signaled into the crayon-shaded air. She must have drawn it.

She shook her head. "Again."

"Da BO-LO-CA-NO," I repeated loudly. Maybe like O-Jiji with the stink ear on his left side, she couldn't hear "We wen' go 'n see da bolocano," I explained confidentially to her. And what a big flat *puka* it was, I thought, ready to tell her the picture made a clear mistake.

"It's the vol-cano," she enunciated clearly, forcing me to watch her mouth move aggressively. She continued with downcast eyes. " 'We went to see the vol-cano.' You can go wait outside, okay?"

Outside I wondered why—if she had seen it for real—she drew it all wrong.

Mama shrugged it off as we trudged home.

"Neva' mind. Get too many stuck shet ladies ova dea. People no need act, Lei. You wait. You gon' get one good education, not like me."

That was how I ended up at Ka'ahumanu School which was non-English Standard. Its front yard sported massive flower beds of glowing red and yellow canna lilies arranged in neat rows, which were weeded and watered daily by the students. Teachers at Ka'ahumanu were large in size, often Hawaiian or Portuguese with only an occasional wiry Chinese or Japanese lady in sight. There was a surprise *haole* teacher who came in to teach art and hug kids. Many teachers wore bright hibiscus blooms stuck into their pugs of upswept hair. They didn't hold back on any emotions as they swept through the main yard like part of a tide of orderliness, lining up their wriggly children into classes. They cuffed the bad and patted the heads of the obedient as they counted us. They were magnetic forces with commanding voices, backbones at full attention and bright flowers perched like flags on the tops of their heads. When we stood in formation, the first ritual of the morning, rumors of all kinds went through our lines. I learned right away that on special holidays the cafeteria might even serve *laulau* and *poi* which we would help to prepare. Now that was worth waiting for.

I had resolved that in Honolulu I would have friends "fo' real." To this goal I studied the children at play and kept a silent watch before venturing in. When I forgot this logic and opened my mouth, it almost cost me my appetite to get educated. Because I occupied a fantasy world of vividly drawn characters from books and people I had made up for the lonely times in Kohala, I could go "off on a toot" and momentarily forget the real ones in front of me. I had gotten used to amusing myself in that way even while other kids swirled in activity around me.

I was in a dreamy mood when I first ran into Mrs. Vincente, who was to be my teacher. As a human being she was an impressive creation, since her bulk was unsettling and her head quite small. As she waddle-walked toward me, I made a fatal error. I mistook her for an illustration in a library book I had grown fond of in Kohala. She was a dead ringer for the character I thought I was seeing right before my nose. And why not? The first day of school was supposed to be the beginning of new and exciting things in my life. Everything so far had been surprising.

Therefore, I squealed out loud in pleasure, "Oh, Mrs. Piggy-Winkle!" at the sight of the pink-fleshed mountain topped by a salad plate-sized orange hibiscus. Did I truly think she would be equally delighted to see me? Mrs. Vincente, as I learned later, would never forget me. At the moment of our meeting, she grabbed me by the back of my neck and shook me fiercely until I blubbered.

Teachers came running; students formed a mob around our frantic struggling, and the school principal, Mrs. Kealoha-Henry, saved me.

As I stood sobbing in shivers from the wild shaking, Mrs. Vincente lectured me and the others on good manners. I shook my head in a no-no-no when she asked in an emotional voice, "Do you understand now?" It took all of Mrs. Kealoha-Henry's counsel to keep Mrs. Vincente away from me.

Grabbing the opportunity, I ran all the way back home where long after she came home from work, Mama found me hiding out in the laundry shed. I didn't return to school for several days after that. But my mother's continual nagging, bribery and my own plain boredom finally wore me down. I vowed not to talk at school, in the name of personal safety. And I would forget imagination.

When I returned, I learned another lesson, although this one, also, started out in confusion. Back at Ka'ahumanu School the white-columned building seemed enormous. Without Mama for support, I needed to report my string of absences to the office. Retreating into passive silence, I stood in the main hallway in front of the office with its impressive counter, convinced I was in trouble. The dark paneling and polished wood flooring came together into a tunnel of cool air where important things happened, and people spoke in official whispers. Hanging high on the wall against the painted white wood, positioned to face the person entering up the broad steps through the columned entrance was a large portrait of Queen Ka'ahumanu, our school's namesake. Someone had placed an offering bouquet of many-colored flowers under the picture. I studied her fully fleshed face, the insignia of rank in the background and her guarded expression. In return her eyes reviewed me, a small girl who wasn't sure what to do next.

As I stalled and paced the corridor, the morning bell rang, and all the other children disappeared. Alone in my patch of indecision, with flashing eyes, I mapped out how and where I would run if I had to. I balanced on one bare foot and then the other, while I studied the ancient lady's clear-eyed regard.

When Mrs. Kealoha-Henry found me, she laughed in surprise.

"So you did come back. And now you have met the Queen. Do you know her story? No? Well, I didn't think so."

The principal, a plump woman who wore old fashioned glasses which dangled from a neckpiece onto the front of her shirtwaist, told me then and there about Queen Ka'ahumanu, the *Kuhina Nui*. I learned that she was a favorite child and a favorite wife, that her hair was called *ehu*, meaning it was reddish unlike that of other Hawaiians of her time, and that she was *hapa*—of mixed blood, probably from Spanish ancestors. Mrs. Kealoha-Henry suspected the conquistadores, whose helmets the Hawaiian *alii* had copied in feathers, had been the first Europeans in Hawai'i. I heard the kindly stranger saying that I, too, must be *hapa*. To test me she tried out some Hawaiian, and when I answered correctly, "*Aloha kakahiaha*," she nodded favorably. She suggested a visit to the school library, where I would be welcome to read more about the Queen and what she did with the tremendous power she held at the end of her life.

Mrs. Kealona-Henry put her hands on my shoulders and turned me in the direction of the polished *koa* wood steps that led to the second floor. She would take care of the absences.

Although I hoped that the principal had not confused me with someone else who was Hawaiian by blood, I was very pleased with the thrilling story. Her comments became the bond between the Queen and me. I felt lucky that I went to a school where a *hapa* was the boss—in fact, commanded tribute. After all, I did have the reddish hair, or some of it, and if I was *hapa* as she said, then that was the reason for my being different from the others. I felt lighter whenever I looked at Queen Ka'ahumanu's portrait from then on. Every day the Queen's round face gave me a signal that I was okay: a small thing, but necessary for someone so hungry for a sign.

Still, no matter how hard I squinted, the hair depicted in the painting showed no sign of being red. Never mind, I told myself, she was right there, up high, and she looked at me affectionately, if I kept up the squint. Whenever I needed to, I found my way back to the hallway to stand in the breeze and acknowledge the power of our kinship.

I had singled out Darleen Nishimura, a sixth grader, as my new model. I wanted to grow up to look just like her, even though she despised me.

Darleen looked so dainty and petite as she completed every action with grace. I tagged along behind her as she received smiles and praises, followed her as she delivered newspapers for her older brothers. But when she saw me, she looked annoyed and tried to shake me. She often escaped by cutting through a yard unknown to me. She made a clippety-clop sound with her merry flopping slippers, a sound which left you with a carefree rhythm. When she laughed, she covered her teeth delightfully with a hand in the way some of the older Japanese women did. I practiced and got nowhere. Never mind that Darleen wouldn't give me the time of day. Now I could forget it. Queen Ka'ahumanu was somber and regal; she never giggled.

One day I spotted another girl, this one chubby and my own age, standing in front of the painting. She quickly placed a white ginger blossom on the *koa* table and disappeared with a smile at me. Later, I heard her name was Monica. When we played in the school yard together, she revealed the secret of her full name: Monica Mahealani Michiko Macadangdang. Happily memorizing it on the spot, I learned that choosing friends wasn't the only way you got them; some chose you, if you were lucky.

Midway through the year I was happy enough to be going to school there, skipping down the streets extra early, eager to help water the taro patch and the red and gold lilies.

Three years later I was a bonafide Ka'ahumanu Kid, as accustomed as any one of my classmates to the school routine. Our neighbor Mrs. Lee, who lived on our block, must have seen my enthusiasm. She entrusted her only son, who had been living in Makawao, Maui, to my care since we were both in the fourth grade. Joseph and I walked to school together on his first day I felt a nudge from one side and a soft pinch from the other.

Just before the first morning bell rang, the whispers traveled around. We were aware that our teacher was moving down the line to study each one of us. Our voices were high, and our faces as busy as the noisy birds in the banyan outside. Always chattering, always in tune with our buddies, always watching, we knew how to move together on our quiet bare feet, without getting caught talking. We studied how to do it.

"Pssssssssst . . ."

"Joseph. Make quick. We gotta line up; no talk. Standupstraight. Sing loud or she gon' make us guys sing one mo' time."

"She checking da guys' clothes first, if clean or what. Bumbye she gon' look our finganail and den check our hair behind da eah, l'dat."

The clanging bell brought us to silent attention.

Joseph looked completely blank. Unconcerned, he, being new, had no understanding of the importance of our morning classroom ritual. He didn't even pretend to mouth the words of Mrs. Vincente's favorite greeting, "Good Morning, Deah Tea-cha, Goooood Mor-ning to Youuu."

"W'at fo' she like check us in da eah?" Joseph's slow whisper tickled.

Before I could answer importantly, 'Cuz got *ukus*, some guys, you stupid doo-doo head," and think, "But not us guys," our teacher was standing right in front of us. Mrs. Vincente looked grim. Her gold-rimmed eyeglasses gave off glints in the pools of sunlight, evidence of real daylight outside, which invaded our dark, high-ceilinged and wood-paneled classroom.

She was the one who taught us to sing "Old Plantation *Nani Ole*" (Oooll . . . Plan-tay-shun . . . Na-ni . . . Ohlay) and "Ma-sa's (never her way, Massa's) in the Cold, Cold Ground," her favorite mournful melodies. She had turned to making us sing in order to drill us on our English skills, so lacking were we in motivation.

Frequently Mrs. Vincente spoke sharply to us about the inappropriate silences of our group. She complained that too often we spoke out of turn but "rarely contributed to the discussion." She must have believed that we didn't absorb anything that she lectured about repeatedly. She confided that she was "disappointed in" us or we had "disappointed Teacher" or she was "sorry to have to disappoint" us, "however," we had done something wrong again.

She was a puzzle.

The oriental kids—for that was our label—in the room knew better than to open their mouths just to lose face, and the part-Hawaiian and Portuguese kids knew they would get lickings one way or another if they talked, so we all firmly agreed that silence was golden.

Never would an adult female loom up as large to me as Mrs. Vincente did then. I could see her face only when I sat at a safe distance with a desk for protection. If she approached—in all her girth she was most graceful moving across her neatly waxed floor—her hands took my complete attention. When they were ready to direct us, I felt the way I did when Mama showed me what the red light at the crosswalk was for. When Teacher stood very near me, I couldn't see her tiny eyes, because the soft underpart of her delicate chin transfixed me so that I could not understand the words she mouthed. I got my mouth wrenched up to be ready for an alert answer, just in case she eyeballed me. Somehow whenever I had to respond to her I managed to get the subject and verb unmatched—"Yes, ma'am. We is ready fo' class"—even though she drilled us on the continual sin of the mixed singular and plural, because it was so fascinating to see her furious reaction to what she called Broken English, which none of us could fix.

Passing outside by Room 103, 1 overheard her passionate argument with another teacher who wanted to introduce the hula in our PE exercises. Mrs. V.'s reasoning escaped me, but I knew she was against it unconditionally. I stayed hidden in the *ti* leaves under her window just to hear the rush of her escaping emotions as she grew angrier and pronounced words more distinctly.

Mrs. Vincente's face was averted from the horrors she saw represented in the existence of our whole class. To her, we were not by any means brought up well, didn't know our p's and q's, often acted in an un-American fashion as evidenced by our smelly home lunches, dressed in an uncivilized manner, and refused moreover to speak properly or respectfully as soon as her back was turned. Her standards were in constant jeopardy.

Our concentrated looks centered on her totally. We followed her every move, a fact which unnerved her briefly each morning. To hide her discomfort, revealed by streams of perspiration, she swabbed her face delicately with a lace-trimmed hankie.

She shook her head at Francene Fuchigami, whose mother made her wear around her neck an amulet in a yellowed cotton pouch which also contained a foul incense and active herbs. The blessed *o-mamori* guaranteed the absence of both slippery vermin and casual friends.

Francene and I competed for Mrs. V's favor, no matter how much we accepted her obvious but peculiar interest in the boys only. She favored them shamelessly, but bullied them at every opportunity.

We brought Mrs. Vincente homegrown anthuriums, tangerines and sticky notes: "Dear Mrs. V., Your so nice. And your so pretty, too," with high hopes. *Maybe she will like me now*, ran the thread of wishful thinking. Winning her favor took all of my attention. I had to stay neat and clean and pretend to be a good girl, somebody who could "make nice-nice" and "talk high *makamak*." To win Mrs. Vincente over, I saw that I would have to be able to speak properly, a complicated undertaking demanding control of all my body parts, including my eyes and hands, which wandered away when my mouth opened up. Therefore, in a compromise with my desire to shine, I resolved to keep absolutely quiet, stand up with the stupid row and ignore the one I wanted to impress.

Mrs. Vincente was one of us, she claimed, because she herself had grown up in our "very neighborhood." Her school, too, she once let out, had been non-English Standard. We were surprised to hear her say that her family was related to the Kahanus who owned the corner grocery store. We knew them, the ones who used to have money. The brothers Eugene and Franklin Teves claimed they knew for sure she couldn't be kin to anyone they recognized, in answer to the other class who called her "The Portagee Teacha." She spoke, dressed and carried herself in a manner that was unlike any of the women I observed at home, but she fit right in with our other teachers who, like her, had gone to Normal School and shared her authoritative ways.

Difficult as she was, we could understand her preoccupation. Getting rid of *ukus* was a tedious job connected with beratings from your mother and lickings from your father. We always knew who carried *ukus* and were swift to leave that child alone. News traveled fast. All the same we could each remember what it felt like to be the "odd man out," which was the name of one of our favorite games.

To have *ukus*, to tell your close friends not to tell the others, and to have them keep the secret: that was the test of friendship. Like the garbage men who worked under the *uku pau* system, which meant that no gang or worker was finished until everybody on that truck helped the final guy unload his very last can, and everybody could quit, *uku* season wasn't over until every kid got rid of every last clinging egg.

At Christmastime, Mrs. Vincente wrapped up a useful comb for each and every one of us. At the end of the year we raced each other to be the first one lined up at her massive desk.

We would each shyly request her autograph with the suggested correct phrases, "Please, Mrs. Vincente," and "Thank you, Teacha," so she must have been what we had grown to expect a teacher to be.

Because of Mrs. Vincente I wanted to become a teacher. I wanted to wield power and know how to get my way. I wanted to be the one who would point out a minute, luminous silver egg sack stuck on a coarse black hair; shake it vigorously with arm held out far away from body, and declare victoriously, "Infestation . . . of . . . pediculosis!"

She would then turn to address the entire class. "This child must go directly to the nurse's office." She would speak firmly but in a softer tone to the kid. "Do not return to our room until you can bring me the white clearance certificate signed by both of your parents."

Completely silent during class, I practiced those words at home while I played school. I turned to the class. I gave the warning to the kid. Mrs. Vincente was not to be taken lightly.

The day Joseph learned about *ukus*, I figured out teachers.

Facing him, Mrs. Vincente demanded to know the new boy's name from his own mouth.

"Joseph Kaleialoha Lee."

"Say ma'am."

"Hah?"

"You must say 'Joseph Kaleialoha Lee, ma'am.'"

"Joseph-Kaleialoha-Lee-ma'am!"

"Hold out your hands, please."

Evidently he had not paid attention, the biggest error of our collective class, one which we heard about incessantly. He had not watched her routine, which included a search for our hidden fingernail dirt. He held his hands palms up. I shuddered.

Mrs. Vincente studied Joseph with what we called the "stink eye," but he still didn't catch on. She must have considered his behavior insubordinate, because he did not seem retarded or neglected as he was wearing his new long, khaki pants and a freshly starched aloha shirt.

She reached into the big pocket of her apron and took out a fat wooden ruler. Our silence was audible. She stepped up a little nearer to Joseph, almost blocking out all the air and light around us so that her sharp features and steely voice cut through to reach our wobbly attention.

"What grade are you in now, young man?"

Joseph was silent as if in deep thought. Why wouldn't he say the answer? I nudged him quickly on his side with the hand nearest his body.

"Fot grade," he blurted in a small, panicky wheeze.

She turned on us all, enraged at our murmurs of anticipation. We knew for sure he would get it now.

Some girl giggled hysterically in a shrill whinny. "Heengheengheeng . . ." Probably Japanese.

"Quiet."

Businesslike, she returned to Joseph with her full attention, peering into his ear. "Say th, th, th. Speak slowly." He heard the warning in her voice.

"Tha, tha, tha." Joseph rippled droplets of sweat.

"Th, th, th . . . everyone, say it all together: the tree!"

We practiced loudly with Joseph leading the chorus, relieved now to be part of the mass of voices.

"Say the tree, not da chree."

"The tree, not da chree."

"Fourth grade, not fot grade."

"Foth grade, not foth grade."

With a rapid searching movement which caught most of us off guard, Mrs. Vincente swung around to face Darcie Ah Sing, whose hand was still stuck in her curly brown hair when she was spotted scratching herself vigorously. Mrs. V. stared blackly into Darcie's tight curls with unshakeable attention. In a matter of seconds, with an upward swoop of her palm, Teacha found the louse at the nape of the exposed neck and pronounced her memorable conclusion, ending with "by both of your parents," indicting Darcie's whole family into the crime.

"March yourself into the office, young lady." Mrs. Vincente wrung a hankie between her pudgy hands with tight motions. Head hanging, Darcie moved out wordlessly to the school nurse's station for the next inspection. We knew that she would be "shame" for a long time and stared at our dusty toes in hopeless sympathy.

When we were allowed to sit at our desks (after practicing the sks sound for desks: "sssk'sss, sssk'sss, dehss-kuss, dehss-kuss, dehss-kuss, not desses, dessess, dessess"), we were hooked into finishing our tasks of busywork and wearing our masks of obedience, totally subdued.

Then she read to us, as she explained that she was "wont to do when the occasion arose," while we sat at our desks with our hands folded quietly as she had trained us. She enunciated each word clearly for our benefit, reminding us that by the time we graduated we would be speaking "proper English" and forgot the *uku* check for the day. Her words stuck like little pearly grains into the folds of my brain. I pondered how to talk *haole* while she continued to lecture.

"The child . . . the school . . . the tree . . ." I could not hear the meaning of her words and scratched my head idly but in secret, my head dodging her line of vision. I yearned to master her knowledge, but dared not make myself the target of her next assault. I was not getting any smarter, but itchier by the minute, more eager than anyone to break free into the oasis of recess.

When the loud buzzer finally shattered the purring motor of her voice, we knew better than to whoop and scatter. We gathered our things formally and waited silently to be dismissed. If we made noise we would have to sit inside in agony, paying attention to the whole endless, meaningless story which sounded like all the ones before and wasted our precious time. Even Joseph caught on.

He said, "Whew, 'as waste time."

Once we were outside, surveying the situation, we saw two teams of the bigger boys who pulled at a heavy knotted rope from opposite ends. Joseph's bare feet dug into the ground right in back of Junior Boy, the tug-of-war captain. Clearly he wouldn't need any more of my guidance if Junior Boy had let him in. Beads of wetness sparkled off their bodies as the tight chain of grunting boys held fast under the bright sun.

Noisy clumps of kids skipped rope and kicked up the grass, twisting bodies and shining faces, all together in motion. Racing around the giant banyan, for no good reason, I scream-giggled, "Wheeeeeha-ha-hah!" Like a wildcat I roared up the trunk of the chree . . . just to see if I could.

Joseph spotted me. "Too good, you!" he yelled.

While the girls played jacks, and the boys walked their board stilts, Joseph and I moved around groups trading milk bottle covers and playing marbles. We wondered aloud to each other. We spread the word.

"Ho, w'atchoo tink?"

"Must be da teacha wen' catch *ukus* befo'."

"Not . . ."

"Not not!"

"Cannot be . . ."

"Can can!"

"Yeah?"

"Ay, yeah. O' how else she can spock' em dat fast?"

That made me laugh, the thought of Mrs. V. picking through her careful topknot. She would have to moosh away the hibiscus to get in a finger. I mimed her by scratching through the hair I let hang down in front of my face. When I swept it back professionally with the palm of my hand, I threw in a cross-eyed crazy look. Joseph pretended to "spock *uku*" in my hair as he took on Mrs. V.'s exaggerated ladylike manner to hold onto one of my ears like a handle and peer into the endless *puka*.

"Ho, man," he proclaimed, "get so planny inside."

The recess bell rang, ending our sweet freedom. We pranced back to the classroom in a noisy herd. Teacha gave us the Look. We grew cautious. We would spend the next hour silently tracking Mrs. Vincente's poised head, while Joseph and I smiled knowingly at each other.

Eyes gleaming, Mrs. Vincente never disappointed any of us, because she always stuck right on her lessons and never let up at all. She stayed mean as ever, right on top of the class. As for us, fourth grade *ukus* could appreciate the effort . . . so much not letting go.

Questions for Reflection and Analysis

1. What strikes you about the story as a whole? Is there a particular aspect of the story that elicits a memory or concern about teaching and learning?

2. How does Mrs. Vincente's attitude toward the children's heritage language and traditions influence her approach to teaching? How, in turn, does her attitude affect how the children feel about themselves?

3. How are the students' school identities similar to or different from their identities outside of the classroom? How do these shifting identities help to explain the children's resistance to or acceptance of Mrs. Vincente and her approach?

4. How does the narrator's response to the story about Queen Ka'ahumanu compare to her response to the classroom lessons? What does her response suggest about the role of culture in the language classroom?

5. What effect does the children's use of their heritage language have on you as a reader? What insight do these instances of language give you into the challenges these children face?

Photograph by Han Nguyen: Hanvp@aol.com

II.

CHILDHOOD TRANSFORMATIONS

The presence of children who are not fully conversant or literate in English presents special challenges for teachers in English-medium classrooms. In these four stories, the authors portray classrooms and home situations in which children are invited or expected to try on new linguistic and cultural identities. We see how the children respond to the idea of learning a new language, how they resist or adapt to their teachers' or parents' expectations, and how they develop as language learners over time. We also observe how teachers' or family members' responses to the children may promote or impede their language and literacy acquisition. In Rudy Wiebe's "Speaking Saskatchewan," a German-speaking Mennonite boy enters an English-language school in Canada. In Francisco Jiménez's "Inside Out," the son of migrant workers from Mexico enters first grade in a U.S. public school. In Andrew Lam's "Show and Tell," a refugee from Vietnam joins an eighth grade U.S. classroom. In Lan Samantha Chang's "The Unforgetting," the son of an immigrant couple from China progresses from fourth grade through high school in a U.S. school system. Together, these stories demonstrate how teachers, parents, and children of different language backgrounds can meet, interact, misunderstand, and ultimately transform one another.

■ *Speaking Saskatchewan*

Rudy Wiebe

(1934–)

Rudy Wiebe was born in Canada. His parents emigrated from the Soviet Union when he was four years old. He did not speak English until age six. His family followed the Mennonite tradition of speaking only German: Low German at home and High German at Church. He received a B.A. and an M.A. in Creative Writing from University of Alberta, Edmonton, where he was a professor of Creative Writing and English from 1967 to 1992. Among his many books are the award-winning *The Temptations of Big Bear* (1973), *A Discovery of Strangers* (1994), and *Of This Earth: A Mennonite Boyhood in the Boreal Forest* (2007).

In summer the thick green poplar leaves clicked and flickered at him, in winter the stiff spruce rustled with voices. The boy, barefoot in the heat or trussed up like a lumpy package against the fierce, silver cold, went alone to the bush where everything spoke: the warm rocks, the flit of quick, small animals, a dart of birds, tree trunks, burning air, ground, the squeaky snow: everything as he breathed and became aware, its language clear as the water of his memory when he lay in the angle of the house rafters at night listening to the mosquitoes slowly find him under his blanket, though he had his eyes shut and only one ear uncovered. Everything spoke, and it spoke Low German.

Like his mother. She would call him long, long into the summer evening when it seemed the sun burned all night down into the north, call long and slow as if she were already weeping and when he appeared beside her she would bend her wide powerful hands about his head and kiss him so hard his eyes rang. "Why don't you answer, you?" she would speak against his hair. "Why don't you ever answer when I call, it's so dark, why don't you ever say a word?" While he nuzzled his face into the damp apron at the fold of her thigh, and soon her words would be over and he heard her skin and warm apron smelling of saskatoon jam and dishes and supper buns love him back.

His sister laughed at his solitary silence. "In school are thirty kids," she would say, "you'll have to talk, and English at that. You can't say Low German there, and if you don't answer English when she asks, the teacher will make you stand in the corner."

"Right in front, of people?" he would ask, fearfully.

"Yeah, in front of every one of them, your face against the wall. So you better start to talk. English too."

And she would try to teach him English names for things, but he did not listen to that. Rather, when he was alone he practiced standing in the corners of walls. Their logs shifted and cracked, talking. Walls were very good, especially where they came together so warm in winter.

But outside was even better, and he followed a quiet trail of the muskrat that had dented the snow with its tail between bullrushes sticking out of the slough ice, or waited for the coyote to turn and see him, its paw lifted and about to touch a drift, its jaw opening on a red tongue laughing with him. In summer he heard a mother bear talk to her cubs among the willows of the horse pasture, though he did not see them, but he found their sluffing paw prints in the spring snow and his father said something would have to be done if they came that close to the pig fence again. The boy knew his father refused to own a gun, but their nearest neighbor west gladly hunted everywhere to shoot whatever he heard about and so he folded his hands over the huge, wet prints and whispered in Low German, "Don't visit here any more. It's dangerous."

The school sat on the corner, just below the hill where the road turned south along the creek to the church and the store. He never looked at the school, the tiny panes of its four huge windows staring at him, just staring. The day before he had to go there every day like his sister, the planes came for the first time.

Their horses were pulling the wagon up the hill as slowly, steadily as they always did and it happened very fast, almost before he looked around. There had been a rumble from somewhere like thunder, far away, though the sky was clear sunlight and his father had just said in a week they could start bindering the oats, it was ripening so well, and his mother sat beside him broad and straight as always, her braided, waist-long hair coiled up for church under her hat when the roaring planes were there as he turned, four yellow-and-black, louder than anything he had ever heard. West over the school and the small grain fields and pastures and all the trees and hills to the far edge of the world. His father would not look around, holding the horses in carefully, muttering, "Now it comes here too, that war training," but the boy was looking at his mother. Perhaps his own face looked like that next morning when the yellow planes roared over the school at recess, so low he saw huge glass eyes in a horrible leather head glare down at him before he screamed and ran inside to the desk where his sister had said he must sit. When he opened his eyes the face of the teacher was there, her gentle face very close, smiling almost up-side-down at him between the iron legs of the desk beneath which he crouched. Her gentle voice.

"Come," she said, "come," and after a moment he scrambled to his feet; he thought she was speaking Low German because he did not yet know that what that word meant was spoken the same in English. Not touching him, she led him between desks to a cupboard against the wall opposite the windows and opened its narrow door. Books. He has never imagined so many books. There may be a million.

She is, of course, speaking to him in English and later, when he remembers that moment again and again, he will never be able to explain how he can understand what she is saying. The open book in her hand shows him countless words: words, she tells him, he can now only see the shape of, but he will be able to hear them when he learns to read, and that the word "READ" in English is the same as the word "SPEAK," *raed*, in Low German and through reading all the people of the world will speak to him from books, when he reads he will be able to hear them, and then he will understand. He is staring at what he later knows are a few worn books on a few shelves, and then staring back at the few visible but as yet unintelligible words revealed in her hands and slowly he understands that there are shelves and shelves of books in great stacks on many, many floors inside all the walls of the enormous libraries of the world where he will go and read: where the knowing she will now help him discover within himself will allow him to listen to human voices speaking from everywhere and every age, saying everything, things both dreadful and beautiful, and all that can be imagined between them; and that he will listen. He will listen to those voices speaking now for as long as he lives.

Questions for Reflection and Analysis

1. What strikes you about the story as a whole? Is there a particular aspect of the story that elicits a memory or concern about teaching and learning?

2. Taking the entire story into account, from beginning to end, what do the boy's responses to the various voices and languages that surround him, human and otherwise, reveal about his inner life and his sensitivity to sounds and words? What do his responses reveal about his language development?

3. Under what circumstances, and why, does the boy listen, remain silent, or speak?

4. What effect does his sister's description of school have on the boy and why? How accurately does his sister's description of school reflect the boy's actual experience in the classroom?

5. How does the teacher's theory about the relationship between reading and understanding English apply to the boy's own experience acquiring English? How might her theory account for the way the boy understands the natural world that surrounds him?

■ *Inside* **O**ut

Francisco Jiménez

(1943–)

Francisco Jiménez was born in Mexico and was four years old when his family migrated illegally to the United States. He spent much of his childhood as a migrant worker alongside his family, with no permanent home or regular schooling. When he was in the eighth grade, his family was deported back to Mexico, but they were able to return to the United States legally. A graduate of Santa Clara University, he attended Harvard University, received a Master's Degree and Ph.D. from Columbia University, and is now a professor of Modern Languages and Literatures at Santa Clara University. His award-winning books include *The Christmas Gift/El regalo de Navidad* (2000) and *Breaking Through* (2001).

"I remember being hit on the wrists with a twelve-inch ruler because I did not follow directions in class," Roberto answered in a mildly angry tone when I asked him about his first year of school. "But how could I?" he continued, "the teacher gave them in English."

"So what did you do?" I asked, rubbing my wrists.

"I always guessed what the teacher wanted me to do. And when she did not use the ruler on me, I knew I had guessed right," he responded. "Some of the kids made fun of me when I tried to say something in English and got it wrong," he went on. "I had to repeat first grade."

I wish I had not asked him, but he was the only one in the family, including Papá and Mamá, who had attended school. I walked away. I did not speak or understand English either, and I already felt anxious. Besides, I was excited about going to school for the first time that following Monday. It was late

---

January and we had just returned, a week before, from Corcoran where my family picked cotton. We settled in "Tent City," a labor camp owned by Sheehey Strawberry Farms located about ten miles east of Santa Maria.

On our first day of school, Roberto and I got up early. I dressed in a pair of overalls, which I hated because they had suspenders, and a flannel checkered shirt, which Mamá had bought at the Goodwill store. As I put on my cap, Roberto reminded me that it was bad manners to wear a hat indoors. I thought of leaving it at home so that I would not make the mistake of forgetting to take it off in class, but I decided to wear it. Papá always wore a cap and I did not feel completely dressed for school without it.

On our way out to catch the school bus, Roberto and I said goodbye to Mamá. Papá had already left to look for work, either topping carrots or thinning lettuce. Mamá stayed home to take care of Trampita, and to rest because she was expecting another baby.

When the school bus arrived, Roberto and I climbed in and sat together. I took the window seat and, on the way, watched endless rows of lettuce and cauliflower whiz by. The furrows that came up to the two lane road looked like giant legs running alongside us. The bus made several stops to pick up kids and, with each stop, the noise inside got louder. Some kids were yelling at the top of their lungs. I did not know what they were saying. I was getting a headache. Roberto had his eyes closed and was frowning. I did not disturb him. I figured he was getting a headache too.

By the time we got to Main Street School, the bus was packed. The bus driver parked in front of the red brick building and opened the door. We all poured out. Roberto, who had attended the school the year before, accompanied me to the main office where we met the principal, Mr. Sims, a tall, red-headed man with bushy eyebrows and hairy hands. He patiently listened to Roberto who, using the little English he knew, managed to enroll me in the first grade.

Mr. Sims walked me to my classroom. I liked it as soon as I saw it because, unlike our tent, it had wooden floors, electric lights, and heat. It felt cozy. He introduced me to my teacher, Miss Scalapino, who smiled, repeating my name, "Francisco." It was the only word I understood the whole time she and the principal talked. They repeated it each time they glanced at me. After he left, she showed me to my desk, which was at the end of the row of desks closest to the windows. There were no other kids in the room yet.

I sat at my desk and ran my hand over its wooden top. It was full of scratches and dark, almost black, ink spots. I opened the top and inside were a book, a box of crayons, a yellow ruler, a thick pencil, a pair of scissors. To my left, under the windows, was a dark wooden counter the length of the room. On top of it, right next to my desk, was a caterpillar in a large jar. It looked just like the ones I had seen in the fields. It was yellowish green with black bands and it moved very slowly, without making any sound.

I was about to put my hand in the jar to touch the caterpillar when the bell rang. All the kids lined up outside the classroom door and then walked in quietly and took their seats. Some of them looked at me and giggled. Embarrassed and nervous, I looked at the caterpillar in the jar. I did this every time someone looked at me.

Miss Scalapino started speaking to the class and I did not understand a word she was saying. The more she spoke, the more anxious I became. By the end of the day, I was very tired of hearing Miss Scalapino talk because the sounds made no sense to me. I thought that perhaps by paying close attention, I would begin to understand, but I did not. I only got a headache, and that night, when I went to bed, I heard her voice in my head.

For days I got headaches from trying to listen, until I learned a way out. When my head began to hurt, I let my mind wander. Sometimes I imagined myself flying out of the classroom and over the fields where Papá worked and landing next to him and surprising him. But when I daydreamed, I continued to look at the teacher and pretend I was paying attention because Papá told me it was disrespectful not to pay attention, especially to grown-ups.

It was easier when Miss Scalapino read to the class from a book with illustrations because I made up my own stories, in Spanish, based on the pictures. She held the book with both hands above her head and walked around the classroom to make sure every one got a chance to see the pictures, most of which were of animals. I enjoyed looking at them and making up stories, but I wished I understood what she was reading.

In time I learned some of my classmates' names. The one I heard the most and therefore learned first was "Curtis." Curtis was the biggest, strongest, and most popular kid in the class. Everyone wanted to be his friend and to play with him. He was always chosen captain when the kids formed teams. Since I was the smallest kid in the class and did not know English, I was chosen last.

I preferred to hang around Arthur, one of the boys who knew a little Spanish. During recess, he and I played on the swings and I pretended to be a Mexican movie star, like Jorge Negrete or Pedro Infante, riding a horse and singing the *corridos* we often heard on the car radio. I sang them to Arthur as we swung back and forth, going as high as we could.

But when I spoke to Arthur in Spanish and Miss Scalapino heard me, she said "NO!" with body and soul. Her head turned left and right a hundred times a second and her index finger moved from side to side as fast as a windshield wiper on a rainy day. "English, English," she repeated. Arthur avoided me whenever she was around.

Often during recess I stayed with the caterpillar. Sometimes it was hard to spot him because he blended in with the green leaves and twigs. Every day I brought him leaves from the pepper and cypress trees that grew on the playground.

Just in front of the caterpillar, lying on top of the cabinet, was a picture book of caterpillars and butterflies. I went through it, page by page, studying all the pictures and running my fingers lightly over the caterpillars and the bright wings of the butterflies and the many patterns on them. I knew caterpillars turned into butterflies because Roberto had told me, but I wanted to know more. I was sure information was in the words written underneath each picture in large black letters. I tried to figure them out by looking at the pictures. I did this so many times that I could close my eyes and see the words, but I could not understand what they meant.

My favorite time in school was when we did art, which was every afternoon, after the teacher had read to us. Since I did not understand Miss Scalapino when she explained the art lessons, she let me do whatever I wanted. I drew all kinds of animals but mostly birds and butterflies. I sketched them in pencil and then colored them using every color in my crayon box. Miss Scalapino even tacked one of my drawings up on the board for everyone to see. After a couple of weeks it disappeared and I did not know how to ask where it had gone.

One cold Thursday morning, during recess, I was the only kid on the playground without a jacket. Mr. Sims must have noticed I was shivering because that afternoon, after school, he took me to his office and pulled out a green jacket from a large cardboard box that was full of used clothes and toys. He handed it to me and gestured for me to try it on. It smelled like graham crackers. I put it on, but it was too big, so he rolled up the sleeves about two inches to make it fit. I took it home and showed it off to my parents. They smiled. I liked it because it was green and it hid my suspenders.

The next day I was on the playground wearing my new jacket and waiting for the first bell to ring when I saw Curtis coming at me like an angry bull. Aiming his head directly at me, and pulling his arms straight back with his hands clenched, he stomped up to me and started yelling. I did not understand him, but I knew it had something to do with the jacket because he began to pull on it, trying to take it off me. Next thing I knew he and I were on the ground wrestling. Kids circled around us. I could hear them yelling Curtis's name and something else. I knew I had no chance, but I stubbornly held on to my jacket. He pulled on one of the sleeves so hard that it ripped at the shoulder. He pulled on the right pocket and it ripped. Then Miss Scalapino's face appeared above. She pushed Curtis off of me and grabbed me by the back of the collar and picked me up off the ground. It took all the power I had not to cry.

On the way to the classroom Arthur told me that Curtis claimed the jacket was his, that he had lost it at the beginning of the year. He also said that the teacher told Curtis and me that we were being punished. We had to sit on the bench during recess for the rest of the week. I did not see the jacket again. Curtis got it but I never saw him wear it.

For the rest of the day, I could not even pretend I was paying attention to Miss Scalapino, I was so embarrassed. I laid my head on top of my desk and closed my eyes. I kept thinking about what had happened that morning. I wanted to fall asleep and wake up to find it was only a dream. The teacher called my name but I did not answer. I heard her walk up to me. I did not know what to expect. She gently shook me by the shoulders. Again, I did not respond. Miss Scalapino must have thought I was asleep because she left me alone, even when it was time for recess and everyone left the room.

Once the room was quiet, I slowly opened my eyes. I had had them closed for so long that the sunlight coming through the windows blinded me. I rubbed my eyes with the back of my hands and then looked to my left at the jar. I looked for the caterpillar but could not see it. Thinking it might be hidden, I put my hand in the jar and lightly stirred the leaves. To my surprise, the caterpillar had spun itself into a cocoon and had attached itself to a small twig. It looked like a tiny, cotton bulb, just like Roberto had said it would. I gently stroked it with my index finger, picturing it asleep and peaceful.

At the end of the school day, Miss Scalapino gave me a note to take home to my parents. Papá and Mamá did not know how to read, but they did not have to. As soon as they saw my swollen upper lip and the scratches on my left cheek, they knew what the note said. When I told them what happened, they were very upset but relieved that I did not disrespect the teacher.

For the next several days, going to school and facing Miss Scalapino was harder than ever. However, I slowly began to get over what happened that Friday. Once I got used to the routine in school and I picked up some English words, I felt more comfortable in class.

On Wednesday, May 23, a few days before the end of the school year, Miss Scalapino took me by surprise. After we were all sitting down and she had taken role, she called for everyone's attention. I did not understand what she said, but I heard her say my name as she held up a blue ribbon. She then picked up my drawing of the butterfly that had disappeared weeks before and held it up for everyone to see. She walked up to me and handed me the drawing and the silk blue ribbon that had a number one printed on it in gold. I knew then I had received first prize for my drawing. I was so proud I felt like bursting out of my skin. My classmates, including Curtis, stretched their necks to see the ribbon.

That afternoon, during our free period, I went over to check on the caterpillar. I turned the jar around, trying to see the cocoon. It was beginning to crack open. I excitedly cried out, "Look, look," pointing to it. The whole class, like a swarm of bees, rushed over to the counter. Miss Scalapino took the jar and placed it on top of a desk in the middle of the classroom so everyone could see it. For the next several minutes we all stood there watching the butterfly emerge from its cocoon, in slow motion.

At the end of the day, just before the last bell, Miss Scalapino picked up the jar and took the class outside to the playground. She placed the jar on the ground and we all circled around her. I had a hard time seeing over the other kids so, Miss Scalapino called me, and motioned for me to open the jar. I broke through the circle, knelt on the ground, and unscrewed the top. Like magic, the butterfly flew into the air, fluttering its wings up and down.

After school I waited in line for my bus in front of the playground. I proudly carried the blue ribbon in my right hand and the drawing in the other. Arthur and Curtis came up and stood behind me to wait for their bus. Curtis motioned for me to show him the drawing again. I held it up so he could see it.

"He really likes it, Francisco," Arthur said to me in Spanish.

"*¿Como se dice 'es tuyo' en inglés?*" I asked.

"It's yours," answered Arthur.

"It's yours," I repeated, handing the drawing to Curtis.

Questions for Reflection and Analysis

1. What strikes you about the story as a whole? Is there a particular aspect of the story that elicits a memory or concern about teaching and learning?

2. How do the narrator's feelings about attending school, shaped in part by his brother's description of his own educational experience, help or hinder his learning?

3. How does Miss Scalapino's response to the narrator's presence during his first days at school compare to the way she later responds to his ability to understand her lessons? What are the advantages or disadvantages of her different responses to the narrator?

4. How do the narrator's inner thoughts and feelings differ from his outward behavior? What insights can you draw from these differences about the way the narrator copes with the academic challenges in school? How might the teacher have behaved differently if she had known his inner thoughts?

5. What do you perceive to be the significance of the title?

■ *Show and Tell*

Andrew Lam

(1964–)

Andrew Lam was born in South Vietnam, the son of an officer in the South Vietnamese army. The family fled Vietnam in 1975 and eventually arrived in the United States. Lam did not learn English until age 12. After a brief career in biochemistry, he decided to become a writer and pursued a graduate degree in Creative Writing. An award-winning journalist, he is now an editor of the Pacific News Service and a regular commentator on National Public Radio's "All Things Considered." Lam co-edited *Once upon a Dream. . . : The Vietnamese-American Experience* (1995) and authored *Perfume Dreams: Reflections on the Vietnamese Diaspora* (2005).

Mr. K. brought in the new kid near the end of the semester during what he called oral presentations and everybody else called eighth grade Show and Tell. This is Cao Long Nguyen, he said, and he's from Vietnam and immediately mean old Billy said cool!

What's so cool about that? asked Kevin who sat behind him and Billy said, Idiot, don't you know anything, that's where my Daddy came back from with this big old scar on his chest and a bunch of grossed out stories. And that's where they have helicopters and guns and VCs and all this crazy shit. Billy would have gone on and on but Mr. K said, Billy, be quiet.

Mr. K. stood behind the new kid and drummed his fingers on the kid's skinny shoulders like they were little wings flapping. He tried to be nice to the new kid, I could tell, but the kid looked nervous anyway. The new kid

Andrew Lam, "Show and Tell." Originally published in *Crab Orchard Review,* 1998. Reprinted by permission of Andrew Lam.

stood like he was waiting to be thrown into the ocean the way he was hugging his green backpack in front of him like a life saver.

Cao Long Nguyen is a Vietnamese refugee, Mr. K. said and he turned around and wrote "Cao Long Nguyen—Refugee" in blue on the blackboard. Cao doesn't speak any English yet but he'll learn soon enough so let's welcome him, shall we, and we did. We all applauded but mean old Billy decided to boo him just for the hell of it and Kevin and a few others started to laugh and the new kid blushed like a little girl. When we were done applauding and booing Mr. K. gave him a seat in front of me and he sat down without saying hello to anybody, not even to me, his neighbor, and I had gone out of my way to flash my cutest smile to no effect. But right away I started to smell this nice smell from him. It reminded me of eucalyptus or something. I was going to ask him what it was but the new kid took out his Hello Kitty notebook and began to draw in it like he'd been doing it forever, drawing and drawing even when Show and Tell already started and it was, I'm sorry to say, my turn.

Tell you the truth, I didn't want it to be my turn. I can be funny and all but I hated being in front of the class as much as I hated anything. But what can you do? You go up when it's your turn, that's what. So when Mr. K. called my name I brought my family-tree chart and taped it on the blackboard under where Mr. K. wrote "Cao Long Nguyen—Refugee" but before I even started Billy said Bobby's so poor he only got half a tree and everybody laughed.

I wanted to say something back real bad right then and there. But as usual I held my tongue on the account that I was a little afraid of Billy. OK, I lie, more than a little afraid. But if I weren't so fearful of that big dumb ox I could have said a bunch of things like Well at least I have half a tree. Some people they only have sorry ass war mongers with big old scars for a Daddy or I could have said what's wrong with half a tree. It's much better than having a quarter of a brain or something like that.

Anyway, not everybody laughed at Billy's butt swipe of a comment. Mr. K., for instance, he didn't laugh. He looked sad, in fact, shaking his head like he was giving up on Billy and saying, Shh Billy, how many times do I have to tell you to be quiet in my class? And the new kid he didn't laugh neither. He just stared at my tree like he knew what it was but I doubt it 'cause it didn't even look like a tree. Then when he saw me looking at him, he blushed and pretended like he was busy drawing but I knew he wasn't. He was curious about my drawing, my half a tree.

If you want to know the awful truth it's only half a tree 'cause my Mama wouldn't tell me about the other half. Your Daddy was a jackass, she said, and so is his entire family and clan. That's all she ever said about him. But Mama, I said, it's for my Oral Presentation project and it's important but she said so what.

So nothing, that's what. So my Daddy hangs alone on this little branch on the left side. He left when I was four so I don't remember him very well. All I remember is him being real big and handsome. I remember him hugging and kissing and reading me a bedtime story once or twice and then he was gone. Only my sister Charlene remembers him well on account that she's three years older than me. Charlene remembers us having a nice house when my Daddy was still around and Mama didn't have to work. Then she remembers a lot of fighting and yelling and flying dishes and broken vases and stuff like that. One night when the battle between Mama and Daddy got so bad Charlene said that she found me hiding in the closet under a bunch of Mama's clothes with my eyes closed and my hands over my ears saying Stop, please, Stop, please, Stop like I was singing or chanting or something. Charlene remembers us moving to California; not long after that Daddy left us. I don't remember any of that stuff. It just feels like my entire life is spent living in a crummy apartment at the edge of the city and that Mama had been working at Max's Diner forever, and that she smoked and drank and cussed too goddamn much and she was always saying we should move somewhere else soon, go back to the South maybe, to New Orleans where we came from, but then we never ever did.

So what did I do? I started out with a big lie. I had rehearsed the whole night for it. I said my Daddy's dead. Dead from a car accident a long, long time ago. I said he was an orphan so that's why there's only half a tree—(so fuck you, Billy). Then I started on the other half. I know the other half real well 'cause all of Mama's relatives are crazy or suicidal and naturally I loved their stories. So I flew through them. There was my great-great-Granddaddy Charles Boyle the third who was this rich man in New Orleans and who had ten children and a big old plantation during the Civil War. Too bad he supported the losing side 'cause he lost everything and he killed himself after the war ended. Then there was my Grandaddy Jonathan Quentin who became a millionaire from owning a gold mine in Mexico and then he lost it all on alcohol and gambling and then he killed himself. And there was my Grandma Mary who was a sweetheart and who had three children and who killed herself before the bone cancer got to her and there were a bunch of cousins who went north and east and west and became pilots and doctors and lawyers and maybe some of them killed themselves too and I wouldn't be a bit surprised 'cause my Mama said it's kinda like a family curse or something. I went on like that for some time, going through a dozen or so people before I got to the best part: See here, that's my great-aunt Jenny Ann Quentin, I said, all alone on this little branch 'cause she's an old maid. She's still alive too, I said, ninety-seven years old and with only half a mind and she lives in this broken-down mansion outside of New Orleans and she wears old tattered clothes and talks to ghosts and curses them Yankees for winning the war. I saw her once when I was young, I told my captive audience. Great-aunt Jenny scared the heck out of me 'cause she had an old shotgun and everything and she didn't pay her electric bills so her big old house was always dark and scary and haunted. You stay overnight and they'll pull your legs or rearrange your furniture. In summary, had we won the war a hundred years ago, we might have all stayed around in the South. But as it is, my family tree has its leaves fallen all over the States. So that's it, there, now I'm done, thank you.

Tommy went after me. He told about stamp collecting and he brought three albums full of pretty stamps, stamps a hundred years old and stamps as far as the Vatican and Sri Lanka. He told how hard it was for him to have a complete collection of Pope John Paul the Second. Then it was Cindy's turn. She talked about embroidery and she brought with her two favorite pillow cases with pictures of playing pandas and dolphins that she embroidered herself and she showed us how she stitches, what each stitch is called and how rewarding it was to get the whole thing together. And Kevin talked about building a tree house with his Daddy and how fun it was. He even showed us the blueprint which he and his Daddy designed together and photos of himself hanging out on the tree house, waving and swinging from a rope like a monkey with his friends and it looked like a great place to hide too if you're pissed off at your Mama or something and then the bell rang.

Robert, Mr. K. said, I wonder if you'd be so kind as to take care of our new student and show him the cafeteria. Why me, I said and made a face like when I had to take the garbage out at home when it wasn't even my turn but Mr. K. said why not you, Robert, you're a nice one.

Oh no I'm not, I said.

Oh yes you are, he said, and wiggled his bushy eye brows up and down like Groucho.

Oh no I'm not.

Oh yes you are.

OK, I said, but just today. OK, though I kinda wanted to talk to the new kid anyway, and Mr. K. said, thank you, Robert Quentin Mitchell. He called the new kid over and put one arm around his shoulders and another around mine. Then he said Robert, this is Cao, Cao, this is Robert. Robert will take care of you. You both can bring your lunch back here and eat if you want. We're having a speed tournament today and there's a new X-Men comic book for the winner.

All right! I said. You're privileged if you get to eat lunch in Mr. K.'s room. Mr. K. has all these games he keeps in the cabinet and at lunch time it's sort of a club and everything. You can eat there if a) you're a straight-A student, b) if Mr. K. likes and invites you which is not often, or c) if you know for sure you're gonna get jumped that day if you play outside and you beg Mr. K. really really hard to let you stay. I'm somewhere in between the b) and c) category. If you're a bad egg like Billy, who is single-handedly responsible for my c) situation, you ain't never ever gonna get to eat there and play games, that's for sure.

So, Kal Nguyen—Refugee, I said, let's go grab lunch then we'll come back here for the speed tournament, what d' you say? But the new kid said nothing. He just stared at me and blinked like I'm some kinda strange animal that he ain't never seen before or something. Com'n, I said and waved him toward me, com'n, follow me, the line's getting longer by the sec', and so finally he did.

We stood in line with nothing to do so I asked him, hey, Kal, where'd you get them funny shoes?

No undostand, he said and smiled, *no sspeak engliss.*

Shoes, I said, Bata, Bata and I pointed and he looked down. *Oh, Ssues*, he said, his eyes shiny and black and wide opened like he just found out for the first time that he was wearing shoes. *Sssues . . . sssues . . . Saigon.* Yeah? I said, I guess I can't buy me some here in the good old U.S. of A then? Mine's Adidas. They're as old as Mrs. Hamilton, prehistoric if you ask me but they're still Adidas. A-di-das, go head, Kal, say it.

Adeedoos Ssues, Kal said, *Adeedoos.*

That's right, I said, very good, Kal. Adidas shoes. And yours, they're Bata shoes, and Kal said *theirs Bata sssues* and we both looked at each other and grinned like idiots and that's when Billy showed up. Why you want them gook shoes anyway, he said and cut in between us but nobody behind in line said nothing 'cause it's Billy. Why not, I said, trying to sound tough. Bata sounds kind of nice, Billy. They're from Saigon.

Bata ssues, the new kid said it again, trying to impress Billy.

But Billy wasn't impressed. My Daddy said them VCs don't wear shoes, he said. They wear sandals made from jeep tires and they live in fuck'n tunnels like moles and they eat bugs and snakes for lunch. Then afterwards they go up and take sniper shots at you with their AK-47s.

He don't look like he lived in no tunnel, I said.

Maybe not him, said Billy, but his Daddy I'm sure. Isn't that right, refugee boy? Your Daddy a VC? Your Daddy the one who gave my Daddy that goddamn scar?

The new kid didn't say nothing. You could tell he pretty much figured it out that Billy's an asshole 'cause you don't need no English for that. But all he could say was *no undohsten* and *ssues adeedoos* and those ain't no comeback lines and he knew it. So he just bit his lip and blushed and kept looking at me with them eyes.

So, I don't know why, maybe 'cause I didn't want him to know that I belonged to the c) category, or maybe 'cause he kept looking at me with those eyes, but I said leave him alone, Billy. I was kinda surprised that I said it. And Billy turned and looked at me like he was shocked too, like he just saw me for the first time or something. Then in this loud singsong voice, he said Bobby's protecting his new boyfriend. Everybody look, Bobby's got a boyfriend and he's gonna suck his VC's dick after lunch.

Everybody started to look.

The new kid kept looking at me too like he was waiting to see what I was gonna do next. What I'd usually do next is shut my trap and pretend that I was invisible or try not to cry like last time when Billy got me in a headlock in the locker room and called me sissy over and over again 'cause I missed the softball at P.E. even when it was an easy catch. But not now. Now I couldn't pretend to be invisible 'cause too many people were looking. It was like I didn't have a choice. It was like now or never. So I said, you know what, Billy, don't mind if I do. I'm sure anything is bigger than yours and everybody in line said Ooohh.

Fuck you, you little faggot, Billy said.

No thanks, Billy, I said, I already got me a new boyfriend, remember?

Everybody said Ooohh again and Billy looked real mad. Then I got more scared than mad, my blood pumping. I thought oh my God, what have I done? I'm gonna get my lights punched out for sure. But then, God delivered stupid Becky. She suddenly stuck her beak in. And he's cute too she said, almost as cute as you, Bobby. A blond and a brunette. You two'll make a nice faggot couple, I'm sure. So like promise me you'll name your first born after me, OK?

So like I tore at her. That girl could never jump me, not in a zillion years. And I'm sure you're a slut, I said, I'm sure you'd couple with anything that moves. I'm sure there are litters of strayed mutts already named after you. You know, Bitch Becky One, Bitch Becky Two, and, let's not forget, Bow Wow Becky Junior and Becky called me asshole and looked away and everyone cracked up, even mean old Billy.

Man, he said, shaking his head, you got some mean mouth on you today. It was like suddenly I was too funny or famous for him to beat up. But after he bought his burger and chocolate milk, he said it real loud so everybody could hear, he said, I'll see you two bitches later. Outside.

Sure, Billy, I said and waved to him, see yah later, and then after we grabbed our lunch the new kid and me, we made a beeline for Mr. K's.

Boy, it was good to be in Mr. K's, I tell you. You don't have to watch over your shoulders every other second. You can play whatever game you want. Or you can read or just talk. So we ate and afterward I showed the new kid how to play speed. He was a quick learner too, if you asked me, but he lost pretty early on in the tournament. Then I lost too pretty damn quickly after him. So we sat around and I flipped through the X-Men comic book and tried to explain to the new kid why Wolverine is so cool 'cause he can heal himself with his mutant factor and he had claws that cut through metal, and Phoenix, she's my favorite, Phoenix's so very cool 'cause she can talk to you psychically and she knows how everybody feels without even having to ask them, and best of all, she can lift an eighteen-wheeler truck with her psycho-kinetic energy. That's way cool, don't you think, Kal. The new kid, he listened and nodded to everything I said like he understood. Anyway, after a while, there were more losers than winners and the losers surrounded us and interrogated the new kid like he was a POW or something.

You ever shoot anybody, Cao Long?

Did you see anybody get killed?

How *long* you been here, Long? (Haha).

I hear they eat dogs over there, is that true? Have you ever eaten a dog?

Have you ever seen a helicopter blown up like in the movies?

No undohsten, the new kid answered to each question and smiled or shook his head or waved his hands like shooing flies but the loser flies wouldn't shoo. I mean where else could they go? Mr. K.'s was it. So the new kid looked at me again with them eyes and I said, OK, OK, Kal, I'll teach you something else. Why don't you say Hey, fuckheads, leave me alone! Go head, Kal, say it.

Hey-fuck-heads, I said, looking at him.

Hee, Foock headss, he said, looking at me.

Leave. Me. Alone! I said.

Leevenme olone! he said. *Hee, Foock headss. Leevenme olone!*

And everybody laughed. I guess that was the first time they got called fuckheads and actually felt good about it, but Mr. K. said Robert Quentin Mitchell, you watch your mouth or you'll never come in here again but you could tell he was trying not to laugh himself. So I said OK, Mr. K., but I leaned over and whispered *hey fuckheads, leave me alone* again in the new kid's ear so he'd remember and he looked at me like I'm the coolest guy in the world. Sthankew Rowbuurt, he said.

Then after school when I was waiting for my bus, the new kid found me. He gave me a folded piece of paper and before I could say anything he blushed and ran away. You'd never guess what it was. It was a drawing of me and it was really really good. I was smiling in it. I looked real happy and older, like a sophomore or something, not like in the 7th grade yearbook picture where I looked so goofy with my eyes closed and everything and I had to sign my name over it so people wouldn't look. When I got home I taped it on my family-tree chart and pinned the chart on my bedroom door and, I swear, the whole room had this vague eucalyptus smell.

Next day at Show and Tell Billy made the new kid cry. He went after Jimmy. Jimmy was this total nerd with thick glasses who told us how very challenging it was doing the New York Times crossword puzzles 'cause you got to know words like ubiquitous and undulate and capricious, totally lame and bogus stuff like that. When he took so long just to do five across and seven horizontal we shot spitballs at him and Mr. K. said stop that. But we got rid of that capricious undulating bozo ubiquitously fast and that was when Billy came up and made the new kid cry.

He brought in his Daddy's army uniform and a stack of old magazines. He unfolded the uniform with the name Baxter sewed under U.S. ARMY and put it on a chair. Then he opened one magazine and showed a picture of this naked and bleeding little girl running and crying on this road while these houses behind her were on fire. That's Napalm, he said, and it eats into your skin and burns for a long, long time. This girl, Billy said, she got burned real bad, see there, yeah. Then he showed another picture of this monk sitting cross-legged and he was on fire and everything and there were people standing behind him crying but nobody tried to put the poor man out. That's what you call self-immolation, Billy said. They do that all the time in 'Nam. This man, he poured gasoline on himself and lit a match 'cause he didn't like the government. Then Billy showed another picture of dead people in black pajamas along this road and he said these are VCs and my Daddy got at least a dozen of them before he was wounded himself. My Daddy told me if it weren't for them beatniks and hippies we could have won, Billy said and that's when the new kid buried his face in his arms and cried and I could see his skinny shoulders go up and down like waves.

That's enough, Billy Baxter, Mr. K. said, you can sit down now, thank you.

Oh, man! Billy said, I didn't even get to the part about how my Daddy got his scar, that's the best part.

Never mind, Mr. K. said, sit down, please. I'm not sure whether you understood the assignment but you were supposed to do an oral presentation on what you've done or something that has to do with you, a hobby or a personal project, not the atrocities your father committed in Indochina. Save those stories for when you cruise the bars when you're old enough.

Then Mr. K. looked at the new kid like he didn't know what to do next. That war, he said, I swear. After that it got real quiet in the room and all you could hear was the new kid sobbing. Cao, Mr. K. said finally, real quiet like, like he didn't really want to bother him. Cao, are you all right? Cao Long Nguyen?

The new kid didn't answer Mr. K. so I put my hand on his shoulder and shook it a little. Hey, Kal, I said, you OK?

Then, it was like I pressed an ON button or something, 'cause all of a sudden Kal raised his head and stood up. He looked at me and then he looked at the blackboard. He looked at me again, then the blackboard. Then he marched right up there even though it was Roger's turn next and Roger, he already brought his two pet snakes and everything. But Kal didn't care. Maybe he thought it was his turn 'cause Mr. K. called his name and so he just grabbed a bunch of colored chalk from Mr. K.'s desk and started to draw like a wild man and Mr. K. he let him.

We all stared.

He was really really good but I guess I already knew that.

First he drew a picture of a boy sitting on this water buffalo and then he drew this rice field in green. Then he drew another boy on another water buffalo and they seemed to be racing. He drew other kids running along the bank with their kites in the sky and you could tell they were laughing and yelling, having a good time. Then he started to draw little houses on both sides of this river and the river ran toward the ocean and the ocean had big old waves. Kal drew a couple standing outside this very nice house and underneath them Kal wrote *Ba* and *Ma*. Then he turned and looked straight at me, his eyes still wet with tears. *Rowbuurt*, he said, tapping the pictures with his chalk, his voice sad but expecting, *Rowbuurt*.

Me? I said. I felt kinda dizzy. Everybody was looking back and forth between him and me now like we were tossing a softball between us or something.

Rowbuurt. Kal said my name again and kept looking at me until I said what, what'd you want, Kal?

Kal tapped the blackboard with his chalk again and I saw in my head the picture of myself taped on my family-tree and then, I don't know how but I just kinda knew. So I just took a deep breath and then I said, OK, OK, Kal, uhmm, said he used to live in this village with his Mama and Papa near where the river runs into the sea, and Kal nodded and smiled and waved his chalk in a circle like he was saying *Go on, Robert Quentin Mitchell, you're doing fine, go on.*

So I went on.

And he went on.

I talked. He drew.

We fell into a rhythm.

He had a good time racing them water buffaloes with his friends and flying kites, I said. His village is, hmm, very nice, and . . . and . . . and . . . at night he goes to sleep swinging on this hammock and hearing the sound of the ocean behind the dunes and everything.

Then one day, I said, the soldiers named VCs came with guns and they took his Daddy away. They put him behind barbed wires with other men, all very skinny, skinny and hungry and they got chains on their ankles and they looked really, really sad. Kal and his mother went to visit his Daddy and they stood on the other side of the fence and cried a lot. Yes, it was very, very sad. Then, hmm, one day his Daddy disappeared. No, he didn't disappear, he died, he died.

And Kal and his mother buried him in this cemetery with lots of graves and they lit candles and cried and cried. After that, there was this boat, this really crowded boat, I guess, and Kal and his Mama climbed on it and they went down the river out to sea. Then they got on this island and then they got on an airplane after that and they came here to live in America.

Kal was running out of space. He drew the map of America way too big but he didn't want to erase it. So he climbed on a chair and drew these highrises right above the rice fields and I recognized the Trans-American building right away, a skinny pyramid underneath a rising moon. Then he drew a big old heart around it. Then he went back to the scene where the man named Ba stood in the doorway with his wife and he drew a heart around him. Then he went back to the first scene of the two boys racing on the water buffaloes in the rice field and paused a little before he drew tiny tennis shoes on the boys' feet and I heard Billy say that's Bobby and his refugee boyfriend but I ignored him.

Kal loves America very much, especially San Francisco, I said, he'd never seen so many tall buildings before in his whole life and they're so pretty. Maybe he'll live with his mother someday up in the penthouse when they have lots of money. But he misses home too and he misses his friends and he especially misses his Daddy who died. A lot. And that's all, I said. I think he's done, thank you.

And he was done. Kal turned around and climbed down from the chair. Then he looked at everybody and checked out their faces to see if they understood. Then in this real loud voice he said, *Hee, Foock headss, leevenme olone!* and bowed to them and everybody cracked up and applauded.

Kal started walking back. He was smiling and looking straight at me with his teary eyes like he was saying *Robert Quentin Mitchell, ain't we a team, or what?* and I wanted to say yes, yes, Kal Long Nguyen—Refugee, yes we are but I just didn't say anything.

Questions for Reflection and Analysis

1. What strikes you about the story as a whole? Is there a particular aspect of the story that elicits a memory or concern about teaching and learning?

2. What does Mr. K.'s behavior reveal about his attitude toward the children in general and toward teaching Cao in particular?

3. What is the relationship between Robert's inner thoughts and feelings and what he shows and tells in the classroom?

4. What do the verbal and nonverbal interactions between Cao and Robert and between Cao and the other children reveal about the factors that impede or enable their communication?

5. How do the various characters' understandings of the war in Vietnam affect their responses to Cao? What does your analysis suggest about the effect of politics on the dynamics of this classroom?

■ *The Unforgetting*

Lan Samantha Chang

(1965–)

Lan Samantha Chang, the daughter of refugees from communist China, was born and raised in the United States. At the time she went to school, her family was one of three Chinese families in a city of about 50,000. Chang received a B.A. from Yale University and an M.F.A. from the University of Iowa. She has taught in the M.F.A. programs at the University of Iowa and Warren Wilson College and is currently director of the University of Iowa Writers' Workshop. An award-winning writer, she is the author of *Hunger: A Novella and Stories* (1998) and *Inheritance: A Novel* (2004).

On the summer day in 1967 when Ming Hwang first saw the eastern Iowa hills, he pulled his car off the road and stopped the engine. He felt overwhelmed, as if he had arrived once more at the sea that he had crossed to reach America and his destiny lay again upon some faraway shore. The neat, green fields rolled out to meet the sky. The narrow strip of highway looked barely navigable. Surely no Chinese man could ever have laid eyes upon this place before.

Beside him, Sansan stirred and squinted into the hazy light. "This is beautiful," she said. "Why did you stop?"

For a minute Ming could not reply. He wanted to say, "This place has nothing to do with us." Instead, he pointed out the windshield. "Do you see that water over there? That's Mercy Lake. The town is only a mile away." He added, "Maybe it will bring us luck."

When she didn't answer, he turned to examine her smooth, brown face and knew that she also was afraid. He looked over his shoulder to make sure that Charles was still asleep and would not hear the conversation. "Is something wrong?" he asked.

"We're getting old," she said. "How will we make the space in our minds for everything we'll need to learn here?"

Without a pause, he answered her, "We will forget."

Sansan's dark eyes flickered; then she nodded. Ming glanced back again at his son. He turned the key in the ignition and fixed his gaze upon the road.

And so the Hwangs forgot what they no longer needed. In the basement, inside the yellow carpetbag that Sansan had carried from Beijing, were six rice bowls that Sansan's mother said had once been used in the emperor's household. They were plain white bowls; Sansan said she thought they were only from the servants' quarters. Still, she had held onto them, imagining that their thin-edged beauty might sustain her when she grew tired of living in the present. But once the Hwangs had settled in Mercy Lake, she never used the bowls; she rarely even mentioned them.

They forgot what they could no longer bear to hope for. In the basement of their house, behind a sliding panel in his desk, stood Ming's old copy of the *Handbook of Chemistry and Physics*. It was the Twenty-sixth Edition, published in 1943, the only book that he had carried in his suitcase out of China. *The Handbook's* deep brown cover was cracked and stained; its information had grown out-dated. Ming had once believed that some day Charles might find it interesting, and so he had saved the heavy volume, even though its Periodic Table listed only ninety-two elements. In 1958, when Charles was born, the table of known elements had grown to 101, and Ming had lost track of chemistry, had given up his hope of studying science. In Mercy Lake he started his new job as a photocopy machine repairman, and the *Handbook* stayed on its shelf.

They learned what they needed to know. Photocopy machines were still so new that people had trouble maintaining them—mostly due to fear. They would call about the slightest problems: a toner cartridge, a paper jam. Ming possessed a delicate touch. He quickly grasped the ins and outs of the different models. He could sense which button or lever to press and how to get at the most difficult jams. While he fiddled around, a clerk or secretary often stood nearby, curious and wary, watching his face and hands, remarking on the infallibility and effectiveness of carbon paper. Ming would listen and nod, affecting sympathy, but privately he disagreed. He needed to believe in the future, when every office would have a new machine. And he found comfort in the presence of such effortless reproduction. He brought home photocopied samples to show Sansan how the machines could trace the shapes of drawings or letters, handwritten or typed. Sometimes, on the weekend, he took Charles to the office. To the inside cover of his logbook he taped a photocopy of Charles's little hand.

When Charles finished fourth grade, the Hwangs received a letter from his teacher, Mrs. Carlsen. She said he was doing excellent work in math and science, but his vocabulary was below average. He also had trouble pronouncing words. Did they speak Chinese in their house? She suggested that they not require him to speak Chinese, for the time being at least.

"I *do* speak English," Ming insisted, after he and Sansan had told Charles his usual bedtime story and sent him off to bed.

Charles had always been quiet and slow to speak. But Ming had assumed that he was cautious, reasoning out what he said. Now Ming began to worry that he might get lost between his two languages. The day after they received the letter, Ming came home early and watched Charles trudge up the driveway, his blue backpack heavy with books he could not read. Sansan kissed him at the door, helped him remove the backpack and poured him a bowl of sweet bean porridge. After his snack, he bent over his reader at the kitchen table. He breathed with effort, sounding out each English word so slowly that Ming did not see how he could remember what he had read.

The sight of him lit a fear in Ming's mind: "If you pay him less attention, he might want to stay in school instead of flying home to you," he told Sansan.

She said, "You don't know about children."

"I was not so coddled by my mother."

"The other children make fun of him."

Ming frowned. He reread the teacher's letter. That evening, when Charles had finished his bath and climbed into Ming and Sansan's bed for his nighttime ritual, Ming told his son there would be no bedtime story.

Charles sat perfectly still. "No story?"

"Daddy thinks we should speak English for a while," Sansan explained.

Ming watched his son's face. Recently, Charles had developed an expression of careful solitude. "I can read to you from your schoolbook," Ming said.

Charles shook his head.

"Do you understand why you need to learn English?" Ming asked.

Charles nodded. In the next few months, he gradually stopped speaking Chinese. Since they did not test him, Ming never knew how long it took for all of those words to be forgotten.

Many other things passed out of memory without their noticing. Sansan stopped reading her Chinese classics and romances. When they first moved to Mercy Lake, she had reread them until their bindings buckled, shredded, and fell off. She had even tried to get Ming to skim the books, so she would have someone to talk to, but Ming was busy at work. Then came Charles's letter from Mrs. Carlsen. Eventually, the tales were pushed into a smaller and smaller part of her mind, until the characters and stories only came up now and then, usually in her dreams, and when they did, she said to Ming, they seemed almost quaint, exotic. The novels found their way onto a shelf, in the basement, where they stood next to a red-bound history text that Ming and Sansan had kept in order to remind themselves of their culture and the importance of their race.

Instead of reading, Sansan practiced her English by watching television. She also took good care of Ming and Charles. She laundered Ming's new work clothes: permanent-press shirts with plastic tabs inserted in the stiff, pointed collars; bright, wide ties. Ming needed to dress well, because he had found a second calling as a salesman. He had discovered that clients were comforted by his appearance and his accent, which went together, in some way, with his efficiency and mechanical know-how. He began persuading them to buy larger, more expensive machines. He asked for and received a commission for each machine he sold. These extra monies, he and Sansan agreed, would go into a savings account for Charles's education at the University of Iowa.

In the kitchen, Sansan learned to cook with canned and frozen foods. She made cream of tomato soup for lunch, and stored envelopes of onion soup mix for meat loaf or quick onion dip. More often as Ming's career improved, Sansan consulted the Betty Crocker cookbook and made something for him to bring to an office party or to entertain a coworker at home. She kept a filebox listing everything she made, with annotations reminding her which dishes the Americans liked and didn't like.

She bought air freshener in a plastic daisy, and a jello mold shaped like a fish. They taught Charles to use a knife and fork and they ate their meals off brittle plastic plates that they had chosen at the discount store: bright, hard disks, flat and cheerful, the color of candy: scarlet, lime green, yellow, and white.

They forgot some things deliberately; they wanted to forget. Ming won a trip for two to Chicago, based on his annual sales, and he did not protest when Sansan bought an expensive new suitcase rather than open her old yellow carpetbag and confront the six white rice bowls. At work, Ming avoided one well-meaning coworker who had once asked, "What was it like in China? It must be different from here." How could he answer that question without remembering the smell of fresh rolls sold on the street, or the scent of his grandfather's pipe?

Ming forgot the delicate taste of his grandfather's favorite fruit, the yellow watermelon. He forgot his grandfather's hopes that he might study hard and rebuild China. He forgot the fact that he had once desired to earn a Ph.D., to work in a laboratory, to discover great things and add to the body of humanity's scientific knowledge.

He replaced such useless memories with thoughts of Charles. It was for Charles that Ming had taken his job in Iowa and bought his house, because he had believed, since Charles was born, that he could make a new life in America. He struggled through clumsy conversations at the office and employee "happy hours," practicing his English. For Charles, he read the local newspaper and mowed the lawn. With Charles in mind, he struggled out of bed on winter mornings, fighting sleepiness and persistent dreams. He maintained the new Chevrolet sedan—changed the oil, followed the tune-up dates, and kept good records of all repairs.

He labored on the yard. They had moved into a neighborhood so new that at certain times the air was redolent of cow, and Ming would dream that he was being watched by large, calm eyes, and that their house had been surrounded by those strange and fragrant animals. The soil itself seemed exotic to Ming; it looked so coarse, so rich and reddish-purple—not exhausted by three thousand years of farming, like the Chinese earth, but exuberant and wild. Ming could sense the rolling fields that pressed upon their house. Mutinous seeds opposed the lawn: tall leaves of pale new wheat, foamy milkweed, Queen Anne's lace. He fussed over his spears of frail bluegrass. In the autumn he reseeded and raked, pruned back the shrubs, hid Sansan's yellow rosebush under its protective cone; but in the spring, when the melting snow lay bare his lawn, he watched and held his breath.

He did not quite trust the land. He did not know what he might find. On warm spring nights, he lay awake and listened to a distant hum amidst the silence; it might have been the wind over ten thousand acres of fields, or the hatching of a thousand insects. He did not want to miss these changes. He wanted nothing taking place behind his back.

Charles's English did improve. To Ming's surprise, he read all the time: after school, in front of the television, on Saturday mornings, over meals, and even, his teachers told Ming and Sansan, during recess. In fifth grade, his teachers were pleased. In sixth grade, they were excited, and by the time he entered seventh grade, his level of achievement was, they said, phenomenal.

Even more, the teachers said, he seemed to find a pure pleasure in learning—an almost obsessive pleasure. He once failed to hear a fire drill bell while reading a biography of Thomas Paine. He wrote his papers, they said, with such articulate and righteous passion that his assignments more than compensated for his lack of class participation. He was drawn to the humanities and he seemed to be developing a passion for examining the past; he possessed a truly unusual mind.

Why the humanities? Ming wondered. What intricate foldings lay behind his son's quiet face; what opinions had formed beneath his stiff-mown hair? The autumn of Charles's eighth-grade year, Ming bought him a wooden desk and a sturdy lamp with a metal shade. He adjusted his chair and bolted a steel pencil sharpener into the wall. Then he and Sansan drove to the discount store and heaped a shopping cart with blue spiral notebooks (his favorite color) as well as blue pencils, a blue cloth-covered binder, and an enormous blue eraser. Charles brought these things to school in his backpack, and after that, Ming glimpsed them only now and then, evidence of his son's mysterious passions.

One winter evening, while Charles was helping his mother set the dining room table, Ming said, "I think I understand your interest in history. I used to like to read the history of science. I used to love science." He allowed his mind a glimpse—only a glimpse—into the basement, through the sliding panel of his desk, at the *Handbook of Chemistry and Physics.* "Do you like science?"

Charles looked up, the silverware clutched in his hand. "Not really," he said quickly. "But in history, I learned about trains." He began to talk about the European and American-born pioneers who had settled the land

and made it into fields and towns. Ming watched him gesture, still holding their three forks in one brown hand, his wrists grown out of his last year's shirtsleeves. He described how the use of trains had sped the populating of the West, and how the transcontinental railroad had been built by Chinese immigrants. Then, to Ming's dismay, he asked, "Why was China so poor that people had to come to the U.S. and work on the railroads?"

Ming did not know how to tackle this enormous question. "Well," he said finally, "I'm not certain of that, but the country has always been poor."

"Why is that? Did you learn about it when you were in school?"

"We studied history."

"Did you like history?"

Ming stood and thought for a moment. "To tell you the truth," he said, "I can't remember."

That careful, lonely look came into Charles's face. He went into the kitchen and left Ming standing at the table, regretting how he had ended the conversation. He found himself envying the easy way that Charles reached for the past. How could he explain to his son that the past was his enemy? That his memories dogged him, filled his thoughts and plans with silt? They rose up in his dreams, the way that in the spring the Mercy Lake flooded through its margins, leaving the fishing huts surrounded by water.

He could not forget the colors of the Beijing sky. At night, in bed, he remembered the burning smell on winter nights from the thousand coal fires that burned in kitchens and under old-fashioned brick beds, the thousand pale streams of smoke that rose into the darkness. He recalled the grit of the spring dust storms catching in his throat, and the loose slat on the wall of the noodle-making shop that had enabled him to peer inside at the man who thinned the noodles by hand.

Ming could not forget one warm and beautiful summer evening in 1932, when he had helped his Uncle Lu pack up his belongings. The family was leaving Beijing, for what they thought would be only a few years, the duration of the war. Uncle Lu, his father's youngest brother, had never taken a real job but had remained in the family house, supported by his brothers and sisters, like an invalid, long after his beard indicated that he should have had a family of his own. As far as Ming could recall, his Uncle Lu was only interested in the practice of calligraphy. He had no other desires, it seemed, but to sit before a well-lit table, the brush upright in his hand, a gentle hand unfit for more practical tasks. That night, when they were not half finished, his uncle had sat down at this desk, helplessly, and looked about his little, room, with tears rolling down his cheeks. Ming had turned away in embarrassment and hurried to pack the precious brushes and rolls of soft, white paper—the only things Uncle Lu wanted brought with him.

Where had those brushes and papers gone? What had become of the scrolls that Lu had painted and saved, so carefully? Nothing remained except Ming's recollection of them. Charles had never even seen a photograph of his great uncle. Like everyone else, Lu had died. He had suffered a stroke the night after the family left Beijing, the first casualty in a long line of lost and missing. Only a few cousins were living now, and they were scattered. Any photographs had been lost. Sometimes, Ming wondered if it were possible—that of the over two dozen members of that household everyone was scattered and gone. He could not believe that of the grandparents, uncles and aunts, cousins, and so many others, that this family had dwindled into the slender thread of his own memory.

By the time Charles entered high school he had impressed his teachers as a young man with a singular determination and potential. They said he needed to relax more, that was all. They said he seemed "like a fish out of water" during lunch period. Academically, he continued to excel. In his World History class, he developed an interest in World War II and, in particular, the Pacific theater.

One spring night Ming went to Charles's room to ask his son if he wanted a bowl of sweet bean porridge. He trudged down the hall, with no particular expectation, but was surprised to find his son's door closed. He stood dumbly for a moment and then, without thinking, he put his hand on the knob. The door was locked.

He knocked, foolishly, a little angry. After a moment, he heard the creak of a mattress, three steps toward the door. The lock clicked open.

"Charles?"

They were of a height, he noticed. Charles was so young that even when weary, he looked fresh. Ming observed his son, in whose narrow face he recognized his own; he noted the smooth, brown skin Charles had inherited from Sansan. What did he have to be weary about? "What are you doing?" Ming asked, despite the fact that he could see the books and papers strewn over the bed.

"What do you mean?"

Ming retreated. "I came up to see if you would like some *lu dou tang.*"

"No, not right now, thanks," With such politeness Ming was thus rebuffed. Charles closed the door in his face and Ming stood there, blank for a moment. Then he turned and went back to the kitchen. Halfway down the hall he heard the lock click shut again.

That night, his dreams kept bringing him down the hallway, and he stood once again before his son's locked door. The next day he could not concentrate at work. The image of the door disturbed him, as if Charles had access to another world inside that room, as if he might disappear at will, might float from their second-story windows and vanish into the shimmering, yellow Iowa light.

He used a Phillips screwdriver to take apart the doorknobs and disable the locks on Charles's bedroom, the bathrooms, and the upstairs closets. Charles said nothing to him. But later Ming heard him ask his mother, "What did Dad do to my lock?" Ming caught these words one morning on his way out and paused to listen. "That's all right," Sansan said. Ming heard the squeak of a kiss. "Things get old sometimes. Don't tell Daddy—you'll make him feel bad."

Later he attempted to defend himself. A family, he told Sansan, should need no windows and no doors. In China there had been no locks on children's rooms. True, they had come to America—but even in this country, what obedient child would *need* to lock his parents from his room? "He doesn't respect me," Ming insisted.

"Of course he does."

"He's my son—I can tell from his voice, the shape of his face. But sometimes I wonder if he's my son!"

"Hush," said Sansan. She cocked her head, gesturing toward Charles's room. They both listened, but the house was absolutely quiet. The comforting odor of fried rice lingered in the air. Ming listened more closely. Beyond the house, from the land, he could hear the distant hum of early spring.

Despite their efforts, they could not forget their language, the musical pitch of Mandarin tones, the shapes of phrases. Over and, over, they reached for certain words that had no equivalents in English. Sansan could find no substitute for the word *yiwei,* which meant that a person "had once assumed, but incorrectly." And no matter how much he drilled himself, Ming could not instinctively convert the measure *wan* to "ten thousand," rather than "a thousand."

In English, Sansan seemed to hide from her more complicated thoughts. "So much is missing," she told Ming. Her English world was limited to the clipped and casual rhythm of daily plans. "Put on your tie." "Did you turn on the rice?" "Be home by five o'clock."

Later that spring, there came a rainy evening when Charles looked up from his book and said, "Tomorrow I can't be home until ten."

"Is there a school event of yours that we should go to?" Ming asked.

"No." Charles flipped his book out of its jacket and folded it back. "It's college night," he said, finally. "The guidance counselor is ordering pizza. Then a man is coming to talk to us about college."

Ming nudged Sansan. "We like you to come home for dinner," Sansan said. "We don't get to see you otherwise."

Charles moved his lips for a moment, then looked up at them. "Sometime I'll have to go to college," he said. Then he stopped.

Ming jumped in. "We've been saving for you to go to college! I wanted to go to college, myself. You know that!" His voice cracked. He frowned at Sansan. "Why are you looking at me like that?"

She said, "Let's talk about this later."

A painful knot, the size of a cherry stone, formed inside Ming's throat and stayed there. Sansan turned on the television. Neither spoke until Charles had gone back to his room. Then they went to their own bedroom and undressed in silence.

In bed, in the dark, Sansan turned to him. "It's funny," she said. "I am very proud of Charles. But lately, I've been thinking it's not enough."

Ming swallowed and nodded in the dark.

"Do you remember the second Taipei flood?" she asked, cautiously, in Mandarin this time.

Ming muttered, "Maybe—not too well. Maybe you should remind me."

Her words, in Mandarin, came slowly at first and then more easily, low and wondering, as if she were marveling at her ability to speak. Her murmuring voice flowed with the steady drumming of the storm.

"Remember how poor we were? We were so poor that we could only afford one vegetable with the rice. We had to live with my mother's old Aunt Green Blossom in her flat over that restaurant, the Drunken Moon. On the day of the storm, the restaurant was serving flounder. A big catch must have just come in. When you got home for lunch, the scent of ginger and garlic sprouts, with oil, had soaked into our room."

He knew she spoke to comfort him, but his eyes had filled with tears.

"The smell from the restaurant made us quarrel with each other," she said. "That afternoon, the rains began; we holed ourselves inside and watched the commotion from the window. It rained until the streets were rivers. And you had a wonderful idea."

He smiled then. "It wasn't wonderful; it was scientific logic. The Drunken Moon was only on step up."

"We waited; we watched the water rise, then trickle over the step. All the customers left. The neighborhood was as flooded as a rice paddy. And then you went downstairs and asked them if they needed a dry place to store their food!" She laughed. "How well we ate that night!"

Ming looked at his wife. He could barely see her profile in the glow from their bedside clock. She lay on her back now, gazing at the ceiling. "Lately," she said, "I've been dreaming about that meal. Over and over. And I wonder why the food we eat now doesn't taste as good."

Their memories seeped under the doors and sifted through the keyhole. They had taken root in the earth itself, as tough and stubborn as the weeds in the garden. It seemed to Ming that after seven years in Mercy Lake, the world of his past had grown every day larger and more vivid until it pressed against his mind, beautiful and shining. And he wondered if perhaps this world had pushed his own son out of his house—if they had lost their son because of their stubborn inability to forget.

One evening he came home early. Sansan had gone to the library. In the mailbox was a letter from the guidance counselor at Charles's high school; he wanted to congratulate Charles's parents for his high test scores, and he was certain that their son would be an excellent student at the prestigious East Coast college that he had applied to, early admission. Ming read this letter; he pushed his glasses up his rose, and read it again, the paper weightless in his hands.

Ming went to his son's room. Everything lay neatly under the lamplight: the desk, the piles of books, the plain blue bedspread. Charles sat at his desk, surrounded by piles of homework. A college brochure lay open before him.

"The best state school is only an hour away," Ming said.

Charles took a deep breath. "But I don't want to go to the state school," he said.

This fact drowned out all sound for a moment, but when Ming's thoughts cleared he grew aware that Charles was still talking. Charles was saying, Did they realize how little he knew about the world? He needed to know what the world was like, the world outside of their house, outside of Iowa, so that for the rest of his life he would not remain entirely lost.

"Why didn't you tell me?" Ming asked.

"I knew you didn't want me to leave."

"Why do you want to leave, then?"

Charles looked at him. "Because I know I have to go," he said.

Ming said nothing. Charles turned his attention to his brochure. After a few minutes Ming realized that his son had ended the conversation. He stood, bewildered, and walked out, closing the door behind him. When he reached the foot of the stairs, he stopped and glanced again at the closed door.

After this, it seemed to Ming that the very passage of days imprisoned him. Each morning, alone in the small bathroom, he cleared his throat and blew his nose—he had developed an allergy to ragweed over the years. His cough rang off the tiles. In the kitchen, his tea steamed sour against his upper lip. He left the house, and climbed into the Chevrolet. These habits built around him a dark and airless riddle. Charles was a part of it; even Sansan was a part of it.

On the day after they learned that Charles had been accepted early to Harvard, Sansan cooked a celebratory dinner. Afterward, they waited all evening for their son to go upstairs, their eyes bright and voices low, deliberate, and harsh. Ming tidied the messy coffee table with shaking hands. Sansan folded laundry, gripping the center of the sheets between her teeth. Charles vanished off to bed, as if he could smell the sulfur in the air. He stepped out of the room so quietly they would never have noticed if they had not been waiting.

Later, they turned off the television and faced each other. The air between them quivered as if they had been waiting to make love.

Sansan shrugged. "What did you expect?" she asked. "Sons in this country leave their parents and make their own homes, with their women." Her voice was tense, accusatory.

Ming took a sharp breath. "And that is all you have to say?"

"Isn't this what you wanted for him? That he should become like them?" Her voice grew higher. "No, I have nothing else to say."

"What *I* wanted?" Ming's voice rose. "So this is all my fault?"

"It is what you wanted! It was your idea to get a job here, in the middle of nowhere—your idea!"

"It's your fault as much as mine!"

She was standing before him, her knees bent and both feet planted, her face distorted, shouting suddenly, "You're lying!" Then, without taking her eyes from him, she moved backward, toward the dishrack. She reached blindly for a brittle, plastic plate, raised it slowly into the air, as if she were casting a spell, then flung it against the kitchen floor.

For a moment Ming stood, arrested by the sight of the red disk hurtling downward, surprised to see it breaking into pieces against the floor. He had not known such goods could shatter. Then he walked slowly to the cabinet, his heavy fingers tingling at his sides.

They broke every plate on the shelf, plus the china pencil holder and the good teapot. Sansan stood with knees bent and both feet planted, near the dishrack, jerking her arm downward to emphasize a point, tears flying as she shook her head from side to side: She shouted, *"You are the cause of this! You have ruined me! You have trapped me into this life!"* "I should go downstairs and get those rice bowls!" Ming threatened. "Go ahead!" she shouted. "Why did we save them, anyway?" The words flew from their mouths, whirled through the kitchen. Colorful disks flew through the air, cracked and bounced against the walls, the chairs, the cabinets.

When they had finished, they stood transfixed, breathing hard, admiring their handiwork. The broken pieces made a bright mosaic on the floor.

A certain quality to the silence made them both look up.

The kitchen door had somehow been left open. There stood Charles in his pajamas, squinting in the light. He whispered, "I wish you would be happy for me."

In that moment, Ming understood that Charles was indeed his son. There was no question about it. The resemblance wasn't in the shape of his face. It was in his look of sorrow.

After Charles left the room, they turned once more toward each other. Sansan's face was rigid and blank. What had happened to them? Ming wondered. What would happen? He had no one to ask—no friends, no parents—no one who could have understood the language of his thoughts.

Now Sansan stood by the back door, holding her jacket. "I want to go back," she said. Her voice was shaking. "Why did you have to bring me here?"

She turned and quietly left the house, clicking the door shut behind her. Ming stood inside. He made out her shape in the dim garage as she got into the Chevrolet, backed it out in one quick motion, and drove west, toward the highway.

For an hour, he sat at the kitchen table. He had switched off the lights, and the blackness soothed his mind. He fixed his gaze upon the square of faint streetlight that lay upon the counter.

He was alone. What kind of cruelty had held him back from saying what she most desired to hear? That he needed her. That even with Charles gone, they would endure.

The Chevrolet moved like a comet in his mind. Sansan, never a confident driver, veering left onto Polk Avenue. The neighborhood houses prim on either side of her, reflecting the pale car in their dark windows. She would list over the centerline and then correct herself. She would enter the freeway, careening down the empty entrance ramp; she would turn north, away from the new commercial area, and toward the country roads that stretched among the winter fields, the dried-up stalks of corn, the earth rich and softly dark, scattered with snow and bits of wheat and chaff from the harvest. He knew his wife. For a long time, he had suspected that a part of her longed simply to disappear into those fields. The car would jounce a bit as she turned onto the gravel, then into the simplest two-tire track in the dirt. And there she might sit amidst the harvested soy beans, surrounded by silence, resting. Why did so many farmers grow soy beans? Ming wondered. No one in a hundred miles would dream of buying soy sauce. He imagined the local people were secure in their desires for steak and milk, protected by their barns, their tractors, and their slumbering cows.

Would she leave him? Perhaps she would leave, now that they had glimpsed their fate. Perhaps she would be able to forget—free and clear, wiped clean at last. Ming imagined her leaving the dirt roads and heading across the local highway to join the night traffic on the interstate, merging silently into the stream of traffic.

But even as he envisioned this, he knew it would not happen. Sansan had nowhere else to go. Nothing remained of the stories and meals and people they'd known, nothing but what they remembered. Their world lived in them, and they would be the end of it. They had no solace, and no burden, but each other.

The next morning, as he warmed up the car, he stooped to examine the tires. He found mud and grains of yellow wheat embedded deep into the treads.

Questions for Reflection and Analysis

1. What strikes you about the story as a whole? Is there a particular aspect of the story that elicits a memory or concern about teaching and learning?

2. How do the use of English and Mandarin, respectively, influence the behavior and thoughts of Sansan and Ming? What do your answers suggest about the relationship between their languages and their identities?

3. What are the fourth grade teacher's assumptions about Charles's use of Chinese at home and its effect on his acquisition of English? What are the immediate and long-term effects of the advice she gives in her letter to Charles's parents? Given the outcome, how would you assess her advice?

4. What do Sansan and Ming feel they need to forget and to learn, and how successful are they in their efforts? What do they gain, and what do they lose?

5. What do you perceive to be the significance of the story's title?

III.

ADULT EDUCATION

The life circumstances of many refugees, immigrants, exiles, and natural-born citizens compel them to learn English as adults. In these five stories, the authors reveal how personal and political histories have shaped the characters' responses to learning the language. We see how these adults subsequently negotiate—in both humorous and sobering ways—the multiple languages that impact their lives. We also observe how members of their families, classrooms, and communities respond to them: what they understand about adult learning and what they fail to recognize. In Leo Rosten's "The Rather Baffling Case of H*Y*M*A*N K*A*P*L*A*N," an immigrant from Eastern Europe challenges the patience of his English instructor with his creative use of language. In Nicholasa Mohr's "The English Lesson," 28 students deliver oral presentations under the watchful eye of their teacher. In Lucy Honig's "English as a Second Language," a refugee from Guatemala attends school five nights a week while working as a hotel maid. In Raquel Puig Zaldívar's "Nothing in Our Hands but Age," a Cuban exile couple enroll in a college philosophy class in the United States. In Lily Brett's "What Do You Know About Friends?" a refugee from Poland enrolls in a university physics class in Australia. Together, these stories show that adult education, for all of its benefits, can result in frustration or confusion when learners' unique experiences—as well as their desire, motivation, or passion for study—remain invisible or misunderstood.

■ The Rather Baffling Case of
H*Y*M*A*N K*A*P*L*A*N

Leo Rosten

(1908–1997)

Leo Rosten was born in Poland and immigrated to the United States with his family at the age of three in 1911. His first language was Yiddish. Rosten attended the University of Chicago, where he earned a Ph.D. While in Chicago, he taught in a nightschool for adult learners. During World War II, Rosten served as director of the MotionPicture Research Project and as deputy director of the Office of War Information. After the war, he worked as a special editorial advisor to *Look* magazine. He published many works—sometimes under the pseudonym of Leonard Q. Ross or simply Leonard Ross—including *The Education of H*Y*M*A*N K*A*P*L*A*N* (1937), *The Joys of Yiddish* (1968) and *Leo Rosten's Carnival of Wit* (1994).

"Mr. Aaron Blattberg."

"Here."

"Miss Carmen Caravello."

"Ina place!"

"Mr. Karl Finsterwald."

"Ratty!"

"Mrs. R. R. Rodriguez."

"*Sí.*"

"Mr, Wolfgang Schmitt."

"*Ja!* "

"Yussel Spitz."

No answer.

"Yussel Spitz?" Mr. Parkhill looked up.

There was no Yussel Spitz.

A growl from Mr. Gus Matsoukas, in the back of the room, preceded the announcement: "He laft class. Gave op. Won't come back. He told me to say."

Mr. Parkhill made a note on his attendance sheet. He was not especially sorry, in all honesty, that Mr. Spitz had given up the ghost of learning. Mr. Spitz was an echoer. He had a startling need to repeat every question directed at him. If asked, "What is the plural of 'child'?" Mr. Spitz was sure to echo, "What is the plural of *child?*"—and offered no answer whatsoever. Even worse, Mr. Spitz had so spacious a temperament that he often repeated questions asked of students two rows in front of him. This upset them. Many members of the beginners' grade had grumbled that their answers had been positively "crippled" by Yussel Spitz's prior requestioning.

"Mrs. Slavko Tomasic."

"Mm."

"Olga Tarnova."

"Da, da."

Besides, Mr. Parkhill thought, it was not unusual for a pupil to drop out of the American Night Preparatory School for Adults. Students came; students went. Some stayed in Mr. Parkhill's class for more than one semester; some left after only one session, or a week's, or a month's. Some enrolled because a father or mother, mate or loved one, had come to Manhattan or Brooklyn or the Bronx. Some departed because a husband's work or a wife's family drew them to another borough or another city. (Last year, a Mrs. Ingeborg Hutschner had disappeared after six weeks of conscientious attendance and commendable progress in both spelling and pronunciation; no one knew where on earth Mrs. Hutschner had gone, or why, or if she still bit her nails.)

"Miss Mitnick."

"Yes, sir," came the soft, shy voice.

And Mr. Parkhill always bore in mind that many of his students entered the portals of the A.N.P.S.A. because of the world's political upheavals: a revolution in Greece, a drought in Italy, a crisis in Germany or Cuba, a pogrom in Poland or a purge in Prague—each convulsion of power on the tormented globe was reflected, however minutely, in the school's enrollment or departures. For immigrants came to the A.N.P.S.A. not only to learn the basic, perplexing ingredients of English; they came to learn the rudiments of Civics, so that they could take the municipal court's examination for that priceless, magical event: admission to citizenship.

"Mrs. Moskowitz."

"Oy."

"Mr. Kaplan."

"Here is Hyman Keplen! In poisson!"

Mr. Parkhill sighed. Mr. Kaplan baffled him. Mr. Kaplan had baffled him more than any other of the thirty-odd members of the beginners' grade ever since the very first class assignment: "Twenty Nouns and Their Plural Forms." After correcting a dozen papers, in his apartment, Mr. Parkhill came to one from which glared:

Nuns		_Pl._
house	makes	houses
dog	"	dogies
library	"	Public library
cat	"	Katz

Mr. Parkhill had read this over several times. Then he put the page aside and tried to sort out his thoughts. He recalled Plaut and Samish's classic _Teaching English to Foreigners_, which again and again warned teachers not to jump to the conclusion that a student was backward, a laggard or "resistant learner," before probing to the core of whatever it was that might be _causing_ the neophyte's errors. Sometimes, for instance, a slow reader needed stronger glasses, not stricter tutelage. Sometimes a poor speller was lazy, not stupid. (Spelling had nothing to do with intelligence, as the historic research of Dr. Tyler B. Ponsonby had proved.) And sometimes a pupil's errors resulted not from ignorance but from confusing _sounds:_ Mr. Parkhill had noticed that some of his students said "chicken" when they meant "kitchen," and "kitchen" when they meant "chicken." The results were mystifying. He had returned to the page before him:

ear	makes	hear
up	"	levator
pan	"	pants

Mr. Parkhill cleared his throat. All doubt now vanished: here, clearly, was a student who, if not given prompt first-aid, might easily turn into a "problem case." Anyone who believed that the plural of "cat" is "Katz" certainly needed special attention. As for transforming nouns into nuns . . .

Mr. Parkhill had run his eye down that unforgettable page, looking for the pupil's name. There was none. That was strange: the other members of the class always wrote their names at the top of the page. But no name was inscribed on the top of this page—not in the middle or at the left- or right-hand corner.

Mr. Parkhill turned the sheet over. The name was there, all right. It was printed, not written, and in large, bold letters. They looked especially bold because each character was executed in red crayon—and outlined in blue; and between every two letters sparkled a star, carefully drawn, in green. The ensemble, as triumphant as a display of fireworks, proclaimed:

H*Y*M*A*N   K*A*P*L*A*N

At the next session of the class, Mr. Parkhill had studied Mr. Kaplan with special interest. He was a plump, apple-cheeked gentleman with blondish hair and merry blue eyes, who always had *two* fountain pens clipped to the breast pocket of his jacket. (Other male pupils advertised their literacy with one.) But it was not these features that most vividly seized Mr. Parkhill's mind. It was Mr. Kaplan's smile—a bland, bright, rather charitable smile. That smile rarely left Mr. Kaplan's face. He beamed even while being corrected for the most dreadful errors in speech or spelling or grammar. He seemed to take pride in both the novelty and the number of his mistakes.

Mr. Parkhill recalled the time, in Vocabulary Building, when he had been calling off new words to the class, words to be used in oral sentences.

To "duty," Mr. Pinsky had responded: "To be a good American, please do all your duty!"

Given "nickname" (a word the pupils greeted with delight), Miss Kipnis had replied: "My name is Clara, but friends are calling me 'Cookie.'"

But presented with "choose," Mr. Kaplan had beamed: "I hate to put on a pair vet choose."

And another time, in a brisk drill on opposites, with Miss Mitnick eliciting admiration for the list she daintily wrote on the blackboard:

pull	push
cry	laugh
fix	brake

and Wolfgang Schmitt winning hosannas for his forceful

work	rest
right	rong
sunshine	moonshine

Mr. Kaplan had stunned Mr. Parkhill with

milk	cream
life	debt
dismay	next June

Why, in one composition drill Mr. Kaplan had described how much he hated violins. It had taken Mr. Parkhill several damp moments to hit upon the fact that when Mr. Kaplan wrote "violins" what he probably had in mind was "violence."

Any lingering doubts about Mr. Kaplan's singular use of English were resolved when he was asked to conjugate the verb "to die." Without a second's reflection, Mr. Kaplan had answered: "Die, dead, funeral."

Mr. Parkhill felt a pang of guilt. He had clearly been remiss; he had not applied himself as diligently as he should have to the case of Hyman Kaplan.

Having completed the roll call, Mr. Parkhill opened the session by announcing, "Tonight, class, let us devote ourselves to—Recitation and Speech."

A symphony of approval, punctuated by moans of dismay and groans of alarm, ascended from the rows before him. Most students enjoyed Recitation and Speech, but those who had moaned preferred writing to speaking (like Miss Valuskas, who came from Finland), and those who had groaned considered public performance of any sort out-and-out torture (like Casimir Scymczak, a plasterer from Danzig).

"Suppose we begin with Mr.,"—Mr. Parkhill tried to sound as if the choice was entirely spontaneous—"Kaplan."

The cherub seated in the chair he always occupied in the exact center of the front row gasped, *"Me?!"*

"Yes," smiled Mr. Parkhill. "Won't you start us off?"

"Gledly!"

"Good," said Mr. Parkhill.

"You valcome," said Mr. Kaplan.

He rose, ecstatic, stumbled over the outstretched legs of Mr. Perez (who uttered an Iberian oath), bumped the knee of Mrs. Yanoff (who hissed, "Mister, you are a fireman?!"), apologized to both colleagues with a debonair "Oxcuse," and hurried to the front of the room. Mr. Parkhill ambled to the back. (He always took a seat in the rear during Recitation and Speech.)

At Mr. Parkhill's desk, Mr. Kaplan turned to face his peers. He placed one hand on the dictionary, as if posing for a statue, raised the other like a Roman reviewing his legions, broke into the sunniest of smiles, and in a ringing tenor declaimed: "Mr. Pockheel, ladies an' gantlemen, fallow mambers of beginnis' grate! For mine sobject I vill tell abot fife Prazidents fromm vunderful U.S.A. Foist, Judge Vashington, de fodder of his contry. Naxt, James Medicine, a *fine* lidder. Den, Ted E. Roosevelt, who made de Spenish Var a soccess. Also, Voodenrow Vilson, he made de voild safe for democrats. An' lest, mine *favorite* prazident, a *great* human bean, a man mit de hot an' soul of an angel: Abram Lincohen! . . . Denk you."

Mr. Kaplan strode back to his chair like a hero.

"That's a *speech*?" protested Mr. Bloom.

"Go-o-o-d-bye English," mourned Olga Tarnova.

"Oy!" That was Mrs. Moskowitz.

Mr. Parkhill cleared his throat. "That—uh—was very good, Mr. Kaplan— in content. But I'm afraid you made a considerable number of mistakes in pronunciation."

"My!" chortled Mr. Kaplan.

"The floor is open for corrections," called Mr. Parkhill. "Anyone?"

The repairs came from everyone.

"I'm *dizzy* from so many mixed-op woids!" announced Aaron Blattberg.

"He pronounces 'v' like 'w'—and 'w' like 'v'!" proclaimed Mr. Marcus.

Miss Rochelle Goldberg advised Mr. Kaplan to monitor his sibilants with greater vigilance, "because you told us, teacher, how it is important to keep the difference between 's's and 'z's, so a 'ssss' shouldn't toin into a 'zzz', and a 'zzz'—God fabid—into a 'sss'!"

Several of Miss Goldberg's cronies broke into applause. This caused Wolfgang Schmitt, who was sensitive about his own sibilants, to exclaim that "beans" are not human, and that the "ham" in President Lincoln's first name had been totally omitted. "'Abram Lincohen' iss not Abra*ham* Lincollen!" was how Mr. Schmitt put it.

"Right!" boomed Mr. Bloom, his bald head gleaming.

"Bravo!" cried Miss Caravello.

"Class . . . please . . . ." Mr. Parkhill saw a tiny hand flutter in the air. "Miss Mitnick."

Miss Mitnick, by all odds the best student in the class, shyly observed, "The speaker can improve in his speaking, I think, if he maybe *listens* to the sounds he is making. Then he will say 'leader', not 'lidder', also 'heart' not 'hot', and '*father*', which is absolutely different than '*fodder*'—which is for horses, not humans."

Mr. Parkhill ignored the guffaw from Mrs. Tomasic and the cackle from Miss Gidwitz. "I agree with Miss Mitnick, Mr. Kaplan. You can greatly improve your *pro*nunciation by being careful about your *e*nunciation. For instance, we say 'fellow students', Mr. Kaplan, not 'fallow students.' We say 'president', not 'pr*a*zident', and 'first', not—er—'foist', which is a wholly different word. And it's '*George*' Washington, Mr. Kaplan, not '*Judge*' Washington. Why, right there is a perfect example of why pronunciation is so important! Washington was a *general*, not a judge." (The news came as a blow to Mr. Kaplan.) "And if we pronounce it 'M*a*dison', Mr. Kaplan, we are uttering the name of a President; but if you say, as you did—er—'Medicine', you are not pronouncing the name of a President, but something we take when we are sick."

The laughter (and Aaron Blattberg's scathing observation that James Madison never owned a drugstore) caused Mr. Parkhill to call on the next student at once.

What most troubled Mr. Parkhill was the fact that throughout the entire barrage of corrections from his colleagues, Mr. Kaplan smiled and chuckled and nodded his head in undisguised admiration. One could not tell whether he was congratulating his colleagues on their proficiency or preening himself on having hatched so many fascinating contributions to the English language. Mr. Parkhill felt distinctly uneasy.

During the weeks that followed, Mr. Kaplan's English showed no improvement. If anything, his mistakes increased in scope and were magnified by his enthusiasm. What made Mr. Parkhill's task doubly difficult was the fact that Mr. Kaplan was such a *willing* student. He adored learning. He never came to school late. He always worked hard. He knit his brows regularly, unfailingly submitted his homework on time, and never, never missed a class.

One evening it occurred to Mr. Parkhill that Mr. Kaplan might improve if he simply was encouraged to be a little less *hasty* in the answers he volunteered with such gusto. That insight was born during a lesson on parts of speech, when Mr. Parkhill asked Mr. Kaplan to "give a noun."

"Door," said Mr. Kaplan.

Mr. Parkhill remarked that "door" certainly was a noun, but had been supplied only a moment earlier, by Miss Ziev. "Can you give us another noun?"

"Another door," said Mr. Kaplan.

No, Mr. Kaplan could not be said to be making progress. Asked to name the opposite of "new," he had replied, "Second-hand." Told to construct a sentence using the word "fright" (which Mr. Parkhill *very* carefully enunciated), Mr. Kaplan responded: "I like fright potatoes more than smashed potatoes." And in an exercise on proper nouns, after the other students simply recited names (Lexington Avenue, Puerto Rico, New "Joisey"), Mr. Kaplan proudly announced, "Ohio!"

"Very good!"

It would have been better had not Mr. Kaplan added, "It sonds like an Indian yawnink."

An Indian yawning . . . the outlandish image haunted Mr. Parkhill as he tossed and turned in his bed half that night.

Or take the pleasant, moon-bright evening Mr. Parkhill was running through a useful list of synonyms and antonyms: "Cheerful . . . Sad. Easy . . . Difficult. Lazy—"

"Kachoo!" sneezed Mrs. Shimmelfarb.

"God blast you," said Mr. Kaplan.

"*Mis*ter Kaplan," gasped Mr. Parkhill. "The expression is 'God *bless* you.' Why, you have confused 'bless' "—he printed BLESS on the board—"with 'blast'" and he printed BLAST right underneath. "The words, though somewhat similar in sound, are *entirely* different in meaning . . . I'm sure you all know what 'bless' means?"

"Sure!"

"Soitinly."

But the sage in the front row, scornful of lazy affirmations, gazed at the ceiling and murmured, " 'Bless' . . . 'Bl*ess*'?" His ruminations were audible in the back row. "Aha!" He beamed upon Mr. Parkhill: " 'Bless'! Dat's an okay fromm God."

Mr. Parkhill straightened his tie. "Y-yes . . . Now, what is the meaning of 'blast'?"

"Past tanse of 'blass'?"

"Oh, no, Mr. Kaplan. Goodness, no! The whole *point* lies in the difference between the short 'e' "—Mr. Parkhill placed the pointer on BLESS—"and the open 'a'!" He slid the pointer down to BLAST. "Who can tell us what this word means?"

"Is 'blast' a relation to gas?" asked Mr. Finsterwald.

"Well—er—gas can set off a blast. So can dynamite, or gasoline. But—"

"I think 'blast' is a type exploding," ventured Miss Mitnick.

"Precisely! *Very* good, Miss Mitnick. A blast *is*, in fact, an explosion."

"Blast gas," Mr. Kaplan decreed, searing Miss Mitnick with a superior glance.

Hard though he tried, Mr. Parkhill could discover no consistent pattern to Mr. Kaplan's many errors. They erupted in totally unpredictable ways and wholly spontaneous improvisations.

Take the evening the class was working on "a one-paragraph composition." Mr. Kaplan submitted the following:

When two people are meating on the street [Mr. Parkhill noted that although Mr. Kaplan wrote "street" correctly, he always pronounced it "stritt"] on going Goodby, one is saying, "I am glad I mat you," but the other is giving answer, "Mutchual."

It had taken twelve minutes for the class to complete its autopsy on that one paragraph.

But it was in Recitation and Speech, which elicited Mr. Kaplan's greatest affection, that that intrepid scholar soared to new and unnerving heights. One night, carried away by his eloquence, Mr. Kaplan referred to America's first First Lady as "Mother Washington." Mr. Parkhill was compelled to employ all his powers of persuasion before he could convince Mr. Kaplan that although George Washington was the father of his country, that did not make Martha the *mother*.

Or take the time Mr. Kaplan followed young Vincente Perez's eulogy to Cervantes, whom he proclaimed the greatest writer "een all the world litterture." Mr. Kaplan cast a scornful eye upon Mr. Perez as he delivered a patriotic rejoinder: "Greatest authors are from U.S." The greatest and most "beauriful" American authors (he had read them, it seemed, in his native tongue) were "Jek Laundon, Valt Vitterman, an' de creator of two vunderful books for grown pipple an' boyiss: 'Hawk L. Barryfeen' an' 'Toms Oyer.'"

Mr. Kaplan explained that he was not conferring laurel wreaths on "Edgar Allen Pope" because that wizard had written mysteries, a genre Mr. Kaplan did not admire, nor on "Hoiman Malville," because "Mopy Dick gives more attantion to fish dan to pipple."

The whole episode had so alarmed Mr. Parkhill that he asked Mr. Kaplan to remain after class, to discuss his disastrous reversals of the open "a" and the short "e" ("A *pat*, Mr. Kaplan, is not a *pet*; nor is a pet a pat!"); his repeated transpositioning of the short "i" and the long "e" (Mr. Kaplan once advised the class to patronize only those dentists who are so skillful that they can "feel a cavity so you don't iven fill it"); his deplorable propensity for converting the hard "g" into the startling "k," and the broad "o" into the short "u" (Mr. Kaplan transformed "dogs" into "dugs," and "sucks" into "socks").

To all these earnest supplications, Mr. Kaplan responded with ardent thanks, abject guilt, and an exuberant promise to "chenge vunce an' for all all mine bed hebits!"

Plaut and Samish contained not one page about a student who wedded such willingness to such unteachability.

Everything, Mr. Parkhill feared, pointed to the likelihood that Mr. Kaplan would have to remain in the beginners' grade for an extra year. How could such a pupil possibly be promoted to Miss Higby's Advanced Grammar and

Civics? The fear was strengthened in Mr. Parkhill's mind the night Mrs. Yanoff read a sentence from the textbook *English for Beginners* about the "vast deserts of Arizona." (Mrs. Yanoff, a lugubrious pupil, always wore black, though Mr. Yanoff was far from dead.) In the discussion that followed, Mr. Parkhill learned that Mrs. Yanoff did not understand the meaning of "vast"; she thought it a misprint for "best."

So Mr. Parkhill turned to the blackboard and there printed VAST. "Well, class," he smiled, "who can tell us the meaning of 'vast'?"

Up shot Mr. Kaplan's hand.

"Yes?"

"Ve have four diractions: naut, sot, yeast, an' vast."

"No, no. That is 'west,' Mr. Kaplan." On the board he printed WEST under VAST. "There is a *considerable* difference in meaning between these two words—apart from the fact that the first is pronounced '*v-v-v*ast,' Mr. Kaplan, and the second '*w-w-w*est.'"

This seemed to flash a new light into Mr. Kaplan's inner world. "Aha! So de void you eskink abot is '*v-v*ast' an' not '*w-w*ast.'"

"'W*est*,'" said Mr. Parkhill, "not 'w*a*st.' You must watch those 'e's and 'a's!"

"Hau Kay. De void you esk is not 'w*e*st' but 'v*a*st'?"

Mr. Parkhill declared that "vast" was indeed the *word* for which he was "*ask*ing."

"So—" Mr. Kaplan beamed. "Ven a man buys a suit, he gats de cawt, de pents, an' de vast."

Mr. Parkhill lowered his chalk. "I—uh—am afraid you have introduced still another word."

Mr. Kaplan awaited the plaudits of the crowd.

"'V*est*,'" frowned Mr. Parkhill, "is an article of clothing, but 'west' . . ."

And then Mr. Kaplan turned Mr. Parkhill's concern into consternation. It came during Open Questions. Open Questions was Mr. Parkhill's own invention, a half-session devoted to answering any questions his students might care to raise about any difficulties with English they might have encountered in the course of their daily work and life. The beginners' grade loved Open Questions. So did Mr. Parkhill. He enjoyed helping his flock with practical problems; he felt ever so much more constructive that way. (Miss Higby often told Miss Schnepfe, secretary to the principal of the A.N.P.S.A., that if ever there was a born Open Questions teacher it was Mr. Parkhill.)

"Questions, anyone? *Any* questions—spelling, grammar, pronun—"

Gus Matsoukas emitted his introductory growl, consulted a dog-eared envelope, and muttered his question. "For furniture: is it 'baboon' or '*bamboon*'?"

"Well, a 'baboon' is a type of—er—ape," said Mr. Parkhill, "whereas 'bamboo' is a certain wood. Bamboo is what is used in furniture. *Baboons* are—er—what you may see in a zoo . . . . Next?"

"The word 'stamp'—for putting on mail. Isn't that masculine?" asked Bessie Shimmelfarb.

"N-no," said Mr. Parkhill, and stressed the difference between the postal and the human. (Mrs. Shimmelfarb had obviously equated "mail" with "male.") "Next question?"

"What is the League of Women Motors?" Miss Gidwitz, a fervent feminist, inquired.

"The League of Women *Voters*," said Mr. Parkhill, "is an organization . . ." His exposition led several women to applaud.

"Who was Madame Pumpernickel?" asked Oscar Trabish, who was a baker. (Mr. Trabish's occupation often affected his diction.)

"Madame *Pompadour*," gulped Mr. Parkhill, "was a famous character in French history. She was King Louis XIV's—er—favorite. She—"

"Pompadour is a type haircut!" protested Barney Vinograd, who was a barber.

"Oh, it is," agreed Mr. Parkhill at once. "The name *comes* from Madame Pompadour, who wore her hair—that way."

"Haddya like that?!" breathed Goldie Pomeranz.

"Aducation, aducation," beamed Hyman Kaplan, tendering gratitude to the wonders of learning.

" 'Merit'!" That was Mrs. Moskowitz.

"I beg your pardon?"

" 'Merit,' " Mrs. Moskowitz repeated. "Why isn't it pernonced the way it's spelt?"

Mr. Parkhill looked puzzled. "But 'merit' is spelled exactly as it is pronounced, Mrs. Moskowitz." He printed MERIT on the board. "Don't you see?"

"I see it, but I don't mean it!" Mrs. Moskowitz complained. "*That* woid I never saw in mine whole life! I mean, if a boy and goil are in love, they get—"

"'Married'!" exclaimed Mr. Parkhill. "Oh, that's an entirely different word, Mrs. Moskowitz." His chalk crowned MERIT with MARRIED.

"Oy," sighed Sadie Moskowitz.

"Next question? . . . Mr. Kaplan."

Mr. Kaplan asked, "Mr. Pockheel, vhat's de minnink fromm 'A big depotment'?"

"It's 'de*part*ment,' Mr. Kaplan," said Mr. Parkhill. "Well, class, I'm sure you have all shopped in a large downtown store." A majority nodded. "Now, in these stores, if you want to buy, say, a shirt, you go to a special *part* of the store, where only shirts are sold: that is called the shirt *department*." The quorum assented. "And if you want to buy, say, a goldfish" —Plaut and Samish approved of lightening a lesson with occasional levity—"you would go to another part of the store, where—er—goldfish are for sale . . . . So, you see, each article is sold, or purchased, in a different, special place. And these different, special places are called—'departments.'" Mr. Parkhill printed DEPARTMENT on the blackboard. "Therefore, a *big* department, Mr. Kaplan, is merely a department which is large—big." He put the chalk down. "Is that clear, class?"

It was perfectly clear to the class—except, apparently, Mr. Kaplan, who was blinking blankly.

"Isn't my explanation clear, Mr. Kaplan?" asked Mr. Parkhill anxiously.

"Ebsolutely! It's a *fine* axplination, Mr. Pockheel. Clear like soda-vater. Foist-class! A number vun! . . . But I don't unnistand vhy I hear dat void in de *vay* I do. Simms to me, it's used in anodder *minnink*."

"There's really only one meaning for 'department.'"

"Maybe it's not 'a' big depotment but '*I* big depotment.'"

Mr. Parkhill surveyed the ceiling. "'*I* big department' does not make *sense*, Mr. Kaplan. Let me repeat my explanation." This time Mr. Parkhill enlisted the aid of a hat department, a pajama department, and "a separate part of the store where, for example, you buy—canaries, or other birds."

Mr. Kaplan hung on to Mr. Parkhill's every word; but at "canaries, or other birds," he shook his head.

"What is it that puzzles you, Mr. Kaplan?"

"Mr. Pockheel, I'm vary sorry, but I don't simm to make mine qvastion clear. So I'll give you de exect vay I hoid dat axpression . . . I'm takink a valk. In de stritt. An' I mit a frand. So I stop to say a few polite voids, like: 'Hollo,' 'Harre you?,' 'How you fill?' An' vhile ve are talkink, along comms somvun alse, pessink by, an' by exident he's givink me a bump. So he says, 'Axcuse me,' no? But *somtimes*, an' dis is vat I minn, he says, 'Oh, I big depotment!'"

For one shameless moment Mr. Parkhill wondered whether he could reconcile it with his conscience if he did promote Mr. Kaplan to Advanced Grammar and Civics. Another three months in the beginners' grade might, after all, be nothing but a waste of Mr. Kaplan's time.

Questions for Reflection and Analysis

1. What strikes you about the story as a whole? Is there a particular aspect of the story that elicits a memory or concern about teaching and learning?

2. Which of Mr. Parkhill's teaching strategies, including his responses to students' English language errors, do you find pedagogically sound or unsound and why? What else might Mr. Parkhill have tried, or how else might he have responded?

3. Why does Mr. Parkhill conclude that Mr. Kaplan's English language errors have "no consistent pattern" (page 110)? Why do you agree or disagree with that assessment?

4. How would you assess Mr. Kaplan's progress in learning English? Given your assessment, how can you account for Mr. Kaplan's attitude toward studying English?

5. Should Mr. Kaplan be kept in the beginner class, or should he be promoted to a more advanced class?

The English Lesson

Nicholasa Mohr

(1935–)

Nicholasa Mohr was born in the United States, of Puerto Rican heritage. An award-winning author, she has written numerous books for readers of all ages, including *Nilda* (1973), *El Bronx Remembered: A Novella and Stories* (1975), *Felita* (1979), *Going Home* (1986), and *A Matter of Pride and Other Stories* (1997). A National Book Award Finalist, she also received a Hispanic Heritage Award and an honorary doctorate from the State University of New York.

"Remember our assignment for today everybody! I'm so confident that you will all do exceptionally well!" Mrs. Susan Hamma smiled enthusiastically at her students. "Everyone is to get up and make a brief statement as to why he or she is taking this course in Basic English. You must state your name, where you originally came from, how long you have been here, and . . . uh . . . a little something about yourself, if you wish. Keep it brief, not too long; remember, there are twenty-eight of us. We have a full class, and everyone must have a chance." Mrs. Hamma waved a forefinger at her students. "This is, after all, a democracy, and we have a democratic class; fairness for all!"

Lali grinned and looked at William, who sat directly next to her. He winked and rolled his eyes toward Mrs. Hamma. This was the third class they had attended together. It had not been easy to persuade Rudi that Lali should learn better English.

"Why is it necessary, eh?" Rudi had protested. "She works here in the store with me. She don't have to talk to nobody. Besides, everybody that comes in speaks Spanish—practically everybody, anyway."

Nicholasa Mohr, "The English Lesson" from *In Nueva New York*. Reprinted by permission of Nicholasa Mohr. Copyright © 1986, 1988.

But once William had put the idea to Lali and explained how much easier things would be for her, she kept insisting until Rudi finally agreed. "Go on, you're both driving me nuts. But it can't interfere with business or work—I'm warning you!"

Adult Education offered Basic English, Tuesday evenings from 6:30 to 8:00, at a local public school. Night customers did not usually come into Rudi's Luncheonette until after eight. William and Lali promised that they would leave everything prepared and make up for any inconvenience by working harder and longer than usual, if necessary.

The class admitted twenty-eight students, and because there were only twenty-seven registered, Lali was allowed to take the course even after missing the first two classes. William had assured Mrs. Hamma that he would help Lali catch up; she was glad to have another student to make up the full registration.

Most of the students were Spanish-speaking. The majority were American citizens—Puerto Ricans who had migrated to New York and spoke very little English. The rest were immigrants admitted to the United States as legal aliens. There were several Chinese, two Dominicans, one Sicilian, and one Pole.

Every Tuesday Mrs. Hamma traveled to the Lower East Side from Bayside, Queens, where she lived and was employed as a history teacher in the local junior high school. She was convinced that this small group of people desperately needed her services. Mrs. Hamma reiterated her feelings frequently to just about anyone who would listen. "Why, if these people can make it to class after working all day at those miserable, dreary, uninteresting, and often revolting jobs, well, the least I can do is be there to serve them, making every lesson count toward improving their conditions! My grandparents came here from Germany as poor immigrants, working their way up. I'm not one to forget a thing like that!"

By the time class started most of the students were quite tired. And after the lesson was over, many had to go on to part-time jobs, some even without time for supper. As a result there was always sluggishness and yawning among the students. This never discouraged Mrs. Hamma, whose drive and enthusiasm not only amused the class but often kept everyone awake.

"Now this is the moment we have all been preparing for." Mrs. Hamma stood up, nodded, and blinked knowingly at her students. "Five lessons, I think, are enough to prepare us for our oral statements. You may read from prepared notes, as I said before, but please try not to read every word. We want to hear you speak; conversation is what we're after. When someone asks you about yourself, you cannot take a piece of paper and start reading the answers, now can you? That would be foolish. So . . ."

Standing in front of her desk, she put her hands on her hips and spread her feet, giving the impression that she was going to demonstrate calisthenics.

"Shall we begin?"

Mrs. Hamma was a very tall, angular woman with large extremities. She was the tallest person in the room. Her eyes roamed from student to student until they met William's.

"Mr. Colón, will you please begin?"

Nervously William looked around him, hesitating.

"Come on now, we must get the ball rolling. All right now . . . did you hear what I said? Listen, 'getting the ball rolling' means getting started. Getting things going, such as—" Mrs. Hamma swiftly lifted her right hand over her head, making a fist, then swung her arm around like a pitcher and, with an underhand curve, forcefully threw an imaginary ball out at her students. Trying to maintain her balance, Mrs. Hamma hopped from one leg to the other. Startled, the students looked at one another. In spite of their efforts to restrain themselves, several people in back began to giggle. Lali and William looked away, avoiding each other's eyes and trying not to laugh out loud. With assured countenance, Mrs. Hamma continued.

"An idiom!" she exclaimed, pleased. "You have just seen me demonstrate the meaning of an idiom. Now I want everyone to jot down this information in his notebook." Going to the blackboard, Mrs. Hamma explained, "It's something which literally says one thing, but actually means another. Idiom . . . idiomatic." Quickly and obediently, everyone began to copy what she wrote. "Has everyone got it? OK, let's GET THE BALL ROLLING, Mr. Colón!"

Uneasily William stood up; he was almost the same height standing as sitting. When speaking to others, especially in a new situation, he always preferred to sit alongside those listening; it gave him a sense of equality with other people. He looked around and cleared his throat; at least everyone else was sitting. Taking a deep breath, William felt better.

"My name is William Horacio Colón," he read from a prepared statement. "I have been here in New York City for five months. I coming from Puerto

Rico. My town is located in the mountains in the central part of the island. The name of my town is Aibonito, which means in Spanish 'oh how pretty.' It is name like this because when the Spaniards first seen that place they was very impressed with the beauty of the section and—"

"Make it brief, Mr. Colón," Mrs. Hamma interrupted, "there are others, you know."

William looked at her, unable to continue.

"Go on, go on, Mr. Colón, please!"

"I am working here now, living with my mother and family in Lower East Side of New York City," William spoke rapidly. "I study Basic English por que . . . because my ambition is to learn to speak and read English very good. To get a better job. Y—y también, to help my mother y familia." He shrugged. "Y do better, that's all."

"That's all? Why, that's wonderful! Wonderful! Didn't he do well, class?" Mrs. Hamma bowed slightly toward William and applauded him. The students watched her and slowly each one began to imitate her. Pleased, Mrs. Hamma looked around her; all together they gave William a healthy round of applause.

Next, Mrs. Hamma turned to a Chinese man seated at the other side of the room.

"Mr. Fong, you may go next."

Mr. Fong stood up; he was a man in his late thirties, of medium height and slight build. Cautiously he looked at Mrs. Hamma, and waited.

"Go on, Mr. Fong. Get the ball rolling, remember?"

"All right. Get a ball rolling . . . is idiot!" Mr. Fong smiled.

"No, Mr. Fong, idio*mmmmmm*!" Mrs. Hamma hummed her *m*'s, shaking her head. "Not an—It's idiomatic!"

"What I said!" Mr. Fong responded with self-assurance, looking directly at Mrs. Hamma. "Get a ball rolling, idiomit."

"Never mind." She cleared her throat. "Just go on."

"I said OK?" Mr. Fong waited for an answer.

"Go on, please."

Mr. Fong sighed, "My name is Joseph Fong. I been here in this country United States New York City for most one year." He too read from a prepared statement. "I come from Hong Kong but original born in city of Canton, China. I working delivery food business and live with my brother and his family in Chinatown. I taking the course in Basic English to speak good and improve my position better in this country. Also to be eligible to become American citizen."

Mrs. Hamma selected each student who was to speak from a different part of the room, rather than in the more conventional orderly fashion of row by row, or front to back, or even alphabetical order. This way, she reasoned, no one will know who's next; it will be more spontaneous. Mrs. Hamma enjoyed catching the uncertain looks on the faces of her students. A feeling of control over the situation gave her a pleasing thrill, and she made the most of these moments by looking at several people more than once before making her final choice.

There were more men than women, and Mrs. Hamma called two or three men for each woman. It was her way of maintaining a balance. To her distress, most read from prepared notes, despite her efforts to discourage this. She would interrupt them when she felt they went on too long, then praise them when they finished. Each statement was followed by applause from everyone.

All had similar statements. They had migrated here in search of a better future, were living with relatives, and worked as unskilled laborers. With the exception of Lali, who was childless, every woman gave the ages and sex of her children; most men referred only to their "family." And, among the legal aliens, there was only one who did not want to become an American citizen, Diego Torres, a young man from the Dominican Republic, and he gave his reasons.

". . . and to improve my economic situation." Diego Torres hesitated, looking around the room. "But is one thing I no want, and is to become American citizen"—he pointed to an older man with a dark complexion, seated a few seats away—"like my fellow countryman over there!" The man shook his head disapprovingly at Diego Torres, trying to hide his annoyance. "I no give up my country, Santo Domingo, for nothing," he went on, "nothing in the whole world. OK, man? I come here, pero I cannot help. I got no work at home. There, is political. The United States control most the industry which is sugar and tourismo. Y—you have to know somebody. I tell you, is political to get a job, man! You don't know nobody and you no work, eh? So I come here from necessity, pero this no my country—"

"Mr. Torres," Mrs. Hamma interrupted, "we must be brief, please, there are—"

"I no finish lady!" he snapped. "You wait a minute when I finish!"

There was complete silence as Diego Torres glared at Susan Hamma. No one had ever spoken to her like that, and her confusion was greater than her embarrassment. Without speaking, she lowered her eyes and nodded.

"OK, I prefer live feeling happy in my country, man. Even I don't got too much. I live simple but in my own country I be contento. Pero this is no possible in the situation of Santo Domingo now. Someday we gonna run our own country and be jobs for everybody. My reasons to be here is to make money, man, and go back home buy my house and property. I no be American citizen, no way. I'm Dominican and proud! That's it. That's all I got to say." Abruptly, Diego Torres sat down.

"All right." Mrs. Hamma had composed herself. "Very good; you can come here and state your views. That is what America is all about! We may not agree with you, but we defend your right to an opinion. And as long as you are in this classroom, Mr. Torres, you are in America. Now, everyone, let us give Mr. Torres the same courtesy as everyone else in this class." Mrs. Hamma applauded with a polite light clap, then turned to find the next speaker.

"Bullshit," whispered Diego Torres.

Practically everyone had spoken. Lali and the two European immigrants were the only ones left. Mrs. Hamma called upon Lali.

"My name is Rogelia Dolores Padillo. I come from Canovanas in Puerto Rico. Is a small village in the mountains near El Yunque Rain Forest. My family is still living there. I marry and live here with my husband working in his business of restaurant. Call Rudi's Luncheonette. I been here New York City Lower East Side since I marry, which is now about one year. I study Basic English to improve my vocabulario and learn more about here. This way I help my husband in his business and I do more also for myself, including to be able to read better in English. Thank you."

Aldo Fabrizi, the Sicilian, spoke next. He was a very short man, barely five feet tall. Usually he was self-conscious about his height, but William's presence relieved him of these feelings. Looking at William, he thought being short was no big thing; he was, after all, normal. He told the class that he was originally from Palermo, the capital of Sicily, and had gone to Milano, in the north of Italy, looking for work. After three years in Milano, he immigrated here six months ago and now lived with his sister. He had a good steady job, he said, working in a copper wire factory with his brother-in-law in Brooklyn. Aldo Fabrizi wanted to become an American citizen and spoke passionately about it, without reading from his notes.

"I be proud to be American citizen. I no come here find work live good and no have responsibility or no be grateful." He turned and looked threateningly at Diego Torres. "Hey? I tell you all one thing, I got my nephew right now fighting in Vietnam for this country!" Diego Torres stretched his hands over his head, yawning, folded his hands, and lowered his eyelids. "I wish I could be citizen to fight for this country. My whole family is citizens—we all Americans and we love America!" His voice was quite loud. "That's how I feel."

"Very good," Mrs. Hamma called, distracting Aldo Fabrizi. "That was well stated. I'm sure you will not only become a citizen, but you will also be a credit to this country."

The last person to be called on was the Pole. He was always neatly dressed in a business suit, with a shirt and tie, and carried a briefcase. His manner was reserved but friendly.

"Good evening fellow students and Madame Teacher." He nodded politely to Mrs. Hamma. "My name is Stephan Paczkowski. I am originally from Poland about four months ago. My background is I was born in capital city of Poland, Warsaw. Being educated in capital and also graduating from the University with degree of professor of music with specialty in the history of music."

Stephan Paczkowski read from his notes carefully, articulating every word. "I was given appointment of professor of history of music at University of Krakow. I work there for ten years until about year and half ago. At this time the political situation in Poland was so that all Jewish people were requested by the government to leave Poland. My wife who also is being a professor of economics at University of Krakow is of Jewish parents. My wife was told she could not remain in position at University or remain over there. We made arrangements for my wife and daughter who is seven years of age and myself to come here with my wife's cousin who is to be helping us.

"Since four months I am working in large hospital as position of porter in maintenance department. The thing of it is, I wish to take Basic English to improve my knowledge of English language, and be able to return to my position of professor of history of music. Finally, I wish to become a citizen of United States. That is my reasons. I thank you all."

After Stephan Paczkowski sat down, there was a long awkward silence and everyone turned to look at Mrs. Hamma. Even after the confrontation with Diego Torres, she had applauded without hesitation. Now she seemed unable to move.

"Well," she said, almost breathless, "that's admirable! I'm sure, sir, that you will do very well . . . a person of your . . . like yourself, I mean . . . a professor, after all, it's really just admirable." Everyone was listening intently to what she said. "That was well done, class. Now, we have to get to next week's assignment." Mrs. Hamma realized that no one had applauded Stephan Paczkowski. With a slightly pained expression, she began to applaud. "Mustn't forget Mr. Paczkowski; everybody here must be treated equally. This is America!" The class joined her in a round of applause.

As Mrs. Hamma began to write the next week's assignment on the board, some students looked anxiously at their watches and others asked about the time. Then they all quickly copied the information into their notebooks. It was almost eight o'clock. Those who had to get to second jobs did not want to be late; some even hoped to have time for a bite to eat first. Others were just tired and wanted to get home.

Lali looked at William, sighing impatiently. They both hoped Mrs. Hamma would finish quickly. There would be hell to pay with Rudi if the night customers were already at the luncheonette.

"There, that's next week's work, which is very important, by the way. We will be looking at the history of New York City and the different ethnic groups that lived here as far back as the Dutch. I can't tell you how proud I am of the way you all spoke. All of you—I have no favorites, you know."

Mrs. Hamma was interrupted by the long, loud buzzing sound, bringing the lesson to an end. Quickly everyone began to exit.

"Good night, see you all next Tuesday!" Mrs. Hamma called out. "By the way, if any of you here wants extra help, I have a few minutes this evening." Several people bolted past her, excusing themselves. In less than thirty seconds, Mrs. Hamma was standing in an empty classroom.

William and Lali hurried along, struggling against the cold, sharp March wind that whipped across Houston Street, stinging their faces and making their eyes tear.

In a few minutes they would be at Rudi's. So far, they had not been late once.

"You read very well—better than anybody in class. I told you there was nothing to worry about. You caught up in no time."

"Go on. I was so nervous, honestly! But, I'm glad she left me for one of the last. If I had to go first, like you, I don't think I could open my mouth. You were so calm. You started the thing off very well."

"You go on now, I was nervous myself!" He laughed, pleased.

"Mira, Chiquitín," Lali giggled, "I didn't know your name was Horacio. William Horacio. Ave María, so imposing!"

"That's right, because you see, my mother was expecting a valiant warrior! Instead, well"—he threw up his hands —"no one warned me either. And what a name for a Chiquitín like me."

Lali smiled, saying nothing. At first she had been very aware of William's dwarfishness. Now it no longer mattered. It was only when she saw others reacting to him for the first time that she was once more momentarily struck with William's physical difference.

"We should really try to speak in English, Lali. It would be good practice for us."

"Dios mío . . . I feel so foolish, and my accent is terrible!"

"But look, we all have to start some place. Besides, what about the Americanos? When they speak Spanish, they sound pretty awful, but we accept it. You know I'm right. And that's how people get ahead, by not being afraid to try."

They walked in silence for a few moments. Since William had begun to work at Rudi's, Lali's life had become less lonely. Lali was shy by nature; making friends was difficult for her. She had grown up in the sheltered environment of a large family living in a tiny mountain village. She was considered quite plain. Until Rudi had asked her parents for permission to court her, she had only gone out with two local boys. She had accepted his marriage proposal expecting great changes in her life. But the age difference between her and Rudi, being in a strange country without friends or relatives, and the long hours of work at the luncheonette confined Lali to a way of life she could not have imagined. Every evening she found herself waiting for William to come in to work, looking forward to his presence.

Lali glanced over at him as they started across the wide busy street. His grip on her elbow was firm but gentle as he led her to the sidewalk.

"There you are, Miss Lali, please to watch your step!" he spoke in English.

His thick golden-blond hair was slightly mussed and fell softly, partially covering his forehead. His wide smile, white teeth, and large shoulders made him appear quite handsome. Lali found herself staring at William. At that moment she wished he could be just like everybody else.

"Lali?" William asked, confused by her silent stare. "Is something wrong?"

"No." Quickly Lali turned her face. She felt herself blushing. "I . . . I was just thinking how to answer in English, that's all."

"But that's it . . . don't think! What I mean is, don't go worrying about what to say. Just talk natural. Get used to simple phrases and the rest will come, you'll see."

"All right," Lali said, glad the strange feeling of involvement had passed, and William had taken no notice of it. "It's an interesting class, don't you think so? I mean—like that man, the professor. Bendito! Imagine, they had to leave because they were Jewish. What a terrible thing!"

"I don't believe he's Jewish; it's his wife who is Jewish. She was a professor too. But I guess they don't wanna be separated . . . and they have a child."

"Tsk, tsk, los pobres! But, can you imagine, then? A professor from a university doing the job of a porter? My goodness!" Lali sighed. "I never heard of such a thing!"

"But you gotta remember, it's like Mrs. Hamma said, this is America, right? So . . . everybody got a chance to clean toilets! Equality, didn't she say that?"

They both laughed loudly, stepping up their pace until they reached Rudi's Luncheonette.

The small luncheonette was almost empty. One customer sat at the counter.

"Just in time," Rudi called out. "Let's get going. People gonna be coming in hungry any minute. I was beginning to worry about you two!"

William ran in the back to change into his workshirt.

Lali slipped into her uniform and soon was busy at the grill.

"Well, did you learn anything tonight?" Rudi asked her.

"Yes."

"What?"

"I don't know," she answered, without interrupting her work. "We just talked a little bit in English."

"A little bit in English—about what?"

Lali busied herself, ignoring him. Rudi waited, then tried once more.

"You remember what you talked about?" He watched her as she moved, working quickly, not looking in his direction.

"No." Her response was barely audible.

Lately Rudi had begun to reflect on his decision to marry such a young woman. Especially a country girl like Lali, who was shy and timid. He had never had children with his first wife and wondered if he lacked the patience needed for the young. They had little in common and certainly seldom spoke about anything but the business. Certainly he could not fault her for being lazy; she was always working without being asked. People would accuse him in jest of over-working his young wife. He assured them there was no need, because she had the endurance of a country mule. After almost one year of marriage, he felt he hardly knew Lali or what he might do to please her.

William began to stack clean glasses behind the counter.

"Chiquitín! How about you and Lali having something to eat? We gotta few minutes yet. There's some fresh rice pudding."

"Later . . . I'll have mine a little later, thanks."

"Ask her if she wants some," Rudi whispered, gesturing toward Lali.

William moved close to Lali and spoke softly to her.

"She said no." William continued his work.

"Listen, Chiquitín, I already spoke to Raquel Martinez who lives next door. You know, she's got all them kids? In case you people are late, she can cover for you and Lali. She said it was OK."

"Thanks, Rudi, I appreciate it. But we'll get back on time."

"She's good, you know. She helps me out during the day whenever I need extra help. Off the books, I give her a few bucks. But, mira, I cannot pay you and Raquel both. So if she comes in, you don't get paid. You know that then, OK?"

"Of course. Thanks, Rudi."

"Sure, well, it's a good thing after all. You and Lali improving yourselves. Not that she really needs it, you know. I provide for her. As I said, she's my wife, so she don't gotta worry. If she wants something, I'll buy it for her. I made it clear she didn't have to bother with none of that, but"—Rudi shrugged—"if that's what she wants, I'm not one to interfere."

The door opened. Several men walked in.

"Here they come, kids!"

Orders were taken and quickly filled. Customers came and went steadily until about eleven o'clock, when Rudi announced that it was closing time.

The weeks passed, then the months, and this evening, William and Lali sat with the other students listening to Mrs. Hamma as she taught the last lesson of the Basic English course.

"It's been fifteen long hard weeks for all of you. And I want you to know how proud I am of each and every one here."

William glanced at Lali; he knew she was upset. He felt it too, wishing that this was not the end of the course. It was the only time he and Lali had free to themselves together. Tuesday had become their evening.

Lali had been especially irritable that week, dreading this last session. For her, Tuesday meant leaving the world of Rudi, the luncheonette, that street, everything that she felt imprisoned her. She was accomplishing something all by herself, and without the help of the man she was dependent upon.

Mrs. Hamma finally felt that she had spent enough time assuring her students of her sincere appreciation.

"I hope some of you will stay and have a cup of coffee or tea, and cookies. There's plenty over there." She pointed to a side table where a large electric coffeepot filled with hot water was steaming. The table was set for instant coffee and tea, complete with several boxes of assorted cookies. "I do this every semester for my classes. I think it's nice to have a little informal chat with one another; perhaps discuss our plans for the future and so on. But it must be in English! Especially those of you who are Spanish-speaking. Just because you outnumber the rest of us, don't you think you can get away with it!" Mrs. Hamma lifted her forefinger threateningly but smiled. "Now, it's still early, so there's plenty of time left. Please turn in your books."

Some of the people said good-bye quickly and left, but the majority waited, helping themselves to coffee or tea and cookies. Small clusters formed as people began to chat with one another.

Diego Torres and Aldo Fabrizi were engaged in a friendly but heated debate on the merits of citizenship.

"Hey, you come here a minute, please," Aldo Fabrizi called out to William, who was standing with a few people by the table, helping himself to coffee. William walked over to the two men.

"What's the matter?"

"What do you think of your paisano. He don't wanna be citizen. I say—my opinion—he don't appreciate what he got in this country. This a great country! You the same like him, what do you think?"

"Mira, please tell him we no the same," Diego Torres said with exasperation. "You a citizen, pero not me. Este tipo no comprende, man!"

"Listen, you comprendo . . . Yo capito! I know what you say. He be born in Puerto Rico. But you see, we got the same thing. I be born in Sicily—that is another part of the country, separate. But I still Italiano, capito?"

"Dios mío!" Diego Torres smacked his forehead with an open palm. "Mira—he turned to William—"explain to him, por favor."

William swallowed a mouthful of cookies. "He's right. Puerto Rico is part of the United States. And Sicily is part of Italy. But not the Dominican Republic where he been born. There it is not the United States. I was born a citizen, do you see?"

"Sure!" Aldo Fabrizi nodded. "Capito. Hey, but you still no can vote, right?"

"Sure I can vote; I got all the rights. I am a citizen, just like anybody else," William assured him.

"You some lucky guy then. You got it made! You don't gotta worry like the rest of—"

"Bullshit," Diego Torres interrupted. "Why he got it made, man? He force to leave his country. Pendejo, you no capito nothing, man . . ."

As the two men continued to argue, William waited for the right moment to slip away and join Lali.

She was with some of the women, who were discussing how sincere and devoted Mrs. Hamma was.

"She's hardworking . . ."

"And she's good people . . ." an older woman agreed.

Mr. Fong joined them, and they spoke about the weather and how nice and warm the days were.

Slowly people began to leave, shaking hands with their fellow students and Mrs. Hamma, wishing each other luck.

Mrs. Hamma had been hoping to speak to Stephan Paczkowski privately this evening, but he was always with a group. Now he offered his hand.

"I thank you very much for your good teaching. It was a fine semester."

"Oh, do you think so? Oh, I'm so glad to hear you say that. You don't know how much it means. Especially coming from a person of your caliber. I am confident, yes, indeed, that you will soon be back to your profession, which, after all, is your true calling. If there is anything I can do, please . . ."

"Thank you, miss. This time I am registering in Hunter College, which is in Manhattan on Sixty-eighth Street in Lexington Avenue, with a course of English Literature for beginners." After a slight bow, he left.

"Good-bye." Mrs. Hamma sighed after him.

Lali, William, and several of the women picked up the paper cups and napkins and tossed them into the trash basket.

"Thank you so much, that's just fine. Luis the porter will do the rest. He takes care of these things. He's a lovely person and very helpful. Thank you."

William shook hands with Mrs. Hamma, then waited for Lali to say good-bye. They were the last ones to leave.

"Both of you have been such good students. What are your plans? I hope you will continue with your English."

"Next term we're taking another course," Lali said, looking at William.

"Yes," William responded, "it's more advance. Over at the Washington Irving High School around Fourteenth Street."

"Wonderful." Mrs. Hamma hesitated. "May I ask you a question before you leave? It's only that I'm a little curious about something."

"Sure, of course." They both nodded.

"Are you two related? I mean, you are always together and yet have different last names, so I was just . . . wondering."

"Oh, we are just friends," Lali answered, blushing.

"I work over in the luncheonette at night, part-time."

"Of course." Mrs. Hamma looked at Lali. "Mrs. Padillo, your husband's place of business. My, that's wonderful, just wonderful! You are all just so ambitious. Very good . . ."

They exchanged farewells.

Outside, the warm June night was sprinkled with the sweetness of the new buds sprouting on the scrawny trees and hedges planted along the sidewalks and in the housing project grounds. A brisk breeze swept over the East River on to Houston Street, providing a freshness in the air.

This time they were early, and Lali and William strolled at a relaxed pace.

"Well," Lali shrugged, "that's that. It's over!"

"Only for a couple of months. In September we'll be taking a more advanced course at the high school."

"I'll probably forget everything I learned by then."

"Come on, Lali, the summer will be over before you know it. Just you wait and see. Besides, we can practice so we don't forget what Mrs. Hamma taught us."

"Sure, what do you like to speak about?" Lali said in English.

William smiled, and clasping his hands, said, "I would like to say to you how wonderful you are, and how you gonna have the most fabulous future . . . after all, you so ambitious!"

When she realized he sounded just like Mrs. Hamma, Lali began to laugh.

"Are you"—Lali tried to keep from giggling, tried to pretend to speak in earnest—"sure there is some hope for me?"

"Oh, heavens, yes! You have shown such ability this"—William was beginning to lose control, laughing loudly—"semester!"

"But I want"—Lali was holding her sides with laughter—"some guarantee of this. I got to know."

"Please, Miss Lali." William was laughing so hard tears were coming to his eyes. "After . . . after all, you now a member in good standing . . . of the promised future!"

William and Lali broke into uncontrollable laughter, swaying and limping, oblivious to the scene they created for the people who stared and pointed at them as they continued on their way to Rudi's.

Questions for Reflection and Analysis

1. What strikes you about the story as a whole? Is there a particular aspect of the story that elicits a memory or concern about teaching and learning?

2. Under what circumstances does Mrs. Hamma's classroom behavior reflect or conflict with her stated pedagogical objectives? Collectively, what do these moments reveal about Mrs. Hamma?

3. Which of Mrs. Hamma's responses to each student's presentation do you find commendable or problematic? What do Mrs. Hamma's different reactions to each student reveal about her underlying assumptions and attitudes?

4. What do the students' reactions and responses reveal about the students' evaluation of Mrs. Hamma's teaching? What do their actual spoken words reveal about their English language progress and proficiency?

5. How extensively is William's theory—that the best way to acquire English is to "talk natural" (p. 125)—enacted in Mrs. Hamma's classroom? How extensively has this advice been enacted in your own experience as a language learner or teacher? Is this good advice?

■ *E*nglish as a *S*econd *L*anguage

Lucy Honig

(1948–)

Lucy Honig holds an M.A. in Teaching English to Speakers of Other Languages and has taught ESOL in university and adult education programs in the United States and elsewhere. For many years, Honig was an associate professor of International Health in the School of Public Health at Boston University. A prize-winning author, her publications include *Picking Up* (1986) and *Open Season* (2002).

Inside Room 824, Maria parked the vacuum cleaner, fastened all the locks and the safety chain and kicked off her shoes. Carefully she lay a stack of fluffy towels on the bathroom vanity. She turned the air conditioning up high and the lights down low. Then she hoisted up the skirt of her uniform and settled all the way back on the king-sized bed with her legs straight out in front of her. Her feet and ankles were swollen. She wriggled her toes. She threw her arms out in each direction and still her hands did not come near the edges of the bed. From here she could see, out the picture window, the puffs of green treetops in Central Park, the tiny people circling along the paths below. She tore open a small foil bag of cocktail peanuts and ate them very slowly, turning each one over separately with her tongue until the salt dissolved. She snapped on the TV with the remote control and flipped channels.

The big mouth game show host was kissing and hugging a woman playing on the left-hand team. Her husband and children were right there with her, and *still* he encircled her with his arms. Then he sidled up to the daughter, a girl younger than her own Giuliette, and *hugged* her and kept *holding* her, asking questions. None of his business, if this girl had a boyfriend back in Saginaw!

"Mama, you just don't understand." That's what Jorge always said when she watched TV at home. He and his teenaged friends would sit around in their torn bluejeans dropping potato chips between the cushions of her couch and laughing, writhing with laughter while she sat like a stone.

Now the team on the right were hugging each other, squealing, jumping up and down. They'd just won a whole new kitchen—refrigerator, dishwasher, clothes washer, microwave, *everything*! Maria could win a whole new kitchen too, someday. You just spun a wheel, picked some words. She could do that.

She saw herself on TV with Carmen and Giuliette and Jorge. Her handsome children were so quick to press the buzzers the other team never had a chance to answer first. And they got every single answer right. Her children shrieked and clapped and jumped up and down each time the board lit up. They kissed and hugged that man whenever they won a prize. That man put his hands on her beautiful young daughters. That man pinched and kissed *her*, an old woman, in front of the whole world! Imagine seeing *this* back home! Maria frowned, chewing on the foil wrapper. There was nobody left at home in Guatemala, nobody to care if a strange man squeezed her wrinkled flesh on the TV.

"Forget it, Mama. They don't let poor people on these programs," Jorge said one day.

"But poor people need the money, they can win it here!"

Jorge sighed impatiently. "They don't give it away because you *need* it!"

It was true, she had never seen a woman with her kids say on a show: My husband's dead. Jorge knew. They made sure before they invited you that you were the right kind of people and you said the right things. Where would she put a new kitchen in her cramped apartment anyway? No hookups for a washer, no space for a two-door refrigerator . . .

She slid sideways off the bed, carefully smoothed out the quilted spread, and squeezed her feet into her shoes. Back out in the hall she counted the bath towels in her cart to see if there were enough for the next wing. Then she wheeled the cart down the long corridor, silent on the deep blue rug.

Maria pulled the new pink dress on over her head, eased her arms into the sleeves, then let the skirt slide into place. In the mirror she saw a small dark protrusion from a large pink flower. She struggled to zip up in back, then she fixed the neck, attaching the white collar she had crocheted. She pinned the rhinestone brooch on next. Shaking the pantyhose out of the package, she remembered the phrase: the cow before the horse, wasn't that it? She should have put these on first. Well, so what. She rolled down the left leg of the nylons, stuck her big toe in, and drew the sheer fabric around her foot, unrolling it up past her knee. Then she did the right foot, careful not to catch the hose on the small flap of scar.

The right foot bled badly when she ran over the broken glass, over what had been the only window of the house. It had shattered from gunshots across the dirt yard. The chickens dashed around frantically, squawking, trying to fly, spraying brown feathers into the air. When she had seen Pedro's head turn to blood and the two oldest boys dragged away, she swallowed every word, every cry, and ran with the two girls. The fragments of glass stayed in her foot for all the days of hiding. They ran and ran and ran and somehow Jorge caught up and they were found by their own side and smuggled out. And still she was silent, until the nurse at the border went after the glass and drained the mess inside her foot. Then she had sobbed and screamed, "Aaiiiee!"

"Mama, stop thinking and get ready," said Carmen.

"It is too short, your skirt," Maria said in Spanish. "What will they say?"

Carmen laughed. "It's what they all wear, except for you old ladies."

"Not to work! Not to school!"

"Yes, to work, to school! And Mama, you are going for an award for your English, for all you've learned, so please speak English!"

Maria squeezed into the pink high heels and held each foot out, one by one, so she could admire the beautiful slim arch of her own instep, like the feet of the American ladies on Fifth Avenue. Carmen laughed when she saw her mother take the first faltering steps, and Maria laughed too. How much she had already practiced in secret, and still it was so hard! She teetered on them back and forth from the kitchen to the bedroom, trying to feel steady, until Carmen finally sighed and said, "Mama, quick now or you'll be late!"

She didn't know if it was a good omen or a bad one, the two Indian women on the subway. They could have been sitting on the dusty ground at the market in San _____, selling corn or clay pots, with the bright-colored striped shawls and full skirts, the black hair pulled into two braids down each back, the deeply furrowed square faces set in those impassive expressions, seeing everything, seeing nothing. They were exactly as they must have been back home, but she was seeing them *here*, on the downtown IRT from the Bronx, surrounded by businessmen in suits, kids with big radio boxes, girls in skin-tight jeans and dark purple lipstick. Above them, advertisements for family planning and TWA. They were like stone-age men sitting on the train in loincloths made from animal skins, so out of place, out of time. Yet timeless. Maria thought, they are timeless guardian spirits, here to accompany me to my honors. Did anyone else see them? As strange as they were, nobody looked. Maria's heart pounded faster. The boys with the radios were standing right over them and never saw them. They were invisible to everyone but her: Maria was utterly convinced of it. The spirit world had come back to life, here on the number 4 train! It was a miracle!

"Mama, look, you see the grandmothers?" said Carmen.

"Of course I see them," Maria replied, trying to hide the disappointment in her voice. So Carmen saw them too. They were not invisible. Carmen rolled her eyes and smirked derisively as she nodded in their direction, but before she could put her derision into words, Maria became stern. "Have respect," she said. "They are the same as your father's people." Carmen's face sobered at once.

She panicked when they got to the big school by the river. "Like the United Nations," she said, seeing so much glass and brick, an endless esplanade of concrete.

"It's only a college, Mama. People learn English here, too. And more, like nursing, electronics. This is where Anna's brother came for computers."

"Las Naciones Unidas," Maria repeated, and when the guard stopped them to ask where they were going, she answered in Spanish: to the literacy award ceremony.

"*English*, Mama!" whispered Carmen.

But the guard also spoke in Spanish: take the escalator to the third floor.

"See, he knows," Maria retorted.

"That's not the point," murmured Carmen, taking her mother by the hand.

Every inch of the enormous room was packed with people. She clung to Carmen and stood by the door paralyzed until Cheryl, her teacher, pushed her way to them and greeted Maria with a kiss. Then she led Maria back through the press of people to the small group of award winners from other programs. Maria smiled shakily and nodded hello.

"They're all here now!" Cheryl called out. A photographer rushed over and began to move the students closer together for a picture.

"Hey Bernie, wait for the Mayor!" someone shouted to him. He spun around, called out some words Maria did not understand, and without even turning back to them, he disappeared. But they stayed there, huddled close, not knowing if they could move. The Chinese man kept smiling, the tall black man stayed slightly crouched, the Vietnamese woman squinted, confused, her glasses still hidden in her fist. Maria saw all the cameras along the sides of the crowd, and the lights, and the people from television with video machines, and more lights. Her stomach began to jump up and down. Would she be on television, in the newspapers? Still smiling, holding his pose, the Chinese man next to her asked, "Are you nervous?"

"Oh yes," she said. She tried to remember the expression Cheryl had taught them. "I have worms in my stomach," she said.

He was a much bigger man than she had imagined from seeing him on TV. His face was bright red as they ushered him into the room and quickly through the crowd, just as it was his turn to take the podium. He said hello to the other speakers and called them by their first names. The crowd drew closer to the little stage, the people standing farthest in the back pushed in. Maria tried hard to listen to the Mayor's words. "Great occasion . . . pride of our city . . . ever since I created the program . . . people who have worked so hard . . . overcoming hardship . . . come so far." Was that them? Was he talking about them already? Why were the people out there all starting to laugh? She strained to understand, but still caught only fragments of his words. "My mother used to say . . . and I said, Look, Mama . . ." He was talking about *his* mother now; he called her Mama, just like Maria's kids called *her*. But everyone laughed so hard. At his mother? She forced herself to smile; up front, near the podium, everyone could see her. She should seem to pay attention and understand. Looking out into the crowd she felt dizzy. She tried to find Carmen among all the pretty young women with big eyes and dark hair. There she was! Carmen's eyes met Maria's; Carmen waved. Maria beamed out at her. For a moment she felt like she belonged there, in this crowd. Everyone was smiling, everyone was so happy while the Mayor of New York stood at the podium telling jokes. How happy Maria felt too!

"Maria Perez grew up in the countryside of Guatemala, the oldest daughter in a family of 19 children," read the Mayor as Maria stood quaking by his side. She noticed he made a slight wheezing noise when he breathed between words. She saw the hairs in his nostrils, black and white and wiry. He paused. "Nineteen children!" he exclaimed, looking at the audience. A small gasp was passed along through the crowd. Then the Mayor looked back at the sheet of paper before him. "Maria never had a chance to learn to read and write, and she was already the mother of five children of her own when she fled Guatemala in 1980 and made her way to New York for a new start."

It was her own story, but Maria had a hard time following. She had to stand next to him while he read it, and her feet had started to hurt, crammed into the new shoes. She shifted her weight from one foot to the other.

"At the age of 45, while working as a chambermaid and sending her children through school, Maria herself started school for the first time. In night courses she learned to read and write in her native Spanish. Later, as she was pursuing her G.E.D. in Spanish, she began studying English as a Second Language. This meant Maria was going to school five nights a week! Still she worked as many as 60 hours cleaning rooms at the Plaza Hotel.

"Maria's ESL teacher, Cheryl Sands, says—and I quote—'Maria works harder than any student I have ever had. She is an inspiration to her classmates. Not only has she learned to read and write in her new language, but she initiated an oral history project in which she taped and transcribed interviews with other students, who have told their stories from around the world.' Maria was also one of the first in New York to apply for amnesty under the 1986 Immigration Act. Meanwhile, she has passed her enthusiasm for education to her children: her son is now a junior in high school, her youngest daughter attends the State University, and her oldest daughter, who we are proud to have with us today, is in her second year of law school on a scholarship."

Two older sons were dragged through the dirt, chickens squawking in mad confusion, feathers flying. She heard more gunshots in the distance, screams, chickens squawking. She heard, she ran. Maria looked down at her bleeding feet. Wedged tightly into the pink high heels, they throbbed.

The Mayor turned toward her. "Maria, I think it's wonderful that you have taken the trouble to preserve the folklore of students from so many countries." He paused. Was she supposed to say something? Her heart stopped beating. What was folklore? What was preserved? She smiled up at him, hoping that was all she needed to do.

"Maria, tell us now, if you can, what was one of the stories you collected in your project?"

This was definitely a question, meant to be answered. Maria tried to smile again. She strained on tiptoes to reach the microphone, pinching her toes even more tightly in her shoes. "Okay," she said, setting off a high-pitched ringing from the microphone.

The Mayor said, "Stand back," and tugged at her collar. She quickly stepped away from the microphone.

"Okay," she said again, and this time there was no shrill sound. "One of my stories, from Guatemala. You want to hear?"

The Mayor put his arm around her shoulder and squeezed hard. Her first impulse was to wriggle away, but he held tight. "Isn't she wonderful?" he asked the audience. There was a low ripple of applause. "Yes, we want to hear!"

She turned and looked up at his face. Perspiration was shining on his forehead and she could see by the bright red bulge of his neck that his collar was too tight. "In my village in Guatemala," she began, "the mayor did not go along—get along—with the government so good."

"Hey, Maria," said the Mayor, "I know exactly how he felt!" The people in the audience laughed. Maria waited until they were quiet again.

"One day our mayor met with the people in the village. Like you meet people here. A big crowd in the square."

"The people liked him, your mayor?"

"Oh, yes," said Maria. "Very much. He was very good. He tried for more roads, more doctors, new farms. He cared very much about his people."

The Mayor shook his head up and down. "Of course," he said, and again the audience laughed.

Maria said, "The next day after the meeting, the meeting in the square with all the people, soldiers come and shoot him dead."

For a second there was total silence. Maria realized she had not used the past tense and felt a deep, horrible stab of shame for herself, shame for her teacher. She was a disgrace! But she did not have more than a second of this horror before the whole audience began to laugh. What was happening? They couldn't be laughing at her bad verbs? They couldn't be laughing at her dead mayor! They laughed louder and louder and suddenly flashbulbs were going off around her, the TV cameras swung in close, too close, and the Mayor was grabbing her by the shoulders again, holding her tight, posing for one camera after another as the audience burst into wild applause. But she hadn't even finished! Why were they laughing?

"What timing, huh?" said the Mayor over the uproar. "What d'ya think, the Republicans put her here, or maybe the Board of Estimate?" Everyone laughed even louder and he still clung to her and cameras still moved in close, lights kept going off in her face and she could see nothing but the sharp white poof! of light over and over again. She looked for Carmen and Cheryl, but the white poof! poof! poof! blinded her. She closed her eyes and listened to the uproar, now beginning to subside, and in her mind's eye saw chickens trying to fly, chickens fluttering around the yard littered with broken glass.

He squeezed her shoulders again and leaned into the microphone. "There are ways to get rid of mayors, and ways to get rid of mayors, huh Maria?"

The surge of laughter rose once more, reached a crescendo, and then began to subside again. "But wait," said the Mayor. The cameramen stepped back a bit, poising themselves for something new.

"I want to know just one more thing, Maria," said the Mayor, turning to face her directly again. The crowd quieted. He waited a few seconds more, then asked his question. "It says here 19 children. What was it like growing up in a house with 19 children? How many *bathrooms* did you have?"

Her stomach dropped and twisted as the mayor put his hand firmly on the back of her neck and pushed her toward the microphone again. It was absolutely quiet now in the huge room. Everyone was waiting for her to speak. She cleared her throat and made the microphone do the shrill hum. Startled, she jumped back. Then there was silence. She took a big, trembling breath.

"We had no bathrooms there, Mister Mayor," she said. "Only the outdoors."

The clapping started immediately, then the flashbulbs burning up in her face. The Mayor turned to her, put a hand on each of her shoulders, bent lower and kissed her! Kissed her on the cheek!

"Isn't she terrific?" he asked the audience, his hand on the back of her neck again, drawing her closer to him. The audience clapped louder, faster. "Isn't she just the greatest?"

She tried to smile and open her eyes, but the lights were still going off—poof! poof!—and the noise was deafening.

"Mama, look, your eyes were closed there, too," chided Jorge, sitting on the floor in front of the television set.

Maria had watched the camera move from the announcer at the studio desk to her own stout form in bright pink, standing by the Mayor.

"In my village in Guatemala," she heard herself say, and the camera showed her wrinkled face close up, eyes open now but looking nowhere. Then the mayor's face filled the screen, his forehead glistening, and then suddenly all the people in the audience, looking ahead, enrapt, took his place. Then, there was her wrinkled face again, talking without a smile. ". . . soldiers come and shoot him dead." Maria winced, hearing the wrong tense of her verbs. The camera shifted from her face to the Mayor. In the brief moment of shamed silence after she'd uttered those words, the Mayor drew his finger like a knife across his throat. And the audience began to laugh.

"Turn it off!" she yelled to Jorge. "Off! This minute!"

Late that night she sat alone in the unlighted room, soaking her feet in Epsom salts. The glow of the television threw shadows across the wall, but the sound was off. The man called Johnny was on the screen, talking. The people in the audience and the men in the band and the movie stars sitting on the couch all had their mouths wide open in what she knew were screams of laughter while Johnny wagged his tongue. Maria heard nothing except brakes squealing below on the street and the lonely clanging of garbage cans in the alley.

She thought about her English class and remembered the pretty woman, Ling, who often fell asleep in the middle of a lesson. The other Chinese students all teased her. Everyone knew that she sewed coats in a sweatshop all day. After the night class she took the subway to the Staten Island Ferry, and after the ferry crossing she had to take a bus home. Her parents were old and sick and she did all their cooking and cleaning late at night. She struggled to keep awake in class; it seemed to take all her energy simply to smile and listen. She said very little and the teacher never forced her, but she fell further and further behind. They called her the Quiet One.

One day just before the course came to an end the Quiet One asked to speak. There was no reason, no provocation—they'd been talking informally about their summer plans—but Ling spoke with a sudden urgency. Her English was very slow. Seeing what a terrible effort it was for her, the classmates all tried to help when she searched for words.

"In my China village there was a teacher," Ling began. "Man teacher." She paused. "All children love him. He teach mathematic. He very—" She stopped and looked up toward the ceiling. Then she gestured with her fingers around her face.

"Handsome!" said Charlene, the oldest of the three Haitian sisters in the class.

Ling smiled broadly. "Handsome! Yes, he very handsome. Family very rich before. He have sister go to Hong Kong who have many, many money."

"*Much* money," said Maria.

"Much, much money," repeated Ling thoughtfully. "Teacher live in big house."

"In China? Near you?"

"Yes. Big house with much old picture." She stopped and furrowed her forehead, as if to gather words inside of it.

"Art? Paint? Pictures like that?" asked Xavier.

Ling nodded eagerly. "Yes. In big house. Most big house in village."

"But big house, money, rich like that, bad in China," said Fu Wu. "Those year, Government bad to you. How they let him do?"

"In *my* country," said Carlos, "government bad to you if you got *small* house, *no* money."

"Me too," said Maria.

"Me too," said Charlene.

The Chinese students laughed.

Ling shrugged and shook her head. "Don't know. He have big house. Money gone, but keep big house. Then I am little girl." She held her hand low to the floor.

"I *was* a little girl," Charlene said gently.

"I *was*," said Ling. "Was, was." She giggled for a moment, then seemed to spend some time in thought. "We love him. All children love—all children did loved him. He giving tea in house. He was—was—so handsome!" She giggled. All the women in the class giggled. "He very nice. He learn music, he go . . . he went to school far away."

"America?"

Ling shook her head. "Oh no, no. You know, another . . . west."

"Europa!" exclaimed Maria proudly. "Espain!"

"No, no, another."

"France!" said Patricia, Charlene's sister. "He went to school in France?"

"Yes, France," said Ling. Then she stopped again, this time for a whole minute. The others waited patiently. No one said a word. Finally she continued. "But big boys in more old school not like him. He too handsome."

"Oooh!" sang out a chorus of women. "Too handsome!"

"The boys were jealous," said Carlos.

Ling seized the word. "Jealous! Jealous! They very jealous. He handsome, he study France, he very nice to children, he give tea and cake in big house, he show picture on wall." Her torrent of words came to an end and she began to think again, visibly, her brow furrowing. "Big school boys, they . . ." She stopped.

"Jealous!" sang out the others.

"Yes," she said, shaking her head "no." "But more. More bad. Hate. They hate him."

"That's bad," said Patricia.

"Yes, very bad." Ling paused, looking at the floor. "And they heat."

"Hate."

"No, they heat."

All the class looked puzzled. Heat? Heat? They turned to Cheryl.

The teacher spoke for the first time. "Hit? Ling, do you mean hit? They hit him?" Cheryl slapped the air with her hand.

Ling nodded, her face somehow serious and smiling at the same time. "Hit many time. And also so." She scooted her feet back and forth along the floor.

"Oooh," exclaimed Charlene, frowning. "They kicked him with the feet."

"Yes," said Ling. 'They kicked him with the feet and hit him with the hands, many many time they hit, they kick."

"Where this happened?" asked Xavier.

"In the school. In classroom like . . ." She gestured to mean their room.

"In the school?" asked Xavier. "But other people were they there? They say stop, no?"

"No. Little children in room. They cry, they . . ." She covered her eyes with her hand, then uncovered them. "Big boys kick and hit. No one stop. No one help."

Everyone in class fell silent. Maria remembered: they could not look at one another then. They could not look at their teacher.

Ling continued. "They break him, very hurt much place." She stopped. They all fixed their stares on Ling, they could bear looking only at her. "Many place," she said. Her face had not changed, it was still half smiling. But now there were drops coming from her eyes, a single tear down each side of her nose. Maria would never forget it. Ling's face did not move or wrinkle or frown. Her body was absolutely still. Her shoulders did not quake. Nothing in the shape or motion of her eyes or mouth changed. None of the things that Maria had always known happen when you cry happened when Ling shed tears. Just two drops rolled slowly down her two pale cheeks as she smiled.

"He very hurt. He *was* very hurt. He blood many place. Boys go away. Children cry. Teacher break and hurt. Later he in hospital. I go there visit him." She stopped, looking thoughtful. "I went there." One continuous line of wetness glistened down each cheek. "My mother, my father say don't go, but I see him. I say, 'You be better?' But he hurt. Doctors no did helped. He alone. No doctor. No nurse. No medicine. No family." She stopped. They all stared in silence for several moments.

Finally Carlos said, "Did he went home?"

Ling shook her head. "He go home but no walk." She stopped. Maria could not help watching those single lines of tears moving down the pale round face. "A year, more, no walk. Then go."

"Go where?"

"End."

Again there was a deep silence. Ling looked down, away from them, her head bent low.

"Oh, no," murmured Charlene. "He died."

Maria felt the catch in her throat, the sudden wetness of tears on her own two cheeks, and when she looked up she saw that all the other students, men and women both, were crying too.

Maria wiped her eyes. Suddenly all her limbs ached, her bones felt stiff and old. She took her feet from the basin and dried them with a towel. Then she turned off the television and went to bed.

Questions for Reflection and Analysis

1. What strikes you about the story as a whole? Is there a particular aspect of the story that elicits a memory or concern about teaching and learning?

2. How do Maria's values, as expressed in the opening scene, differ from those of the new culture? How do her values differ from those of her children? How do these differences in values affect her relationships with her family members in the new country?

3. What factors account for Maria's thoughts and reactions at the award ceremony?

4. How are the teacher's interactions with students in the classroom scene at the end of the story different from the mayor's interactions with Maria? What does your analysis suggest about the kinds of behaviors that enable or impede genuine communication in a second language?

5. How does your knowledge of Maria's background in Guatemala, rendered through flashback, affect your understanding of Maria's reactions to her experiences in the United States?

Nothing in Our Hands but Age

Raquel Puig Zaldívar

(1950–)

Raquel Puig Zaldívar was born in Cuba and moved with her family to the United States in 1961, two years after Fidel Castro came to power. After studying journalism and education, she received an M.A. in Spanish literature. In 1974, Zaldívar began teaching at Miami Dade Community College. She eventually graduated law school and continues to teach as well as practice law. She is the author of *Roberto Goes Fishing—Roberto Va De Pesca* (1992) and *Women Don't Need to Write: A Novel* (1999).

"And since I have realized that many people go through life without thinking, my most important goal in this course will be to teach you to think, and, hopefully, help you make a habit of it." I paused to catch my breath and the door behind me clacked to announce the arrival of a new student. The first day of classes it is very difficult to gather all of them at the same time. They cruise in and out of several wrong rooms before they finally reach the proper destination. I was quiet without looking back. As usually, I expected the student to sit down before continuing my lecture. The door did not clack back right away and I had to turn around.

A heavy set, dark-haired woman was holding the door open, waiting for someone else to come in. She had an over-sized flowery plastic bag hanging from her arm and a fairly large brown paper bundle firmly grasped with her hand. At this point the whole class was interested in who or what was finally

---

Raquel Puig Zaldívar, "Nothing in Our Hands but Age" from *Hispanics in the United States: An Anthology of Creative Literature* (1980), G. Keller and F. Jímenez (Eds.). Reprinted by permission of Bilingual Press/Editorial Bilingüe, Arizona State University, Tempe, AZ.

going to enter. The door, with a personality of its own, struggled with the woman's arm, but she was victorious. A frail-looking man, dragging his feet, entered and glanced at us triumphantly a little out of breath. The woman let go of the door and approached me energetically. The man I suspected to be her husband trailed along with much effort, unable to keep up. "Alicia Pérez de Roca"; she pronounced every syllable carefully and pointed to herself as she opened her enormous eyes even wider. "Antonio Roca," she said pointing to her husband who had not quite reached us.

The group was starting to get restless. Some were speaking to their friends and others were just staring at the newcomers and laughing. I glared at them and for once it worked. They straightened up and looked respectful once more. Then I turned my attention to the couple:

"Mrs. Roca," I began.

"Pérez de Roca," she interrupted; "Alicia Pérez de Roca, Antonio Roca," she added pointing to her husband.

"All right, Mrs. Pérez de Roca, please sit down and I will speak to you again after class." I tried my best to be calm.

It took them five more minutes to settle down. I was able to add a few comments about the grading system and the books that were required for the course, but it was time to leave before I realized it.

"If you have any questions please come to my office. If not, I'll see you Thursday. Have a nice day."

One by one the students gathered their belongings and emptied the room, all of them except the Roca couple, who were standing up and slowly making it to the front. I was waiting for them and felt an unexpected gush of tenderness. Alicia was not very tall, somewhat wide around the hips and the bustline. She was probably past sixty but had a very white, clear complexion on which the years had not cared to leave too many traces. Antonio could have been approximately ten years her senior. He was obviously weak but did not lack enthusiasm. His small eyes glowed with excitement; they were younger than the rest of him and very ill-matched with the multiple folds surrounding his eyes and lips and the wart that sat ungraciously on his nose.

Their attire was spotless, old but well-preserved. It had been ironed and starched with careful, experienced hands. She wore a long black skirt with a pleat in the back. Her white blouse was completely embroidered in the front with what had been colorful threads, the type of work that was imported years ago from the Canary Islands. He wore a firmly starched *guayabera* with long sleeves, four pockets and tiny pleats, the kind Cubans used to wear on grand occasions. There was no doubt in my mind that they were my countrymen.

"You see, professor," she automatically emphasized her *r*'s, "wee come from Cuba and my hoosband was a pharmacist and I was a doctor of pheelosophee and we come to the Junited States of America to find freedom and the social worker tell us we can come to the school for the, the, revalidation of our title . . . ," she looked uncertain.

"Degree," I corrected; "you want to study to revalidate your degrees to continue in your professions." Smiling she nodded profusely; Antonio followed doubtful. "Do you wish to speak Spanish? I'm Cuban, too. I can understand."

"Oh no," she shook her head back and held the heavy plastic bag with both her hands in front of her stomach. "Wee want to comprehend English better, wee have to revalidate in English. This is pheelosophee, correct?"

"Yes."

"My hoosband and me have mooch experience of many years with pheelosophee, we love it very mooch and we want to do good in yourr class."

"Do you know the titles of the books?" I asked.

"Mmmmmm, wee were not able to grasp those names. The vision I don't have it very well and you speek too fast. Wee may come to yourr offiz, yes?"

"Of course, come right up and I'll give you all the details."

I smiled and left the room ahead of them. Where did these people get their energy? They apparently were honest about the whole thing and were seriously considering a new beginning at a point when most individuals are realizing they have to face the end. I wondered how they would pass my course, but decided not to worry about it so soon.

My office was locked. I opened the door, turned on the lights and barely had time to sit down when they appeared at the threshold and asked permission to come in.

"Of course, come right in and sit down," I said as cheerfully as I knew how. They accepted my invitation and looked at me with all their attention.

"Mrs. Roca."

"Pérez de Roca. You know, professor, in Cuba the married ladies keep the father's name. That for me is Pérez."

"Mrs. Pérez de Roca and Mr. Roca, this is a course divided in two parts: philosophy and drama."

"Excellent, excellent," said Antonio and smiled.

"It is not an easy course," I stressed; "you will have to read a lot."

"No problem, we have a good bilingual dictionary," she said.

"There will be weekly quizzes." Mrs. Pérez de Roca wrote everything I said in her new notebook. They could not be dissuaded.

"Alicia, ¿no se to parece a la niña?" The old man's expression became very soft and he looked at me insistently. I understood him perfectly, but:

"My hoosband says you are alike that our daughter." I smiled at him; he was obviously pleased.

"Is your daughter here?" I asked not knowing what else to say.

"In Cuba, in Cuba." Antonio understood for the first time.

"Wee come to the school for her. She come here very soon and then she is goin to need our help."

"When did you see her last?"

"Oh, fifteen years ago, but now she is goin to come very, very soon."

Weeks later Alicia barely passed the first test and Antonio failed miserably but neither of them became discouraged. It was close to impossible for them to understand the lectures. The terminology was difficult and I know I went too fast for them. I realized, however, that they enjoyed the small group sessions the most. Once a week the students were supposed to meet with me in groups of no more than twelve to discuss the assignments. It was here where Alicia gave all her comments and Antonio listened attentively. Most of the students didn't mind them, but others expressed their disgust very openly, and disagreed with them constantly.

"I don't think men need goals," said Matt discussing a passage from *Siddhartha*. "Why can't we just live and take things as they come, and not worry? We spend too much time planning for the future and forget our present."

"I disagree," answered Alicia. Her husband nodded faithfully in the back. "When I was a young woman I wanted to care for my family the best way and wanted to teech history. I had a goal and that made me continue in life and do thins and brin out a family and be happy."

"But what for? We all can do something but without living only for that," insisted the younger man. "In our society we waste our lives in futile things."

"Futile?" asked Alicia. A student who sat next to her translated the word into Spanish.

"Well, maybe goals should be there, we must have one, but we shouldn't devote all our lives to them. Don't you think, Mrs. Morales?" asked another student.

"I don't want to influence your opinions. I know what I believe in, but I want you to do your own thinking."

"Futile not!" refuted Mrs. Pérez de Roca with conviction. "No goals and when you arrive to be as old as me, you see yourr life behind you and you don't have . . . Mmmmm . . . How is it that you say? Anythin to show."

"Is that so?" said Matt sarcastically; "then what do you have to show? If your goals had worked you wouldn't be here. Your circumstances have put you here, goals or no goals. Goals, what they do is chain you, don't let you be free."

"Goals do not chain, they direct," Alicia turned very solemn.

"Well," I interrupted; "we're beginning to talk in circles and besides our time is up. Read the next ten pages for Monday and have a nice day."

The students left immediately. Alicia and Antonio stayed behind as usual. They took a little longer standing up and picking up their belongings. I felt a bit attached to these two souls. They came from the country to which I belong, but of which I have no memory. Sometimes they came to my office and talked to me about the street vendors, the *guajiros* or peasants and the tall palm trees, always in "carrreful" English. More than one time their tales made me smile.

"Do not worry about the commentaries this children make. Wee are not offended. Wee know wee are too old but wee talk because wee have somethin to . . . Mmmmmm!! . . . How do you say? Compart?"

"Share," I corrected.

"Correct, 'share'. Wee share, they share too. This new method of teachin is very new and it function well. When I was a teacher I only taught from the outside. You teech from the inside also."

While the woman talked, Antonio looked at me with affection. Often, as I left, I heard him discuss with his wife how much I resembled their daughter.

"Where do you live, Alicia?" I asked one morning.

"In the block of apartments in Seventh and Thirteen. Nice place but no good to stay there all the day. Very sad, many old people with no family. Wee are not sad," she explained. "Wee have our daughter. She is far away but she is close here." She indicated her heart and nodded resolutely opening her eyes and smiling.

"Did she arrive yet?"

"No, not yet, but she is comin soon. Wee don't see her since fifteen years ago. She cannot write often. It's a little problem. But when she come, we're goin to help an awful mooch."

"An awful lot, Alicia."

"Da's correct," she stopped as if looking for the right words. "You know, wee already bought for her all for the house. All new thins. Wee save and wee buy little by little. Pillows and mantels . . . "

"Tablecloths."

"Correct! and dishes and towels. Everysin, her father and me buy it for her. When she comes."

"Is she married?" I asked.

"No, she had all prepared. You know," she smacked her lips in a sorrowful gesture; "but she was prisioned, you know, to the . . . Mmmmm . . . How do you say it?"

"Jail."

"Dat is it, to the jail. She is forty years old now. It happened fifteen years ago on March. But she is gettin out on dis year. Then she is comin to us. She is our family, you know? Nobody else," she shook her head.

They weren't as disturbed by their jailed daughter as I was. The idea was already part of them and nothing mattered but the fact that she would be free again next March. Fifteen years! My body went cold with the thought.

Humanities 202 continued as usual. The Rocas were never absent. They knew they were slow settling down and they made it a point to arrive early. When I got to class they were usually excited, with new questions and comments to make. The course was more than halfway through when we began discussing *Macbeth*.

"Well, class, how could you describe the character of Macbeth?"

"Imaginative," said Justo.

"Courageous," answered another student.

"Ambitious," exclaimed Alicia.

"What was it that he most desired?"

"Power," explained Justo.

"Why do you suppose he wanted power?" Sometimes it was very hard to make the students talk.

"He wanted to control others and make them do what he wanted," said the young man.

"He was willing to go to any extreme to achieve this," added another one.

"He assessinated the king and his friend B . . . B . . . Bbb . . ."

"Banquo," I said, helping Alicia. She nodded. "Does he represent men of his time or mankind as a whole?"

"Menkind," Alicia was quick to reply. "Dere are," she rolled her *r*'s mercilessly, "men in our world today dat are equal to Macbeth. For example, you know in Cuba know, wee have a man in the power dat kills many people to be powerfool and dominate the whole nation." I knew the subject matter was getting touchy but it was my policy to accept any comments students made and I had to listen and pray the situation wouldn't get out of hand.

"It's not at all the same," answered Jenny; "Macbeth did it to satisfy his own desire. In Cuba it's being done for a purpose, to help the poor." I wished I could have stopped them but I couldn't. That would have been going against my own rules. I remained quiet.

"No, Jenny, you are mistaken," said another one. "Killing and destruction are wrong. We mustn't consider the purpose for which those things are committed."

"You know, people, what I consider is valuable?" Justo was wondering out loud. "My freedom to express any disagreement, man." Several classmates assented.

"Well, that's necessary," Jenny was quick to reply; "but that's allowed in Cuba today, any fool knows that."

"I am not in accordance." This time Alicia stood up as she always did when she was going to say something she considered important. "Nobody can express his opinions in my country today."

"Oh, there she goes again!" I heard someone whisper in boredom. Alicia paid no heed. She wasn't excited; her voice was soft, her words paused. Only a competent observer could have noticed she trembled a little. Antonio usually sat motionless behind her. He knew enough English to realize that things were getting rough for his wife.

"You know, Miss, I know a young woman who was only a little bit older dat you and very pretty also," she smiled and nodded; "and she has espent many years in a prision for the only mistake dat she did not want to teech the wrong way to little childrens."

"Ah!" Jenny exclaimed with exaggerated disgust. "We have learned enough in this class to know that words like 'wrong' are relative." Alicia simply ignored her.

"She went to the country, you know, with the farmers, to teech dem the grammar and the aritmetic and the oder sings importants. She did not desire to teech Communist doctrine." The class became very quiet. "She said dis to her chief and asked to leave the country and she was incarcelated, in prision, you know? For fifteen years."

"Well, that's all a nice tale, a story," answered Jenny stubbornly; "but they are always things that people make up. Rumors. How do you know they are true?" The whole class, including me, was paying close attention to the discussion. We followed with our heads the words that, like arrows, went from one end of the room to the other.

"Dat is not correct. Dis is not a rumor. It is a true story." Alicia's words were paused.

"That's what they always say," rebutted Jenny.

"I know dis is true," the old woman's tone was forgiving, not defiant. "You see, I am espeakin about my daughter."

Everyone was still. Any movement would have wounded the woman's solemn declaration. Moments later other students began trying to enter the room for their next class and we had to leave. Nobody, however, even bothered to speak.

Cuba was never again discussed in that class. We finished with Shakespeare, with Ibsen, with Bernard Shaw, but Cuba was never again touched. Justo, Jenny and the others were sensitive enough to imagine the burden the old couple bore. They stopped raising their eyebrows and sighing hard enough to be noticed every time Alicia spoke. A certain respect grew out of that experience and even though the discussions continued and the disagreements were frequent, the atmosphere of the class was less tight, more pleasant.

Mrs. Pérez de Roca passed the course with few problems. Her test grades were very humble, but throughout the discussions she showed me that she read the material. Her husband Antonio didn't make it. I wondered what tests, group discussions and classes like mine were supposed to mean when a man like Antonio Roca, a college graduate, a man who had supported his family with dignity so many years, did not manage to pass it. I blamed his age but quickly dismissed from my mind the "F" I entered in the gradebook.

When the last class was over, they came to my office one morning.

"Mrs. Morales, wee want to show our appreciation for yourr pacience and help." She sounded as if she had memorized the lines the night before. "Yesterday I ovened some pastries."

"Baked," I said.

"Correct; baked some *guayaba* pastries for you and yourr family. Wee learned very mooch in yourr class. Our grades are not so good but wee learned English, and wee learned what young people sink today and many, many sings, Mrs. Morales. Wee are grateful." Antonio assented and handed me the homemade pastries wrapped in wax paper.

"Wee want to ask one last question."

"By all means, Alicia, and please don't say the last, I hope you come back and visit me very often." Both of them smiled.

"Our friend told us dat somesin very useful for a teacher is a en-cy-clo-pe-dia. It is somesin good to have in the home and check a correct date or find out somesin important. Is that correct?"

"Of course! An encyclopedia is something very useful to own, even if you are not a teacher. The information is right there all the time."

"Exactly like ourr friend says. You know, wee want to buy one for ourr daughter which is comin very soon. You know, it is already April so she must be gettin everysin ready now. Wee sent her all the money and everysin wiz an agency and she is goin to need a en-cy-clo-pe-dia. Correct? When she wants to be a teacher again."

"It is a very good idea." I looked at both of them and thought there was something beautiful in their hopeful, wrinkled stares.

We shook hands and they left. Alicia, as usual, walking ahead with her determined attitude, her very clean embroidered old blouse, and Antonio trailing not too close behind with his spotless *guayabera* and shiny laced shoes.

At the beginning of the fall term it was Jenny who telephoned me one morning and said Antonio had died.

"I heard it over the radio, the Spanish radio station announces such things," she said.

"I know. When did you hear it?"

"Oh, it was last week but I couldn't call you then. You weren't in school and I didn't know your home number. Know what?"

"What is it, Jenny?"

"I'd sure like to go and visit Alicia. Do you know where she lives?"

"She said once that she lived in those government projects on Seventh and Thirteenth. Yes, it must be there."

"Wanna come and look for her?"

"Sure!" I was happy to see the young girl taking an interest.

"Pick you up at lunch time tomorrow?"

"At twelve thirty," I answered.

Alicia opened the door the following afternoon looking the same as always. Her big eyes, less energetic perhaps, were grateful yet silent. She stepped aside; wiping her hands in her apron, she asked us in. It was a very small efficiency apartment with the kitchen and the bedroom separated from the main living area by tall wooden superimposed walls. The tiny coffee table was monopolized by a picture of a young woman—"their daughter," I thought—with lively dark eyes looking far away. In one of the corners of the picture, Alicia secured to the frame an instant shot of Antonio sitting in a rocking chair, wearing a *guayabera*.

There was a map of Cuba hanging from a wall and on top of the sewing machine a statue of Our Lady of Charity, Cuba's patron saint, with lit candles in front of it. By far the most spectacular piece in the room was a very simple bookcase with the complete set of the *Encyclopaedia Britannica*.

"Sit down, pliz. Sank you very mooch for comin, Jenny," she looked at her. "Mrs. Morales," she said facing me, "it is very sad for me, therefore do not say you are sorry. It is all right, Antonio was an old man."

"You are not alone, Alicia. You are an energetic woman. You have a lot to give and you can still help other people," Jenny said.

"You are not alone. Your daughter will be coming soon and she will need you to help her begin. Life is important you know." Everything I said was unfit and I was concerned.

"Correct. Wee know all about estarting all over. You know when Antonio married me I was a telephone operator and he was a estudent. Wee lived in a esmall room. Oh yes, esmaller dan dis. I helped him become a pharmacist and when he was finished I began estudyin at the University to become a professor. Of history," she didn't look at us, she stared at her lap. "It was a very hard task. He worked and saved penny after penny. I finished when ourr daughter was born. Wee had an apartment at that time. It was in La Víbora.

Do you know La Víbora? Nice place. Wee were happy. When my daughter went to school, I too worked teachin history of Cuba. Many years pass and den wee had enough money to buy a pharmacy. Antonio was a good man. He was happy with the new pharmacy."

I was wondering why she didn't cry. She stared at her black skirt but not a drop fell.

"Wee were honest people, dat is why wee could not underestand dat the government came and dey took the pharmacy, and two houses wee had bought for, you know, how is it dat you say? gainin money I sink. It was so eslow, when wee woke up one day it was the law dat wee couldn't have nosing. Only ourr careers, ourr titles, degree like you say, Mrs. Morales. Wee were there because ourr daughter, you know, she like the system and she was happy dat the rich was sharin with the poor and . . . Well she was ourr daughter and wee love her very mooch and wee want to be wiz her. Den she left for the country and she saw what she did not like and complained and when the chiefs did not hear her complaints she was a counter-revolutionary. She was put in prision, for fifteen years, in a prision with oders bad womans and little food and all dirty. . . . One friend tol us to come to the Junited States and save all the money we can get to send ourr daughter the passage—she meant the ticket—when she was out of the prision. Ourr daughter said yes, one day when wee saw her. Wee were old, the government did not want us, we lef. Here wee estart, like when wee were young, nosing in our hand, but wee had the age, very important and very bad. You know, Mrs. Morales. I tol you when I was yourr estudent."

"You are really praiseworthy, Alicia, both you and your husband. You still have such energy, desire to become a better person." I wanted to sound convincing because I meant what I said. "Forget the past, forget . . ." I knew I was telling her to forget her whole life and I felt ridiculous. ". . . what you lost. Think ahead, think of how you will help your daughter, you are the only thing she has here. Don't lose your spirit, your vitality."

"You see, it is difficult to be the same. One month ago, a woman prisoner dat was inside with my daughter. She has liberty now, she wrote and she tells us that ourr daughter is no longer alive." Alicia looked at us, put her hand on the encyclopedia and tightened her lips.

Questions for Reflection and Analysis

1. What strikes you about the story as a whole? Is there a particular aspect of the story that elicits a memory or concern about teaching and learning?

2. What impact do Mrs. Morales' classroom policies and teaching approaches have on the classroom interactions? What examples from Mrs. Morales' teaching show that she is teaching "from the inside" as opposed to teaching "from the outside" (p. 149)?

3. What do you perceive to be Mrs. Morales most effective strategies, in or out of the classroom, for attempting to integrate Alicia and Antonio into the course? How fully do Alicia and Antonio become integral members of the classroom?

4. How do you account for Antonio's performance in the class? Could Mrs. Morales have done anything differently?

5. How does the final scene in the Rocas' apartment shed light on their motivation for studying at the university and on Mrs. Roca's contributions to the class discussions?

What Do You Know About Friends?

Lily Brett

(1946–)

Lily Brett was born in a displaced persons camp in Germany. Her parents were survivors of the Lodz Ghetto and the Auschwitz concentration camp. The family moved to Australia when she was two years old. In the 1960s Brett began her writing career as a music journalist. She currently lives in the United States. An award-winning writer, Brett's publications include *The Auschwitz Poems* (1986), *What God Wants* (1991), *Too Many Men* (1999), and *You Gotta Have Balls: A Novel* (2006).

In Renia Bensky's world, people were pigs. "Don't be a greedy pig," she would say when Lola reached for another potato. Renia's neighbour, Mrs. Spratt, was "a dirty pig." Her favourite grandchild was "a little piggy," her cousin Adek "a big pig."

Josl chauffeured his two daughters around every Saturday morning. To the city, to the dressmaker, to the hairdresser. On the way home he liked to stop and buy himself a double chocolate gelato. "What a pig!" Renia said when they arrived home.

When Renia talked about Josl's father, who had died in the ghetto, she said, "such a pig." Sometimes she would say a bit more, although the past, their lives before they came to Australia, was definitely out of bounds, their own private territory. Sometimes a small sliver of detail would slip out. "Such a pig he was. In the ghetto he cried because he was so hungry. Children were dead in the streets and he was crying because he was hungry."

Until she was twenty Lola had never seen a pig. When she saw her first pigs, she was fascinated by how unself-conscious they were. They snorted their way through their food, big and pink and bulky. They weren't holding their stomachs flat or sucking in their cheeks. They weren't expecting judgments. They seemed quite happy to be pigs.

If people weren't pigs, then they were idiots. Even when she was quite small Lola knew that Mrs. Bensky was an authority on pigs and idiots. "Such an idiot!" Mrs. Bensky would shout. "Such an idiot is that Mrs. Berman. An idiot, an i-d-i-o-t. She thinks she speaks a perfect English. In the butcher I heard her say 'Cut me in half please.' Such a perfect English!"

Mrs. Berman had been Mrs. Bensky's friend. Until Mrs. Berman left Mr. Berman and Mrs. Bensky could no longer be friends with her, the two women had baked cakes in Mrs. Bensky's kitchen on Saturday afternoons. Mrs. Berman made her honeycake and rugelachs and Mrs. Bensky baked her lakech. Working in the kitchen together, they looked like good friends.

"Friends," Mrs. Bensky said to Lola. "What do you know about friends? Friends, pheh! You can trust only your family."

And what did Lola know? She had watched the Benskys and their friends, their "company," as they called themselves. The company went to the pictures together every Saturday night and then to supper afterwards. On Sunday evenings they played cards. If there was a good show on, sometimes they went out during the week. They celebrated each other's birthdays, anniversaries, bar-mitzvahs, engagements and weddings, and were present at the operations, illnesses and funerals.

Lola thought that the company were family. She called them Uncle and Aunty and believed that they would always care about her. What did Lola know?

Mrs. Bensky hated Mrs. Ganz. She was irritated by the way that Mrs. Ganz kept inviting her to fashion parades, card afternoons and charity luncheons. Couldn't Mrs. Ganz see that she was very busy? Every day Mrs. Bensky had to wash six sheets, four pillow cases, three eiderdown covers and seven towels. She had to scrub and polish the floors, and vacuum the carpets. And on top of this she had to cook and to wash up. She was not the kind of woman who had time to go to a fashion parade. Why couldn't Mrs. Ganz understand this?

Mrs. Bensky thought that Mrs. Ganz had always been spoilt. In the ghetto Mrs. Ganz's father had been a Jewish "policeman." Their family had rarely been hungry. In 1943 they were smuggled out of the ghetto and spent the rest of the war hiding in a cellar. Mrs. Bensky often chatted to Mrs. Pekelman on the phone. She felt that Genia Pekelman had her problems, but above all she had a good heart. Mrs. Bensky advised Mrs. Pekelman about which clothes suited her best, how to cook a good gulah, where to buy the freshest Murray Perch. She also shared some beauty tips with her, including the fact that if you rinsed your hair with a bit of beer after washing it the waves stayed in much longer. Renia Bensky and Genia Pekelman, both non-drinkers, often trailed an alcoholic air around with them.

Lola learnt about friendship from listening to the two women on the phone. Last week Mrs. Bensky had said in an affectionate tone, "Genia darling, I bumped into Yetta Kauffman in the city. Such an ugly face that woman has got. You think you are ugly, Genia darling? Next to Yetta Kauffman you are a big beauty."

This may have seemed harsh to an outsider, but Lola knew that it was affectionate and well-intentioned. In this company one of the friendliest and most enthusiastic responses to anything was: "What, what, you are crazy or something?"

Things cooled off between Renia Bensky and Genia Pekelman when Genia took up dancing lessons. She was forty-seven. At thirteen, Genie had been a promising young dancer. She had won a ballet scholarship to study in Paris. She was counting the days to her fourteenth birthday, waiting to leave for Paris, when the Germans arrived in Warsaw.

Now, Mrs. Pekelman was learning Indian dance. She went to dancing classes twice a week. She was taught by Madame Sanrit. Mrs. Pekelman wore leotards under her sari and practised at home every afternoon. She loved to dance and danced at every opportunity.

If a group of women were having a charity luncheon, Mrs. Pekelman asked if she could dance at the lunch. When Mrs. Pekelman learnt that Mrs. Small was taking a group of voluntary Jewish Welfare kitchen helpers on a tour of the Victorian National Gallery, she begged her to bring the group to her home, where she would dance for them.

Some of the company were embarrassed by Genie Pekelman and her dancing. Mrs. Small was furious. She said to Mrs. Bensky, "Look at her! She is so big and fat and ugly, and she wants to dance for everybody. When she moves her big tuches around the room it is shocking."

"She can't help it," Mrs. Bensky replied. "She doesn't know how she looks. She is not so intelligent."

As well as pigs and idiots, Mrs. Bensky knew about intelligence. She dismissed most people as "not intelligent." One year Mrs. Small, who spoke Russian, Polish, Yiddish, French and English, interpreted for the members of the Moscow Circus when they came to Melbourne. Mrs. Bensky was clenched with anger for the entire season.

"She thinks she is such a big intelligence," Mrs. Bensky railed. "What does she read, this big intelligence, this Mrs. Intelligentsia? Maybe a *Women's Weekly* under the hair dryer once a week? I remember her mother delivered our milk in Lodz. Two big cans across her shoulders, she walked from house to house in bare feet. And both daughters finished school at twelve. Now, suddenly, Ada Small is a genius. She tells everybody that she matriculated in Poland. Soon she will say she was almost a doctor. Everybody who came here after the war was almost a doctor. Mrs. Ada Intelligentsia thinks she is important because she is translating for an acrobat."

Mrs. Bensky did know about intelligence. She was the only one of the group who had been at university. She still kept her student card in her handbag. In 1972, Mrs. Bensky enrolled at Melbourne University. She did one semester of "Physics In The Firing Line." Lola had suggested that Mrs. Bensky study Russian or German, languages she was fluent in. Lola thought that this would have been a gentler introduction to university life, but Mrs. Bensky insisted on "Physics In The Firing Line." Science had been Mrs. Bensky's great love in Lodz. When she spoke about Copernicus and the planets, Mrs. Bensky was at her most tender. It was science that Mrs. Bensky wanted to go back to.

In Lodz, Mrs. Bensky came top of her class every year. She was every teacher's favourite student. Her curiosity was as immense as her ambition. Other people in the neighbourhood laughed at her father for wasting his money on a daughter. "You'll make her too clever for a husband," one neighbour repeated regularly.

At the University of Melbourne, Renia Bensky was so tense she could hardly hear the lecturer. His words flew around the auditorium. Mrs. Bensky had to grab each word and put it in its correct place. Sometimes she lost a few words and the sentence didn't make sense. She sat in a sweat through most of the professor's speeches. Later she learnt that this heat was menopausal.

Renia worked feverishly on her first assignment, "Molecules and The Future." At last it was finished. Fifteen pages on bright yellow notepaper. Lina corrected the English, and they hired a professional typist to type the essay.

Mrs. Bensky got a "C" for "Molecules and The Future." She wept and wept.

Mr. Bensky tried to comfort her. "This assignment, Renia darling, is out of this world. Something special. There is no question about it. It is perfect, believe me." But Mrs. Bensky went on weeping.

Mrs. Small gave Mrs. Bensky her sympathy and support. "I think it is anti-Semitism," she said. "For what other reason would he give such a beautiful piece of work only a 'C'? He is an anti-Semite, for sure."

Most of the company called around to offer their condolences. They knew it wasn't Mrs. Bensky's fault. A "C" for Renia Bensky, whoever heard of such a thing? Everybody knew she was too intelligent. But Mrs. Bensky was inconsolable.

She rang her tutor, a young, pale-faced boy of twenty-five, to ask if maybe it was her English that wasn't perfect. Maybe that was why she had got a "C."

"Excuse me, tutor," she began. "I want to know if you have made a mistake with my essay. I think the English was very good. My young daughter who is a lawyer with an honours degree did correct my writing, so it couldn't be my bad English. And my English is very good. She didn't find many mistakes at all. I understand you did give young John Matheson an 'A.' Well, he told me himself that I did understand the molecules much better than him. In fact, I explained some of the facts to him. So, he got an 'A' and I got a 'C'? Maybe I shouldn't have hired a typist? Maybe you think I have got money to burn or to throw away that I hired a typist? My husband worked very hard for fifteen years in factories so I could afford a typist. Maybe you were prejudiced against my typing? Did Mr. Matheson type his essay? I'm sure not. As a matter of fact I know his mother, Mrs. Matheson. She told me he was talking about how much I know about molecules. You know, I, myself, don't think you are an anti-Semite. My friend Mrs. Small does, but she is not intelligent. She doesn't see we are in a modern world and this is not Poland.

"So, do you have an answer, Mr. Tutor? Do you know how many years I dreamed of going to university? Do you know this? I dreamed of studying at university when I was a small girl. And I kept dreaming. Even in Auschwitz, when I didn't dream any more, sometimes when I was standing in roll-call for six hours, barefoot in the snow, I would try to think about what subjects I could study one day."

Now Mrs. Bensky was crying. "Do you have an answer, Mr. Tutor? When I came to Australia my sister-in-law said to me that all women work in Australia. She said to me I should have considered if I could afford to have a baby before I got pregnant. So I took my baby every day to Mrs. Polonsky, a woman in Carlton. I had never been apart from my baby. Sometimes I vomited on the tram on the way to the factory. I felt so frightened. Josl told me that Mrs. Polonsky was a good woman and nothing would happen to little Lola, but I couldn't stop being frightened. When I finished work I picked Lola up. Mrs. Polonsky lived just next to the university, and when I stopped vomiting, I made myself a promise that one day I would go there. Did you hear me, Mr. Tutor?"

Mrs. Bensky left "Physics In The Firing Line" six weeks after she had begun. She left the University of Melbourne a wiser person. The rest of the company acknowledged this and accorded her new respect. "She studied at Melbourne University," they now said when they spoke of her.

Questions for Reflection and Analysis

1. What strikes you about the story as a whole? Is there a particular aspect of the story that elicits a memory or concern about teaching and learning?

2. What is Renia Bensky's attitude toward her friends? What role might the events of Mrs. Bensky's past, before she immigrated to Australia, have played in shaping her attitude?

3. How do Renia Bensky's own expectations and abilities help to explain her reaction to the grade she receives on her first assignment? What different reasons are offered in the story to explain the grade? What reason would you offer to account for the grade she

receives? What are the consequences of the grade? What could the tutor have said in response to Renia's questioning that might have resulted in a different outcome?

4. Why do you think the narrator characterizes Mrs. Bensky as "a wiser person" (p. 162) after she left the university? Do you agree with this assessment? Why do you agree or disagree?

5. How would you answer the question raised by the title of the story?

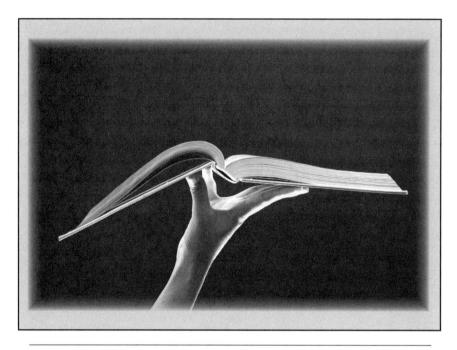

Photograph by Han Nguyen: Hanvp@aol.com

IV.

PRIVATE LESSONS

Learning English privately poses special challenges and benefits. In these five stories, the authors portray adult language learners who are studying or preparing to study with a tutor or by themselves. We observe how a lack of progress can result in frustration for both tutor and student, how secrecy can exacerbate existing tensions, and how isolation can impede learning. We also see how these factors—frustration, secrecy, and isolation—can give way to success and pride in accomplishment. In Bernard Malamud's "The German Refugee," a journalist who has escaped Nazi Germany is tutored by a college student. In Lindsley Cameron's "Private Lesson," an inexperienced teacher from the United States works with a student in Japan. In Shauna Singh Baldwin's "English Lessons," a Sikh refugee from Punjab awaits the arrival of her English tutor. In Frances Khirallah Noble's "Albert and Esene," an immigrant from the Middle East studies in secret. In Linh Dinh's "Prisoner with a Dictionary," a young man studies alone, with an English-only dictionary as his sole resource for learning a new language. Together, these stories reveal how life circumstances can significantly affect the acquisition of language in a private setting and how, in turn, such private lessons can profoundly affect a person's life.

■ The German Refugee

Bernard Malamud

(1914–1986)

Bernard Malamud was born in the United States to Jewish refugees from Czarist Russia. His first language was Yiddish. Malamud received a B.A. from the City College of New York and an M.A. in literature from Columbia University. To support his writing career, he tutored Jewish refugees from Nazi Germany and taught English in evening classes for adult immigrant learners before becoming a college professor. An award-winning author, his many books include *The Natural* (1952), *The Magic Barrel* (1958), *The Fixer* (1966), and *God's Grace* (1982).

Oskar Gassner sits in his cotton-mesh undershirt and summer bathrobe at the window of his stuffy, hot, dark hotel room on West Tenth Street while I cautiously knock. Outside, across the sky, a late-June green twilight fades in darkness. The refugee fumbles for the light and stares at me, hiding despair but not pain.

I was in those days a poor student and would brashly attempt to teach anybody anything for a buck an hour, although I have since learned better. Mostly I gave English lessons to recently-arrived refugees. The college sent me, I had acquired a little experience. Already a few of my students were trying their broken English, theirs and mine, in the American market place. I was then just twenty, on my way into my senior year in college, a skinny, life hungry kid, eating himself waiting for the next world war to start. It was a goddamn cheat. Here I was palpitating to get going, and across the ocean. Adolf Hitler, in black boots and a square mustache, was tearing up and spitting out all the flowers. Will I ever forget what went on with Danzig that summer?

Times were still hard from the Depression but anyway I made a little living from the poor refugees. They were all over uptown Broadway in 1939. I had four I tutored—Karl Otto Alp, the former film star; Wolfgang Novak, once a brilliant economist; Friedrich Wilhelm Wolff, who had taught medieval history at Heidelberg; and after the night I met him in his disordered cheap hotel room, Oskar Gassner, the Berlin critic and journalist, at one time on the *Acht Uhr Abenblatt*. They were accomplished men. I had my nerve associating with them, but that's what a world crisis does for people, they get educated.

Oskar was maybe fifty, his thick hair turning gray. He had a big face and heavy hands. His shoulders sagged. His eyes, too, were heavy, a clouded blue; and as he stared at me after I had identified myself, doubt spread in them like underwater currents. It was as if, on seeing me, he had again been defeated. I had to wait until he came to. I stayed at the door in silence. In such cases I would rather be elsewhere but I had to make a living. Finally he opened the door and I entered. Rather, he released it and I was in. "Bitte,"[1] he offered me a seat and didn't know where to sit himself. He would attempt to say something and then stop, as though it could not possibly be said. The room was cluttered with clothing, boxes of books he had managed to get out of Germany, and some paintings. Skar sat on a box and attempted to fan himself with his meaty hand. "Zis heat," he muttered, forcing his mind to the deed. "Impozzible. I do not know such heat." It was bad enough for me but terrible for him. He had difficulty breathing. He tried to speak, lifted a hand, and let it drop like a dead duck. He breathed as though he were fighting a battle; and maybe he won because after ten minutes we sat and slowly talked.

Like most educated Germans Oskar had at one time studied English. Although he was certain he couldn't say a word he managed to put together a fairly decent, if sometimes comical, English sentence. He misplaced consonants, mixed up nouns and verbs, and mangled idioms, yet we were able at once to communicate. We conversed in English, with an occasional assist by me in pidgin-German or Yiddish, what he called "Jiddish." He had been to America before, last year for a short visit. He had come a month before

---

[1]*Bitte*: Please

Kristallnacht, when the Nazis shattered the Jewish store windows and burnt all the synagogues, to see if he could find a job for himself; he had no relatives in America and getting a job would permit him quickly to enter the country. He had been promised something, not in journalism, but with the help of a foundation, as a lecturer. Then he returned to Berlin, and after a frightening delay of six months was permitted to emigrate. He had sold whatever he could, managed to get some paintings, gifts of Bauhaus friends, and some boxes of books out by bribing two Dutch border guards; he had said goodbye to his wife and left the accursed country. He gazed at me with cloudy eyes. "We parted amicably," he said in German, "my wife was gentile. Her mother was an appalling anti-Semite. They returned to live in Stettin." I asked no questions. Gentile is gentile, Germany is Germany.

His new job was in the Institute for Public Studies, in New York. He was to give a lecture a week in the fall term, and during next spring, a course, in English translation, in "The Literature of the Weimar Republic." He had never taught before and was afraid to. He was in that way to be introduced to the public, but the thought of giving the lecture in English just about paralyzed him. He didn't see how he could do it. "How is it pozzible? I cannot say two words. I cannot pronounziate. I will make a fool of myself." His melancholy deepened. Already in the two months since his arrival, and a round of diminishingly expensive hotel rooms, he had had two English tutors, and I was the third. The others had given him up, he said, because his progress was so poor, and he thought he also depressed them. He asked me whether I felt I could do something for him, or should he go to a speech specialist, someone, say, who charged five dollars an hour, and beg his assistance? "You could try him," I said, "and then come back to me." In those days I figured what I knew, I knew. At that he managed a smile. Still, I wanted him to make up his mind or it would be no confidence down the line. He said, after a while, he would stay with me. If he went to the five-dollar professor it might help his tongue but not his stomach. He would have no money left to eat with. The Institute had paid him in advance for the summer but it was only three hundred dollars and all he had.

He looked at me dully. "Ich weiss nicht wie ich weiter machen soll."[2]

I figured it was time to move past the first step. Either we did that quickly or it would be like drilling rock for a long time.

---

[2]*Ich weiss nicht wie ich weiter machen soll*: I don't know how I will go on.

"Let's stand at the mirror," I said.

He rose with a sigh and stood there beside me, I thin, elongated, red-headed, praying for success, his and mine; Oskar, uneasy, fearful, finding it hard to face either of us in the faded round glass above his dresser.

"Please," I said to him, "could you say 'right'?"

"Ghight," he gargled.

"No—right. You put your tongue here." I showed him where as he tensely watched the mirror. I tensely watched him. "The tip of it curls behind the ridge on top, like this."

He placed his tongue where I showed him.

"Please," I said, "now say right."

Oskar's tongue fluttered. "Rright."

"That's good. Now say 'treasure'—that's harder."

"Tgheasure."

"The tongue goes up in front, not in the back of the mouth. Look."

He tried, his brow wet, eyes straining, "Trreasure."

"That's it."

"A miracle," Oskar murmured.

I said if he had done that he could do the rest.

We went for a bus ride up Fifth Avenue and then walked for a while around Central Park Lake. He had put on his German hat, with its hatband bow at the back, a broad-lapeled wool suit, a necktie twice as wide as the one I was wearing, and walked with a small-footed waddle. The night wasn't bad, it had got a bit cooler. There were a few large stars in the sky and they made me sad.

"Do you sink I will succezz?"

"Why not?" I asked.

Later he bought me a bottle of beer.

2.

To many of these people, articulate as they were, the great loss was the loss of language—that they could not say what was in them to say. You have some subtle thought and it comes out like a piece of broken bottle. They could, of course, manage to communicate but just to communicate was frustrating. As Karl Otto Alp, the ex-film star who became a buyer for Macy's, put it years later, "I felt like a child, or worse, often like a moron. I am left with myself unexpressed. What I know, indeed, what I am, becomes to me a burden. My tongue hangs useless." The same with Oskar it figures. There was a terrible sense of useless tongue, and I think the reason for his trouble with his other tutors was that to keep from drowning in things unsaid he wanted to swallow the ocean in a gulp: Today he would learn English and tomorrow wow them with an impeccable Fourth of July speech, followed by a successful lecture at the Institute for Public Studies.

We performed our lessons slowly, step by step, everything in its place. After Oskar moved to a two-room apartment in a house on West 85th Street, near the Drive, we met three times a week at four-thirty, worked an hour and a half, then, since it was too hot to cook, had supper at the 72nd Street Automat and conversed on my time. The lessons we divided into three parts: diction exercises and reading aloud; then grammar, because Oskar felt the necessity of it, and composition correction; with conversation, as I said, thrown in at supper. So far as I could see, he was coming along. None of these exercises was giving him as much trouble as they apparently had in the past. He seemed to be learning and his mood lightened. There were moments of elation as he heard his accent flying off. For instance when sink became think. He stopped calling himself "hopelezz," and I became his "bezt teacher," a little joke I liked.

Neither of us said much about the lecture he had to give early in October, and I kept my fingers crossed. It was somehow to come out of what we were doing daily, I think I felt, but exactly how, I had no idea; and to tell the truth, though I didn't say so to Oskar, the lecture frightened me. That and the ten more to follow during the fall term. Later, when I learned that he had been attempting with the help of the dictionary, to write in English and had produced "a complete disahster," I suggested maybe he ought to stick to German and we could afterwards both try to put it into passable English. I was cheating when I said that because my German is meager, enough to read simple stuff but certainly not good enough for serious translation; anyway, the idea was to get Oskar into production and worry about translating later. He sweated with it, from enervating morning to exhausted night, but no matter what language he tried, though he had been a professional writer for a generation and knew his subject cold, the lecture refused to move past page one.

It was a sticky, hot July and the heat didn't help at all.

3.

I had met Oskar at the end of June and by the seventeenth of July we were no longer doing lessons. They had foundered on the "impozzible" lecture. He had worked on it each day in frenzy and growing despair. After writing more than a hundred opening pages he furiously flung his pen against the wall, shouting he could no longer write in that filthy tongue. He cursed the German language. He hated the damned country and the damned people. After that what was bad became worse. When he gave up attempting to write the lecture, he stopped making progress in English. He seemed to forget what he already knew. His tongue thickened and the accent returned in all its fruitiness. The little he had to say was in handcuffed and tortured English. The only German I heard him speak was in a whisper to himself. I doubt he knew he was talking it. That ended our formal work together, though I did drop in every other day or so to sit with him. For hours he sat motionless in a large green velours armchair, hot enough to broil in, and through tall windows stared at the colorless sky above 85th Street, with a wet depressed eye.

Then once he said to me, "If I do not this legture prepare, I will take my life."

"Let's begin, Oskar," I said. "You dictate and I'll write. The ideas count, not the spelling."

He didn't answer so I stopped talking.

He had plunged into an involved melancholy. We sat for hours, often in profound silence. This was alarming to me, though I had already had some experience with such depression. Wolfgang Novak, the economist, though English came more easily to him, was another. His problems arose mainly, I think, from physical illness. And he felt a greater sense of the lost country than Oskar. Sometimes in the early evening I persuaded Oskar to come with me for a short walk on the Drive. The tail end of sunsets over the Palisades seemed to appeal to him. At least he looked. He would put on full regalia—hat, suit coat, tie, no matter how hot or what I suggested—and we went slowly down the stairs, I wondering whether he would ever make it to the bottom. He seemed to me always suspended between two floors.

We walked slowly uptown, stopping to sit on a bench and watch night rise above the Hudson. When we returned to his room, if I sensed he had loosened up a bit, we listened to music on the radio; but if I tried to sneak in a news broadcast, he said to me, "Please, I can not more stand of world misery." I shut off the radio. He was right, it was a time of no good news. I squeezed my brain. What could I sell him? Was it good news to be alive? Who could argue the point? Sometimes I read aloud to him—I remember he liked the first part of *Life on the Mississippi*. We still went to the Automat once or twice a week, he perhaps out of habit, because he didn't feel like going anywhere—I to get him out of his room. Oskar ate little, he toyed with a spoon. His dull eyes looked as though they had been squirted with a dark dye.

Once after a momentary cooling rainstorm we sat on newspapers on a wet bench overlooking the river and Oskar at last began to talk. In tormented English he conveyed his intense and everlasting hatred of the Nazis for destroying his career, uprooting his life after half a century, and flinging him like a piece of bleeding meat to the hawks. He cursed them thickly, the German nation, an inhuman, conscienceless, merciless people. "They are pigs mazquerading as peacogs," he said. "I feel certain that my wife, in her heart, was a Jew hater." It was a terrible bitterness, an eloquence almost without vocabulary. He became silent again. I hoped to hear more about his wife but decided not to ask.

Afterwards in the dark Oskar confessed that he had attempted suicide during his first week in America. He was living, at the end of May, in a small hotel, and had one night filled himself with barbiturates; but his phone had fallen off the table and the hotel operator had sent up the elevator boy who found him unconscious and called the police. He was revived in the hospital.

"I did not mean to do it," he said, "it was a mistage."

"Don't ever think of it again," I said, "it's total defeat."

"I don't," he said wearily, "because it is so arduouz to come back to life."

"Please, for any reason whatever."

Afterwards when we were walking, he surprised me by saying, "Maybe we ought to try now the legture onze more."

We trudged back to the house and he sat at his hot desk, I trying to read as he slowly began to reconstruct the first page of his lecture. He wrote, of course, in German.

4.

He got nowhere. We were back to nothing, to sitting in silence in the heat. Sometimes, after a few minutes, I had to take off before his mood overcame mine. One afternoon I came unwillingly up the stairs—there were times I felt momentary surges of irritation with him—and was frightened to find Oskar's door ajar. When I knocked no one answered. As I stood there, chilled down the spine, I realized I was thinking about the possibility of his attempting suicide again. "Oskar?" I went into the apartment, looked into both rooms and the bathroom, but he wasn't there. I thought he might have drifted out to get something from a store and took the opportunity to look quickly around. There was nothing startling in the medicine chest, no pills but aspirin, no iodine. Thinking, for some reason, of a gun, I searched his desk drawer. In it I found a thin-paper airmail letter from Germany. Even if I had wanted to, I couldn't read the handwriting, but as I held it in my hand I did make out a sentence: "Ich bin dir siebenundzwanzig Jahre treu gewesen."[3] There was no gun in the drawer. I shut it and stopped looking. It had occurred to me if you want to kill yourself all you need is a straight pin. When Oskar returned he said he had been sitting in the public library, unable to read.

Now we are once more enacting the changeless scene, curtain rising on two speechless characters in a furnished apartment, I, in a straightback chair, Oskar in the velours armchair that smothered rather than supported him, his flesh gray, the big gray face, unfocused, sagging. I reached over to switch on the radio but he barely looked at me in a way that begged no. I then got up to leave but Oskar, clearing his throat, thickly asked me to stay. I stayed, thinking, was there more to this than I could see into? His problems, God knows, were real enough, but could there be something more than a refugee's displacement, alienation, financial insecurity, being in a strange land without friends or a speakable tongue? My speculation was the old one; not all drown in this ocean, why does he? After a while I shaped the thought and asked him, was there something below the surface, invisible? I was full of this thing from college, and wondered if there mightn't be some unknown quantity in his depression that a psychiatrist maybe might help him with, enough to get him started on his lecture.

He meditated on this and after a few minutes haltingly said he had been psychoanalyzed in Vienna as a young man. "Just the jusual drek," he said, "fears and fantazies that afterwaards no longer bothered me."

"They don't now?"

"Not."

"You've written many articles and lectures before," I said. "What I can't understand, though I know how hard the situation is, is why you can never get past page one."

He half lifted his hand. "It is a paralyzis of my will. The whole legture is clear in my mind but the minute I write down a single word—or in English or in German—I have a terrible fear I will not be able to write the negst. As

---

[3] *Ich bin dir siebenundzwanzig Jahre treu gewesen*: I was faithful to you for twenty-seven years.

though someone has thrown a stone at a window and the whole house—the whole idea, zmashes. This repeats, until I am dezperate."

He said that fear grew as he worked that he would die before he completed the lecture, or if not that, he would write it so disgracefully he would wish for death. The fear immobilized him.

"I have lozt faith. I do not—not longer possezz my former value of myself. In my life there has been too much illusion."

I tried to believe what I was saying: "Have confidence, the feeling will pass."

"Confidenze I have not. For this and alzo whatever elze I have lozt I thank the Nazis."

5.

It was by then mid-August and things were growing steadily worse wherever one looked. The Poles were mobilizing for war. Oskar hardly moved. I was full of worries though I pretended calm weather.

He sat in his massive armchair with sick eyes, breathing like a wounded animal.

"Who can write aboud Walt Whitman in such terrible times?"

"Why don't you change the subject?"

"It mages no differenze what is the subject. It is all uzelezz."

I came every day, as a friend, neglecting my other students and therefore my livelihood. I had a panicky feeling that if things went on as they were going they would end in Oskar's suicide; and I felt a frenzied desire to prevent that. What's more, I was sometimes afraid I was myself becoming melancholy, a new talent, call it, of taking less pleasure in my little pleasures. And the heat continued, oppressive, relentless. We thought of escape into the country but neither of us had the money. One day I bought Oskar a second-hand fan—wondering why we hadn't thought of that before—and he sat in the breeze for hours each day, until after a week, shortly after the Soviet-Nazi non-aggression pact was signed, the motor gave out. He could not sleep at night and sat at his desk with a wet towel on his head, still attempting to write his lecture. He wrote reams on a treadmill, it came out nothing. When he slept out of exhaustion he had fantastic frightening dreams of the Nazis inflicting tortures on him, sometimes forcing him to look upon the corpses of those they had slain. In one dream he told me about, he had gone back to Germany to visit his wife. She wasn't home and he had been directed to a cemetery. There, though the tombstone read another name, her blood seeped out of the earth above her shallow grave. He groaned aloud at the memory.

Afterwards he told me something about her. They had met as students, lived together, and were married at twenty-three. It wasn't a very happy marriage. She had turned into a sickly woman, physically unable to have children. "Something was wrong with her interior strugture."

Though I asked no questions, Oskar said, "I offered her to come with me here but she refused this."

"For what reason?"

"She did not think I wished her to come."

"Did you?" I asked.

"Not," he said.

He explained he had lived with her for almost twenty-seven years under difficult circumstances. She had been ambivalent about their Jewish friends and his relatives, though outwardly she seemed not a prejudiced person. But her mother was always a violent anti-Semite.

"I have nothing to blame myself," Oskar said.

He took to his bed. I took to the New York Public Library. I read some of the German poets he was trying to write about, in English translation. Then I read *Leaves of Grass* and wrote down what I thought one or two of them had got from Whitman. One day, towards the end of August, I brought Oskar what I had written. It was in good part guessing but my idea wasn't to write the lecture for him. He lay on his back, motionless, and listened utterly sadly to what I had written. Then he said, no, it wasn't the love of death they had got from Whitman—that ran through German poetry—but it was most of all his feeling for Brudermensch, his humanity.

"But this does not grow long on German earth," he said, "and is soon deztroyed."

I said I was sorry I had got it wrong, but he thanked me anyway.

I left, defeated, and as I was going down the stairs, heard the sound of someone sobbing. I will quit this, I thought, it has gotten to be too much for me. I can't drown with him.

I stayed home the next day, tasting a new kind of private misery too old for somebody my age, but that same night Oskar called me on the phone, blessing me wildly for having read those notes to him. He had got up to write me a letter to say what I had missed, and it ended by his having written half the lecture. He had slept all day and tonight intended to finish it up.

"I thank you," he said, "for much, alzo including your faith in me."

"Thank God," I said, not telling him I had just about lost it.

6.

Oskar completed his lecture—wrote and rewrote it—during the first week in September. The Nazis had invaded Poland, and though we were greatly troubled, there was some sense of release; maybe the brave Poles would beat them. It took another week to translate the lecture, but here we had the assistance of Friedrich Wilhelm Wolff, the historian, a gentle, erudite man, who liked translating and promised his help with future lectures. We then had about two weeks to work on Oskar's delivery. The weather had changed, and so, slowly, had he. He had awakened from defeat, battered, after a wearying battle. He had lost close to twenty pounds. His complexion was still gray; when I looked at his face I expected to see scars, but it had lost its flabby unfocused quality. His blue eyes had returned to life and he walked with quick steps, as though to pick up a few for all the steps he hadn't taken during those long hot days he had lain torpid in his room.

We went back to our former routine, meeting three late afternoons a week for diction, grammar, and the other exercises. I taught him the phonetic alphabet and transcribed long lists of words he was mispronouncing. He worked many hours trying to fit each sound into place, holding half a matchstick between his teeth to keep his jaws apart as he exercised his tongue. All this can be a dreadfully boring business unless you think you have a future. Looking at him I realized what's meant when somebody is called "another man."

The lecture, which I now knew by heart, went off well. The director of the Institute had invited a number of prominent people. Oskar was the first refugee they had employed and there was a move to make the public cognizant of what was then a new ingredient in American life. Two reporters had come with a lady photographer. The auditorium of the Institute was crowded. I sat in the last row, promising to put up my hand if he couldn't be heard, but it wasn't necessary. Oskar, in a blue suit, his hair cut, was of course nervous, but you couldn't see it unless you studied him. When he stepped up to the lectern, spread out his manuscript, and spoke his first English sentence in public, my heart hesitated; only he and I, of everybody there, had any idea of the anguish he had been through. His enunciation wasn't at all bad—a few s's for th's, and he once said bag for back, but otherwise he did all right.

He read poetry well—in both languages—and though Walt Whitman, in his mouth, sounded a little as though he had come to the shores of Long Island as a German immigrant, still the poetry read as poetry:

> *And I know the spirit of God is the brother of my own,*
> *And that all the men ever born are also my brothers,*
>   *and the women my sisters and lovers,*
> *And that the kelson of creation is love . . .*

Oskar read it as though he believed it. Warsaw had fallen but the verses were somehow protective. I sat back conscious of two things: how easy it is to hide the deepest wounds; and the pride I felt in the job I had done.

7.

Two days later I came up the stairs into Oskar's apartment to find a crowd there. The refugee, his face beet-red, lips bluish, a trace of froth in the corners of his mouth, lay on the floor in his limp pajamas, two firemen on their knees, working over him with an inhalator. The windows were open and the air stank.

A policeman asked me who I was and I couldn't answer.

"No, oh no."

I said no but it was unchangeably yes. He had taken his life—gas—I hadn't even thought of the stove in the kitchen.

"Why?" I asked myself. "Why did he do it?" Maybe it was the fate of Poland on top of everything else, but the only answer anyone could come up with was Oskar's scribbled note that he wasn't well, and had left Martin Goldberg all his possessions. I am Martin Goldberg.

I was sick for a week, had no desire either to inherit or investigate, but I thought I ought to look through his things before the court impounded them, so I spent a morning sitting in the depths of Oskar's armchair, trying to read his correspondence. I had found in the top drawer a thin packet of letters from his wife and an airmail letter of recent date from his anti-Semitic mother-in-law.

She writes in a tight script it takes me hours to decipher, that her daughter, after Oskar abandons her, against her own mother's fervent pleas and anguish, is converted to Judaism by a vengeful rabbi. One night the Brown Shirts appear, and though the mother wildly waves her bronze crucifix in their faces, they drag Frau Gassner, together with the other Jews, out of the apartment house, and transport them in lorries to a small border town in conquered Poland. There, it is rumored, she is shot in the head and topples into an open tank ditch, with the naked Jewish men, their wives and children, some Polish soldiers, and a handful of gypsies.

Questions for Reflection and Analysis

1. What strikes you about the story as a whole? Is there a particular aspect of the story that elicits a memory or concern about teaching and learning?

2. How does Oscar characterize his spoken English? How does his tutor, Martin, characterize Oscar's spoken language? How do you account for the different characterizations?

3. Why does Martin adopt or abandon certain strategies for teaching English? What do his choices reveal about his understanding of language learning and the language learner? How can you account for Martin's changing attitude toward Oscar's language learning?

4. What factors may account for Oscar's failure to write the lecture in either English or in German? What factors lead Oscar to overcome his writer's block?

5. Taking the entire story into account, from beginning to end, how might you answer the questions Martin raises on page 173: "His problems, God knows, were real enough, but could there be something more than a refugee's displacement, alienation, financial insecurity, being in a strange land without friends or a speakable tongue? My speculation was the old one; not all drown in this ocean, why does he?"?

■ *Private Lesson*

Lindsley Cameron

(1948–)

Lindsley Cameron is from the United States and has traveled widely. A contributor to *The New Yorker* and the *New York Times,* she has written about East Asian arts and culture, and she briefly taught English while living in Japan. Cameron is the author of the short-story collection, *The Prospect of Detachment* (1988) and the non-fiction study, *The Music of Light: The Extraordinary Story of Hikari and Kenzaburo Oe* (1998).

Mrs. Longo has no aptitude for teaching, and she finds it disagreeable. Mr. Takahashi, whom she is coaching (tête-à-tête) at the moment, seems to her to have no aptitude for learning, and shows every sign of martyrdom.

But no sympathy, no mercy, no affection dilute the rigor of her pedagogical efforts. It is not merely that Mr. Takahashi lacks charm for Mrs. Longo. Her antipathy is grounded in something larger. Mr. Takahashi is a representative of every class of being Mrs. Longo finds herself resenting these days.

1. *He is young.*

"She is young."

"Wrong, Mr. Takahashi, *he* is young. *Read* the sentence, please."

But she *is* young, although she is not as young as Mr. Takahashi. She is twenty-two; she is five years older than he is. If she were not young, she believes, she would have known better than to make what she now sees as the series of mistakes that have brought her to this classroom where, today, her youth is being wasted on Mr. Takahashi.

He (despite *his* youth) has been studying her language for the past ten years of his life, yet still he uses the feminine pronoun for a masculine antecedent. Why can't he get this he/she stuff straight? In the four and a half months she has known him, Mrs. Longo must have reminded him a thousand times of the necessity of distinguishing between masculine and feminine (not to mention singular and plural). But his imprecision in these matters cannot be attributed to his personal failings, for it is widely shared—not only by all of Mrs. Longo's students at the Dorodarake Special English High School but also by its faculty, who have had far more time, incentive, and opportunity to master the personal pronouns in question.

2. *He is a young man.*

"She is young man."

Mrs. Longo sighs. "Wrong." (She says that often. Her students, including Mr. Takahashi, refer to her behind her back as "Mrs. Wrong-O"—and, since they cannot pronounce the letter "l," that is also what they call her to her face. But they don't know that, since they don't know they can't pronounce the letter "l.") "*He*—not *she*—is young, but, 'He is *a* young man.'"

In being a young man, Mr. Takahashi resembles most of the people who render Mrs. Longo's life oppressive: all the rest of her students, and Mr. Longo, twenty-four, whose fault it is that she is here. On the morning of the day they were married, that young man received an offer from Dorodarake Prefecture—an offer of three teaching positions, to be held simultaneously. As soon as he read the letter, he searched for Dorodarake in an atlas, and discovered it way down at the bottom of the Japanese archipelago, far from any place he'd ever heard of, though he was quite knowledgeable about Japan. He did try calling his fiancée, then, but she was already at the hairdresser's, having orange blossoms stuck in her curls. He had not been able to restrain himself from writing and mailing his acceptance before leaving for the church. He did not tell her what he had done until she had become his wife. "Guess where we're going?" he'd asked her at the altar, with shining eyes.

3. *He is Japanese.*

"She is Japanese."

" '*He* is Japanese,' Mr. Takahashi. We are still talking about the young man. A young man cannot be a 'she.'"

Mrs. Longo has nothing against anyone's being Japanese, of course. But now that she is in Japan, she finds she prefers people to be Japanese on the other side of the world from herself, or at any rate far enough away from her to be unable to thrust uncongenial responsibilities upon her.

"He is *a* Japanese man, but, 'He is Japanese,'" Mrs. Longo tells Mr. Takahashi, rashly. As she might have known, this departure from the text has confused him. He does not seem to know what she expects of him now. Her husband, who knows a lot about Japanese culture, has assured her that the whole thing is based on everyone's knowing what is expected of them at all times.

Mrs. Longo's experiences in the Dorodarake Special English High School—where she herself has no choice but to improvise—have tended to confirm this theory of her husband's.

3. *He is a student.*

"She —"

"*He*," Mrs. Longo leaps in hastily.

"She is student."

"She is *a* student."

Mr. Takahashi may be a student, but so what, when he doesn't learn? She is, in fact, no teacher. Doesn't the foregoing prove it? She has just let her student get away with a "she" that should have been a "he." How can what she is doing be called teaching, when none of her students are learning?

She not only hates teaching, but knows nothing about it. The three educational institutions in Dorodarake Prefecture that banded together to import her husband over-assigned his time, scheduling him simultaneously to teach classes in the Dorodarake Special English High School and to hold seminars at Dorodarake University. A meeting was held at which representatives of the three institutions decided that the best way of resolving this schedule conflict was for Mrs. Longo to take the classes at the High School. Her husband told her that, while this decision was reached by consensus, the original suggestion had been Mr. Mutsu's. That is one reason that Mrs. Longo hates Mr. Mutsu, who is the principal of Dorodarake Special English High School, and she suspects it is also one reason why Mr. Mutsu hates her. He had not yet met her when he made that fateful suggestion.

She is *trying* to teach. ("*He* is *a* student," she tells Mr. Takahashi, very firmly.) Her husband is a teacher. He holds a doctorate, and he has taken courses in the teaching of English as a foreign language. He has taught. His students have learned from him. They have made a point of telling him so.

His wife, however, is inexperienced and uncertified. She has nothing to guide her in her endeavors at the Dorodarake Special English High School but her memories of the foreign-language teachers of her own adolescence. She remembers three spinsters who taught Latin in her boarding school as particularly imposing. They were all very tall. And although she never thought to find herself sharing even a single attribute with these sere and celibate classicists—after all, she does. For, although of exactly average height for an American woman, she is, in Japan, gigantic enough to intimidate her students just by standing next to them.

Like everyone else entering the portals of Dorodarake Special English High School, Mrs. Longo sheds her shoes at the door and shuffles around in heelless school slippers that do nothing to augment her height, but she has heard her students sniggering over the drill on comparatives that includes the question "Is she taller than they are?" Although Mr. Takahashi is considered tall for his age, he does not quite come up to her chin, and she towers over Mr. Mutsu by a satisfying foot and a half.

She is trying to acquire other attributes in common with the teachers she remembers as pedagogical beyond all challenge. She is cultivating a donnish sense of humor: "Those who do not know grammar, Mr. Takahashi, are condemned to repeat it." She follows this aphorism—which Mr. Takahashi cannot, of course, be expected to appreciate—with a snorting, melancholy laugh based on an otherwise unmemorable physics teacher's.

Mrs. Longo turns grimly to the blackboard. "MR. MUTSU IS A PRINCIPAL," she writes. "HE IS A PRINCIPAL." Having written these sentences, she enunciates them at Mr. Takahashi with menacing precision. She raises the chalk again.

"MR. TAKAHASHI IS A STUDENT," she writes. "Now, suppose I want to replace Mr. Takahashi with a pronoun." (She smiles—not happily—at the thought of how very much she would like to replace Mr. Takahashi with a pronoun, or, indeed, anything else that might happen to be handy.) She cancels "MR. TAKAHASHI" with a large X, savoring her power. His lips part in alarm. It is the only sign he gives of comprehension.

She stares at him in relentless expectation. Beneath the X, she taps (long, short-short, long) demandingly with her piece of chalk. She has reproduced the rhythm of the song of the cicada (which, as the poet tells us, little intimates how soon it must die). It is also, she notices as she taps, the rhythm of the sentences "He is a fool," and "She is a fraud," and of the phrase "stuck in Japan," and even of the question "Where is my man?" though she cannot account for its presence in her mind, since she knows quite well that her husband is at Dorodarake University, giving a seminar on translation to three ravishing (that is his word for them) graduate students.

Mr. Takahashi appears to have grasped what is required of him. "She is student," he mutters, closing his eyes as though exhausted by this effort.

"*He*, Mr. Takahashi, '*He* is *a* student.'" As she says this, Mrs. Longo writes "HE" under the X, pressing so hard in her exasperation that the chalk breaks. Half of it rolls under Mr. Takahashi's desk. No effort is made to retrieve it.

With the remaining half, Mrs. Longo writes "MRS. LONGO IS A TEACHER." Abruptly, as though to rectify this misstatement, she effaces her name with an egalitarian X. Under this X, she writes "SHE." Inspired, she wags the chalk significantly between the S in "MRS." and the S in "SHE," as if the mystery of yin and yang could be thus laid bare.

Pointing to the appropriate sentences in a parody of patience, she explains. "Mr. Mutsu is a *man*. We must call him 'he.' *You*, Mr. Takahashi, are a man. So we must call you 'he,' too. I"—here she pauses dramatically—"am a *woman*, so—"

Mr. Takahashi looks down, blushing slightly as if embarrassed by his teacher's constant harping on sex. He is, in fact, consulting his watch. Following his eyes, Mrs. Longo sees that their ordeal will be over in four minutes.

The atmosphere in the classroom becomes almost comfortable for a moment. "'MR. MUTSU IS A PRINCIPAL,'" Mrs. Longo reads encouragingly from the board. "'HE IS A PRINCIPAL.' 'MR. TAKAHASHI IS A STUDENT.'" To make an inquiring face, she raises her eyebrows.

Mr. Takahashi appears willing to let bygones be bygones. "She is student," he says impassively.

Mrs. Longo points to the words on the board and reads them aloud. "'*HE* IS *A* STUDENT.' Just *read* the words, Mr. Takahashi," she suggests plaintively.

He looks at the words as she points to them again. But he says, again, "She is student," nodding a little self-righteously as he does so.

Is it possible, Mrs. Longo wonders, that all those students and teachers think they are saying "he" when they say "she"? "It is four-thirty, Mr. Takahashi," she points out, although it isn't yet, not quite.

"*Shitsurei sh'imasu,*"[1] her pupil mumbles by way of goodbye, bowing, gathering up his books.

Mrs. Longo begins arranging her own. Her teaching is done for the day, but she is not happy. Other ordeals lie before her.

As abruptly as her arrival in Japan made Mrs. Longo tall, it made her mute and illiterate. When she forgets to ask her husband to translate her shopping list into Japanese, misadventure is inevitable. Once, driven to nihilistic extravagance by her desperation for salad oil and her inability to communicate with an ancient clerk, she went home with the four likeliest-looking containers in the shop. These proved to contain rice vinegar, soy sauce, dishwashing liquid, and shampoo. All of them had, on their labels, pictures of salad vegetables.

She has since learned that salad oil is identified with pictures of kewpie dolls, Betty Boop, or bubbles. Since so many surprising substances are to be found lurking behind Betty Boop and the even more versatile kewpie doll, she sticks to the bubbles. (Cynically, she eschews the cans with *green* bubbles, having concluded that because, in their greenness, they suggest salad, they cannot possibly signify salad. Actually, they do, so she has been unwittingly using frying oil to mix her salad dressings.)

Not that she hasn't made progress in identifying food-stuffs. She knows by now that butter is not to be found in either of the rectangular cardboard boxes with pictures of cows on them, but in a squat cylindrical can with a picture of a snowflake on it (although it is not refrigerated). It's usually out of stock anyway, which she has come to think may be just as well since she has been told that *batakusai* ("reeking of butter") is a viciously insulting way to refer to foreigners, especially Americans.

Mrs. Longo makes a decision. She will find her colleague, Miss Miyagaki, and ask her for help with her shopping list. She does not share Miss Miyagaki's determined friendliness, but she sees no reason not to exploit Miss Miyagaki's ability (apparently unique among the faculty) to understand spoken English, even fairly sophisticated forms of it.

But then Mrs. Longo raises her eyes to the classroom door and spots Mr. Mutsu on the threshold. He enters; she watches and smells his approach. The chalk dust in her nostrils mingles with the sweet fumes of his hair oil.

---

[1]*Shitsurei sh'imasu:* Excuse me

Mrs. Longo is sure that by the time she is free of him, Miss Miyagaki will be gone. So much for her shopping list. (One does not ask one's nemesis for help like that.)

"So, Wrong-o-San, just now you have teached private lesson to Taka-hashi-Kun, *ne*?"

"You could put it that way," she tells him with determined inscrutability. (Life offers Mrs. Longo few satisfactions these days. Baiting the principal is one of them.)

"So what are you thinking?" Mr. Mutsu asks. Then he makes his question more specific. "Is Takahashi-Kun going to pass the examinations for Tokyo University?"

"Not unless their standards are singularly inexacting," Mrs. Longo informs him, flushing guiltily with the pleasure of spite. She looks forward to his attempts to extract information from her without admitting that he has not understood what she has said.

"Mmmmm," he hums, "Todai standards are very, very . . ."

Mrs. Longo is disappointed in herself. With a little more effort, she thinks, she could have found a more obscure word than "standards." To penalize herself, she finishes Mr. Mutsu's sentence for him: "High?"

"Exactly so," the principal confirms.

Now it is Mrs. Longo's move again. "How regrettable for Mr. Takahashi," she ventures.

Behind his thick lenses, Mr. Mutsu blinks. "If he can become a doctor, it will make his mother happy," says Mr. Mutsu.

"No doubt," Mrs. Longo tells him, her perverse elation augmented by a grudging admiration of Mr. Mutsu's skill at this game, "but his astonishing incompetence is liable to blight his medical career."

"I am glad to hear you say that," Mr. Mutsu informs her.

She cannot enjoy her victory. Not only were there no spectators, but it was too easy. She would have preferred a longer volley. Perhaps she will have to make new rules for herself: no taking advantage, say, of the confusion between "r" and "l."

"Why?" she inquires, but without real relish. "Don't you like his mother?"

"Mrs. Takahashi has plenty of money," Mr. Mutsu remarks.

Mrs. Longo knows all about Mrs. Takahashi's fortune. It came to her from her father, a plastic surgeon whose curious specialty was the restoration of ruptured hymens. (Miss Miyagaki has explained to Mrs. Longo that the old doctor's skill had been in great demand in the postwar decade.) Mrs. Takahashi evidently believes that her only son is most likely to replicate her father's prosperity by imitating his academic career, and to this end she has had him educated, coached, and tutored unrelentingly.

Mr. Mutsu resumes caution. It appears to Mrs. Longo that he is even now unaware of his defeat, but he seems to suspect that something is amiss. "When her son has acceptance from Tokyo University, Mrs. Takahashi will give us a language lab."

Mrs. Longo finds she has no appetite for a second round. "Mr. Mutsu," she says, "Tokyo's entrance exams are the most difficult in this country, aren't they?"

Mr. Mutsu throws back his small, fragrant head and opens his mouth very wide. Mrs. Longo does not know whether he is overcome by relief at having understood every single word of one of her sentences or whether he is dramatizing his inability to express the surpassing difficulty of Tokyo University's entrance exams.

She looks away, rejecting intimacy with Mr. Mutsu's bridgework. She goes on. "Mr. Takahashi is the worst student I have." As a kind of mocking consolation for the disappointment she must just have occasioned him, she decides to present Mr. Mutsu with an example of what he morbidly calls "living English." "He doesn't have a snowball's chance in hell."

"How can this be?" Mr. Mutsu asks. He looks surprised, which surprises Mrs. Longo.

Mr. Mutsu has informed Mrs. Longo on previous occasions that he is on record (in an article in *The Journal of Southern Japanese Educators*) as having great respect for the analytical capacities of the Western mind. He seems to listen passionately as Mrs. Longo itemizes: "He is stupid. He doesn't study. He doesn't learn. He doesn't seem to know how." (But as she says these things, her mind provides a counterpoint: She is stupid. She doesn't teach. She doesn't seem to know how.)

"He *only* studies," Mr. Mutsu protests. "He don't do nothing else. Every day after school she goes to English classes in *juku*, she comes home at nine o'clock in the night, then there is a private tutor coming to his house. And every weekend it is the same thing."

Mrs. Longo sees that the distinction between learning and being taught is as meaningless to Mr. Mutsu as that between "he" and "she." And yet Mrs.

Longo knows for a fact that this man holds two doctorates, one in Education and one in English Literature. He boasts, moreover, of having spent a semester at Southern Methodist University.

"So when does Mr. Takahashi do his homework?" she asks.

"In the night, with that private tutor." Mr. Mutsu glares at Mrs. Longo, as though she should have figured that out for herself.

She sighs. She thinks, So Mr. Takahashi has never been left alone, unchaperoned, with a piece of information. No wonder he doesn't learn. But she does not say these things.

"Mrs. Longo," Mr. Mutsu says, "if Mr. Takahashi does not pass the entrance examination for Tokyo, there might be some serious consequences."

"Maybe someone else will give you a language lab," Mrs. Longo says, hoisting her shoulder bag. But conversations with Mr. Mutsu are not so easily ended.

"The rate of suicide among children in Japan is the very highest in the world, isn't it so?" he persists.

Mrs. Longo has heard Mr. Mutsu boast about many of the global superlatives Japan has established, from the smallest average bust measurement to the greatest per-capita distribution of both eyeglasses and violins, but it seems to her that he is really scraping the bottom of the barrel of preeminence now. Then she sees why he has dragged out this statistic, and is annoyed. "Mr. Takahashi isn't about to kill himself," she asserts, wondering as she does so why she is saying it—Mr. Takahashi's character is utterly opaque to her. (Although she made the statement with confidence, she finds she is afraid.)

The principal hastens to document his assertion. He extracts a newspaper clipping from his pocket. "Twelve years old," he says, although the clipping looks quite recent. Since the story is in Japanese, Mrs. Longo cannot read it. Instead, she stares at the photograph that illustrates it, and decides Mr. Mutsu is referring to this girl. "She does look a little bit like Mr. Takahashi," she observes. "Heavyset."

"Using gas. Thirty-two persons in that building also died because of that explosion. She wrote a letter to say that she killed herself because she was ashamed to the spirits of her ancestors since she failed the examination for middle school."

Mrs. Longo cannot imagine Mr. Takahashi doing anything newsworthy, even to assuage the presumably implacable spirit of the renovator of maidenheads. "I have done my best with him," she assures Mr. Mutsu dryly.

"Ah, so?" Exuding these syllables, the principal puts the clipping back in his pocket. "Maybe if he don't pass the examination this year, next year he will try again. 'If at first you don't succeed, try, try, try again.'"

Mrs. Longo is afraid he will go on to identify this saying as "living English," but he does not. Instead, he says, "So maybe next year you can do a private lesson to Mr. Takahashi for three hours every day."

Mrs. Longo feels the floor of the classroom shaking beneath her feet. She grips the edge of the desk, which trembles, eluding her grasp. She attributes these phenomena to her extreme dismay at the possibility Mr. Mutsu has just mentioned until, observing the framed face of the Minister of Education lurching away from the map of the world on the wall, she realizes that an earthquake is taking place.

Proust-like, Mrs. Longo is invaded by memory: The sensations of a terrible undergraduate party repossess her. The punch, which she remembers as smelling something like Mr. Mutsu's hair oil, was harsh and even looked garish, but she could not stop drinking it, because the young man who would be but was not yet her husband would not stop dancing with a smug and inexplicably popular anthropology major called Mary Jane Becker. Then, as now, the room and its furnishings wavered and shifted around her: With painful intensity, she remembers how much she wanted him to take her home. She glares accusingly at Mr. Mutsu. *(Mr. Mutsu is a man.)*

"That was a small, everyday kind of earthquake," he informs her. He looks up at her, a nervous laugh escapes him. "Take no notice, dear lady."

"I will not be here next year," she hears herself saying.

"Maybe so," Mr. Mutsu concedes.

"My husband's contract is for one year," she hears herself saying.

"Maybe Dorodarake will renew that contract," the principal speculates, adding, "Do we say 'to renew'?"

Mrs. Longo takes no notice. Tears start to her eyes. Her husband would not do that to her, he couldn't. But look what he has already done.

Dainty little Miss Miyagaki glides by the door of the classroom, her pale gauze sleeves flapping like the wings of a good fairy. Mrs. Longo's shopping list, at least, is not a lost cause after all. "Excuse me, Mr. Mutsu, I must speak to Miss Miyagaki."

Mrs. Longo does not particularly want to share a soggy and chemical éclair in the café called Moscow in the neighboring town of Shizunde (an overgrown fishing village, really), but there is no place to go for a snack near the high school. Besides, for some reason Miss Miyagaki seems extremely eager for the excursion, and since it will probably result in Miss Miyagaki's actually doing Mrs. Longo's shopping for her, Mrs. Longo agrees to go. The bus to Shizunde is filled with the gloomy uniforms of Dorodarake Special English High School, so it is not until the two women are seated on the squat but spindly imitation brass café chairs, picking delicately at the ersatz éclair, that Mrs. Longo feels free to tell Miss Miyagaki, "Mr. Mutsu is such a *creep!*"

"But he perseveres," Miss Miyagaki says mildly.

Mrs. Longo looks at her blankly. "Are you sure that's what you mean to say?" she asks at last.

Miss Miyagaki, blushing, removes an aging dictionary—twice as thick as her delicate wrist—from her bag. "*Ganbaru*," she reads, "to persevere, to keep at it, to continue."

"I wish he wouldn't," Mrs. Longo tells her.

Miss Miyagaki giggles delightedly. She is happily conscious of the interest her exotic companion evokes in the other women in the pâtisserie. She masticates her mouthful ostentatiously, to let Mrs. Longo know how much she is enjoying this cosmopolitan occasion.

Mrs. Longo winces at the consequent sights and sounds. A cultural abyss seems to gape between her and her colleague. She knows that Miss Miyagaki is regarded as a model of deportment, but Mrs. Longo will never, never, never get used to Japanese table manners. Somehow in a person of Miss Miyagaki's delicacy, refinement, and intelligence, they are all the more distressing.

Mrs. Longo does not know why Miss Miyagaki is laughing, since what she just said about Mr. Mutsu was not intended as a joke. She needs to vent her indignation. She tries again. "You know what he was telling me, in the classroom just now when you walked by?"

"I did not hear him, tell it to me, please, I would be delighted," Miss Miyagaki requests carefully, unfortunately deciding to augment the encouraging politeness of her words by sipping her tea very loudly. "And then I will tell you something, too."

"He told me that if that Takahashi idiot doesn't pass the Tokyo entrance exams, next year I might—" In mid-sentence, Mrs. Longo realizes that she cannot very well go on as she is about to. How can she tell Miss Miyagaki *(She is Japanese. She is a teacher)* how homesick she is, how much she hates teaching, how awful the prospect of another year here is to her? Never mind: She has no shortage of grounds for denouncing Mr. Mutsu. "He told me he might kill himself. And he sort of implied that if he did, it would be my fault."

"*Hora!*" Miss Miyagaki exclaims. "Maybe you should stop teasing him."

"*Teasing him?*" Mrs. Longo is sure that in all her dealings with Mr. Takahashi she has shown the patience of a particularly forbearing saint. "Get out that dictionary again."

Miss Miyagaki, her tiny hand trembling under the weight of the heavy book, looks up the word and reads, frowning, "Tease, make mock of, make fun of."

"I have never *teased* Mr. Takahashi," Mrs. Longo says, trying to straighten her back without engulfing her head in the vermilion Plexiglas shade of the low-hanging lighting fixture.

"Not Mr. Takahashi, Mr. Mutsu," Miss Miyagaki explains, hoping that this confusion has not arisen because she expressed herself incorrectly. She looks a little put-upon. Her enthusiasm for the English language is great but not boundless.

Mrs. Longo attempts to restore some semblance of communication to their conversation. "Mr. *Mutsu*? Why would Mr. Mutsu kill himself because Mr. Takahashi flunked an exam?"

"Of course," Miss Miyagaki amplifies, "he would not really kill himself because Mr. Takahashi did not pass that examination; he would really kill himself because you have been teasing him and he has lost face very much when you teased him. But if he explains that that is *why* he is killing himself, then he will lose still more face. So he needs some excuse for killing himself, and if Mr. Takahashi fails that examination, he will have that excuse. People will say it is a very noble—a very elegant?—reason for suicide." Miss Miyagaki is a little breathless after all these complex English sentences. She hopes she has made herself clear.

Mrs. Longo is quite overwhelmed. She has come to trust Miss Miyagaki's assessments of things. And Miss Miyagaki's predictions—even when they are extremely improbable, like the one about the shortage of toilet paper and the fact that several consumers would be trampled to death when it reappeared in supermarkets—have always come true. So it seems it is actually possible that the game she has improvised for her private amusement could drive a man to suicide.

She hates Mr. Mutsu, but not with that kind of hatred. She certainly doesn't want to compass his death. "Do you really think he would?" she asks frantically.

"Maybe so."

"And you're saying I would be responsible?"

"Don't worry," Miss Miyagaki murmurs. "I will tell no one. I think"—here she lowers her bright eyes modestly, perhaps to disavow the inherent boastfulness of her assertion—"I am the only one who can see that you talk on purpose so he won't understand." Raising her eyes again, she sees the distress in Mrs. Longo's. "I will tell no one," she repeats.

Dizzying sequences of lethal causality unfurl in Mrs. Longo's imagination. If it is possible—as it seems to be—that Miss Miyagaki is right about Mr. Mutsu's putative suicide, then is it also possible that Mr. Mutsu is right about Mr. Takahashi's?

She seeks clarification. "Are you saying that Mr. Mutsu might kill himself—because I've humiliated him—if Mr. Takahashi just flunks, or will Mr. Takahashi have to kill himself?"

"Don't worry," Miss Miyagaki insists soothingly. "This will not happen."

"Didn't you just say it might?"

"But Mr. Takahashi will pass the examination, so Mr. Mutsu won't have that excuse for killing himself. Nevertheless, I think maybe you should stop teasing him—if you don't want him to kill himself—because some other excuse might happen. You don't eat this éclair?"

Mrs. Longo stares reproachfully at Miss Miyagaki. "But Mr. Takahashi *can't* pass that examination. Not the English part. Believe me—I know, I teach him every day."

"But I am his teacher too," Miss Miyagaki protests. "Advanced English Grammar. And English Reading Comprehension. I know that he will pass. Mr. Takahashi has many advantages. In our school he has many, many more hours of English classes than students in some ordinary high school. And he has still more in *juku* after school. He has a tutor, too, I mean more than you, yet another one."

"Mr. Mutsu told me. Given all that, he's really amazingly bad at English."

"No, no, he is not so bad. I know very well about Mr. Takahashi, I was giving him private lessons too, at one time. Poor Mr. Takahashi. He seems to be more stupid than he is, because he is often falling asleep. I was going to his house from eight o'clock to ten-thirty at night. He was sleeping sometimes with his eyes open, saying crazy words from his dreams. I was asking him about maybe the gerund and the predicate adjective, and he was all at once yelling something about spiders. This happened four years ago, he was a little boy. I felt so sorry for him, I could not awaken him. One time his mother came in and saw that he was sleeping, and she poured a glass of water on his head. And then she told Mr. Mutsu to find another tutor, because I was a thief, to take her money and let her son sleep.

"But he can pass that exam, I am sure. You see, you have no way of knowing about that because you do not speak Japanese."

"The English exam is in *Japanese*?" Mrs. Longo asks limply.

"Of course there are some examples in English . . . I am not sure if he will pass this year. If not, he can next year, for sure. Poor Mr. Mutsu, then."

Mrs. Longo's mind, wearied by Miss Miyagaki's revelations, pains her. Her long American legs hurt too, cramped by the diminutive furniture. "If you think Mr. Takahashi is going to pass this exam, why do you say 'poor Mr. Mutsu'?"

"Oh." Miss Miyagaki, enjoying the éclair, is expansive. "Then Mrs. Takahashi will give Mr. Mutsu a language lab. *Imagine* that. In some big room, there will be maybe one hundred tape recorders with foreigners' voices talking all day, and Mr. Mutsu will understand very little. For Mr. Mutsu, it will be as if one hundred of Mrs. Longo were teasing him forever. That is why I say 'Poor Mr. Mutsu.' Especially now that Mr. Mutsu has helped—"

Miserably, Mrs. Longo interrupts her colleague. "If that happens, it won't be my fault."

Miss Miyagaki follows her reasoning. "You have not been teaching Mr. Takahashi to pass exams," she agrees.

"I have taught him *nothing*." Mrs. Longo snorts.

"That is all right," Miss Miyagaki soothes. "You are not supposed to teach him nothing. No one expects you to. Really."

"Then what am I supposed to be doing with all those students, if I'm not expected to teach them anything?"

Miss Miyagaki finds this question difficult, but she is no coward. She flattens the paper doily in front of her with the tines of her gold plastic fork. "In a way, of course, there is no point in having a native speaker to teach these children. They are not ready to learn English from a native speaker. But in another way, it is good. It is most important for them to see that you are human beings, too. We don't have foreigners in Dorodarake Prefecture. So we only see how foreigners look in pictures or movies—like big hairy barbarians, you know? How can we see how foreigners are people just like us Japanese, after all, strange eyes and strange customs nevertheless?" As she speaks, Miss Miyagaki hears herself making mistakes, but they do not distress her. She glows with the awareness that what she is expressing, however awkwardly, is beautiful. "So I am so happy you are here." Tears come into her eyes, she is so moved by what she has just said.

Mrs. Longo nods. "But I'm not expected to teach them any *English*?"

"You teach them English, a little bit—maybe some idioms?—but even if they don't learn in your class, it is not really wasting their time."

"*Their* time?" Mrs. Longo growls.

Miss Miyagaki is startled by her tone. Her glow vanishes abruptly. What was wrong with the sentence she just uttered? "*Her* time?" she guesses wildly, but even as this preposterous emendation flies from her mouth, she realizes that she had used the pronoun correctly. But what else is Mrs. Longo growling at? She is sure she can say "waste time"; it occurs in an example sentence she uses frequently in drills. "Time . . ." she falters, then is inspired to squint at her watch. She jumps to her feet; her sleeves flutter ethereally. "Mrs. Longo, we are now missing the last bus!"

The two women dash, panting, through the maze of Shizunde's shopping arcade. Miss Miyagaki bangs on the bus's closing doors, and breathlessly urges the driver to open them for the foreigner who is staggering toward his vehicle. Clutching her side, she smiles, seeing this gesture reproduced on a larger scale by Mrs. Longo, as though in a magnifying mirror. The truth of the assertion she has just made about their common humanity seems vividly exemplified.

By the time the bus deposits them in front of Dorodarake Special English High School, the shops nearby (such as they are) will be shut. "Oh, Miss Miyagaki, what will I do? I was hoping you could help me with my shopping; I have nothing to give my husband for dinner." Mrs. Longo gasps, sinking onto a jouncing seat.

Miss Miyagaki's delicate hand rummages in her bag, extracts a parcel. "Please take this. It is excellent, very fresh, I bought it today."

"Oh, I couldn't possibly—"

"Oh, you must have something for Professor Longo to eat for dinner! I have another thing to give to my mother. You take that, please."

Mrs. Longo peeks into the parcel. She sees purple tentacles pimpled with grayish-white suckers. She does not, and she doubts that her husband will, eat octopus—especially since she has no idea of how to cook it. "It's very kind of you, Miss Miyagaki, but—"

Miss Miyagaki will not let Mrs. Longo refuse her gift. Beaming, she slips it into Mrs. Longo's bag. "Now you have everything you need!"

Mrs. Longo is at a loss for words.

Miss Miyagaki takes advantage of this unusual condition. "Mr. Mutsu is a big fool, everybody knows that," Miss Miyagaki remarks abruptly, "but he is a kind man. He is arranging a marriage for me. I am very grateful, because my mother is poor and cannot do it. And I cannot be unmarried any longer." She peers shyly up into Mrs. Longo's face. "We don't do that in Japan. We must be married. I think it is very different in America." She giggles. "I will learn about America, if I marry this man Mr. Mutsu has found for me. He lives in Kitakyushu now, but next year he will go to teach Japanese children in New York, and if I marry him, I must go with him. It is not yet arranged; I have not yet met this man, but I want to tell you about it now, because if that happens, I will be just like you, then, isn't it so?"

Mrs. Longo notices that her mouth is open, and shuts it. Then she opens it again, but all that comes out of it is "Oh, Miss Miyagaki—"

"I have never visited any foreign country. Or any very big city, even in Japan," Miss Miyagaki tells her. "Do you think I will like to live in New York?"

Mrs. Longo remembers the words she so thoughtlessly threw at Mr. Mutsu: "a snowball's chance in hell." Because although Mrs. Longo thinks of New York often and with intense longing, now, trying to imagine Miss Miyagaki living there, she can think only of its squalor, its cruelty, its ever-present possibilities of violence. "This man you would be marrying—?" she hears herself ask.

"I do not have his photograph here. In some way, I think I know him, although I have not met him. He is a teacher of English, too; he has written some books that we use in school." Miss Miyagaki pulls an English text from her bag.

Mrs. Longo knows it well; it has brightened many a bad day for her. At the end of every chapter, in dialogues called "Sample Conversations," characters with names like Mr. Brown and Miss Johnson greet each other with sentences like "Excuse me, you look familiar. Didn't I meet you in the bathtub last night?"

Miss Miyagaki will be facing New York with no one to help her but the author of these dialogues. "Oh, Miss Miyagaki . . ." Mrs. Longo hears herself trail off again, for what can she possibly say? But something is certainly called for: Though the gesture doesn't seem adequate, she lunges gently down, intending to plant a sisterly kiss on her colleague's cheek.

The bus veers sharply, and the kiss lands instead on Miss Miyagaki's mouth, with much more force than Mrs. Longo had intended. Drawing back, she is horrified at the expression (like an international graphic for shocked disgust) that is disfiguring Miss Miyagaki's dainty features as she wipes her mouth reflexively with the edge of a fluttering sleeve.

"I'm sorry, I didn't mean . . ." Mrs. Longo scans Miss Miyagaki's face anxiously for signs of returning self-possession.

"You mean something good, I know," Miss Miyagaki assures her eventually, in an unsteady voice. "But we never do that in Japan."

Bouncing helplessly on the seat of the lurching bus, crushing her shrinking colleague against the window, wondering what she is going to do about dinner, Mrs. Longo watches Miss Miyagaki's eyes taking a shamed, furtive survey of the fellow passengers who have observed this disgrace. They begin standing up; so does Miss Miyagaki. Mrs. Longo rises too, and is aware, as usual, of being much taller than anyone around her. Nevertheless, and for the first time in this country, she feels extremely small.

Questions for Reflection and Analysis

1. What strikes you about the story as a whole? Is there a particular aspect of the story that elicits a memory or concern about teaching and learning?
2. What personal factors account for Mrs. Longo's emotional state? What situational factors account for her attitude toward teaching in Japan?

3. How successful is Mrs. Longo's approach to teaching English? How do you account for the results? What do her pedagogical efforts reveal about her assumptions about language teaching and learning?

4. How are Mrs. Longo's expectations and assessments of English language learners similar to or different from other characters' expectations and assessments? How do you account for the similarities or differences?

5. What cultural or cross-cultural assumptions do Miss Miyagaki and Mrs. Longo bring to their interaction in the café, and how do these assumptions shape their perspectives? How do language and language differences contribute to confusion or misunderstanding in their exchange? How does their interaction contribute to Mrs. Longo's sense that, "for the first time in this country," she feels "extremely small" (p. 195)?

English Lessons

Shauna Singh Baldwin

(1962–)

Shauna Singh Baldwin was born in Canada to Sikh refugee parents from the Punjab, a state in northwest India. Her family moved back to India in 1972. After receiving an M.B.A. from Marquette University in the United States, she returned to Canada for three years. She now lives in the United States. An award-winning writer, Baldwin's publications include *What the Body Remembers* (1999), *A Foreign Visitor's Survival Guide to America* (1992), and *The Tiger Claw* (2005).

I told Tony—that is what he likes me to call him in America—I told Tony I will take English lessons till my green card comes. Valerie says there are English teachers who will teach me for free, and she will find a good one who will come to the apartment so that I do not have to go outside. Tony says OK, and then he leaves for work at the cardboard factory.

I pick up the breakfast dishes and Suryavir's toys. No one can say his name here—I will tell them at the school to call him Johnny, like Tony's Johnny Walker Whisky.

The phone rings and my heart starts to pound—dharak, dharak. Our answering machine message has Valerie's voice, and I follow the words with her accent.

"We're naat here right naow, but if you leeev a mehsej, weell get right baak to you." But it is only Valerie herself. "Pick up the phone, Kanwaljit. I want to know if you're home so I can drop the kids off for the day."

"Hello," I say. "I am here. You come."

Valerie is a nice person, but you cannot be too careful. Tony says we cannot meet anyone from India till my green card comes, so Valerie is the only one who sees me. I call her Grocery Store Valerie to myself, because she answered my card in the grocery store, and now I babysit her two strong and unruly boys. What farmers they would have made in Punjab! My son is not so strong. More than two years of women's company. I spoilt him while we were waiting for Tony to get his citizenship, but what was I to do? If I had disciplined him, Tony's parents would have been angry—he is their only grandson.

Valerie's boys don't listen to love or scolding. But they go to school, and Valerie says it is the law, I have to send Suryavir to school. So I went there with her to register him and on the form I wrote the address I had memorized from Valerie's cheques, not ours. Still, Tony was worried in case anyone who might report us saw me. He makes me dress in pants so that I look Mexican, and says it is only a short while now. I hope so.

But first I will learn English. It's not that I don't understand it, but it has too many words. Get it. Put it. I am stuffed. Pick up your stuff. On the other hand. Hand it to you. I learned English in school, passed my matriculation examination, too. We learned whole passages of translation by heart—I had a good memory. Now Tony says I must speak English to pass my immigration interview and to memorize my amnesty story.

A knock. Someone is standing far away from the peephole—why are they doing that? Oh, it's Valerie; she was bending down to tie a shoelace for little Mark.

"Hello, hello. Come in. How-are-you?"

Valerie has found an English teacher who will come to the apartment and teach me for free. But Tony and I are afraid. This English teacher is from India and we did not want to meet any people from India. Valerie said she told the teacher I am Tony's girlfriend and that Suryavir is our son. She said the English teacher was surprised. Indian couples do not usually live together, she told Valerie. Tony says to tell Valerie we don't need this teacher. But I took her phone number to please Valerie. I may call her just to speak in Punjabi for a while.

I told Valerie I will change my name. I asked her to call me Kelly. No one here can say Kanwaljit. And Kanwaljit is left far away in Amritsar, before the fire.

Some nights I lie next to Tony, here in America where I live like a worm avoiding the sunlight, and I wonder if he knows. And is it only because it was his brother that he does not sense that another man's body has come between us, or is it that he cannot remember the fire we felt in those early days. We only had three weeks in which Suryavir was made. Then he was gone.

If I had been able to return to my parents until he told me to come to America, I would not have been so weak. But to do so would have smelled of disgrace, and I am not shameless. Nor was it a matter of a month or two, Tony told me after six months, when I was becoming big with his son; it would take him two more years.

I tell myself it is not only another man's body that invades our bed, but another woman's too. And yet, that is different. I hear her tearful voice on our answering machine. Her anger follows us from city to city—Fremont, Dallas, Houston, Miami, New York, Chicago—threatening to report us to Immigration. He lived with her for two years, shared her bed, paid her our life savings for a marriage certificate. I will ask the English teacher how to say, "Is not two years of our life enough? Is not my worm existence, my unacknowledged wifehood, enough for you? Enough that I call myself his girlfriend, my son his bastard?"

But she does not have form, no substance in our bed. I cannot imagine him with her black body—and if I can, what of it? Many men pay prostitutes. This one's price was higher and she lasted longer. And he got his green card after two years. Thus am I here.

The other man in bed with us—he has form. He looks like Tony, only younger. And he still laughs at me, waving pictures of Tony with her. Telling me Tony left me for an untouchable, a hubshi. Threatening to tell my parents if I would not open my legs to him.

I did. Rubba-merey, I did.

I thought some force would come upon us then and tear him from my flesh before the act was done. Save me, as the virtue of Dropadi was saved. And it did. Too late for virtue but soon enough for vengeance.

The police came looking for him. Oh, not for my protection—no. They were rounding up all Sikh boys between the ages of fifteen and twenty-five for "questioning." Tony's parents knew what was in store and they hid him in the servant's quarter, a concrete room on the flat roof of the house.

They told the police he was with Tony in America. That made them angry. One sinewy fellow with a whisky smell took a can of gasoline and slowly, as we watched from the rooms around, and as Suryavir's eyes grew larger, poured it in a steady dribble all round the centre courtyard. They all walked to the door and, almost as an afterthought, the sinewy policeman threw a lit match and the world exploded from silence into horror.

I took no chances. I gave Suryavir to Tony's mother and they climbed out of the back window. His father was blinded by tears and I pushed him after them. Then I ran up the narrow steep staircase to the servant's quarter on the roof.

And I locked it.

And ran back through lung-searing smoke and purifying flame. I was given vengeance, and I took it as my due.

But still he comes between us—the half-dead only half a world away.

I called the English teacher today. She speaks Punjabi with a city accent. I will have to ask Tony, but I think it will be, like Americans say, "fine, fine" for her to come and teach me.

Her family on her father's side is from Rajasansi, just outside Amritsar. And she is married to a white guy so she is probably not part of the Gurdwara congregation; they have all heard of Tony's Green-Card Wife. (These matters travel faster than aeroplanes fly between cities.) I will tell Tony I will take English lessons, and that she will be my teacher.

Tony was finishing breakfast when Mrs. Keogh, the English teacher, arrived. She knocked and I let her in. Then I asked her to sit down, offered her some tea and listened while she and Tony spoke English.

"Thank you very much. My girlfriend is just new from India. As soon as her green card comes we will be getting married, so till then I think English lessons will help her pass the time."

The English teacher did not remark on "my girlfriend." Good. Not a prying woman. She said, "I am glad to help you and your fiancée."

Tony continued, "I will not like it if you teach her more than I know. But just enough for her to get a good paying job at Dunkin' Donuts or maybe the Holiday Inn. She will learn quickly, but you must not teach her too many American ideas."

The English teacher smiled at me.

Tomorrow, I will ask her where I can learn how to drive.

Questions for Reflection and Analysis

1. What strikes you about the story as a whole? Is there a particular aspect of the story that elicits a memory or concern about teaching and learning?

2. Why do the various characters in the story change their names or the names of their children?

3. What societal norms and expectations do Tony's and Kanwaljit's past experiences reflect? What is the effect of these past experiences on Kanwaljit's current living situation, state of mind, and choice of tutor?

4. How are Tony's reasons similar to or different from Kanwaljit's reasons for taking private English lessons? What does Tony's ultimate response suggest about his expectations with regard to their respective gender roles?

5. What are the "English Lessons" to which the title refers?

■ Albert and Esene

Frances Khirallah Noble

(1945–)

Frances Khirallah Noble was born and raised in California. She received her J.D. degree from the University of Southern California Law School in 1972. She left the practice of law in 1997 to write fiction and to teach creative writing. Her short-story collection, *The Situe Stories* (2000), chronicles the experiences of immigrants to the United States from what is now Syria and Lebanon. She has also written *The New Belly Dancer of the Universe Contest: A Novel* (2007).

They sat side by side in the living room of the small duplex, their short, white legs without demarcation for ankle or calf—identical legs, except that one pair was plump and the other, thin—hanging over the side of the couch. Their feet barely grazed the floor. In a rare convergence, they had agreed that the occasion called for their good black dresses. Amelia and Safiyah, in dignity and forbearance, visiting Esene.

The husband of Esene had died two weeks before. His sisters, also widows, had come to console. And to have lunch. Already the smells for which Esene was known floated from her kitchen to reassure her neighbors that she was recovered enough to cook.

Esene carried two mugs of coffee into the living room.

"Did you put cream and sugar?" asked Saliyah.

"I know how you like it," answered Esene.

"I don't see how you can drink coffee in this heat," complained Amelia, her vast and magnificent bosom rising like bread dough above her dropped neckline. "Usually it wakes me up, but in this heat, it makes me so tired."

"If anyone should be tired," Safiyah said, "it should be me. I drove us all the way up here."

"You slam on the brakes every time you see a car," Amelia accused, and she inclined toward Esene, pretending to be confidential. "People were honking and shouting at us the whole trip and she didn't notice. Stop. Start. Stop. Start. She stops twenty feet before every intersection." Then she turned to Safiyah. "This is the last time I let you drive me anywhere."

"He who digs a pit is likely to fall into it," Safiyah answered, subsiding into her sweetened coffee. "Who'll drive you if I don't?" And she clutched the cup with her bony hands, her perfect red fingernails, like pyracantha berries blazing against the white glass, her diamond rings weighting her fingers.

"At any rate," Amelia began again, "now we're all the same. Floating in the same boat, eh, Esene? Safiyah and I, we can tell you what it's like to be a widow."

Esene. Who'd taken the armchair by the window, stepping past the pile of unfolded newspapers and untouched magazines that tilted against the leg of the television. Esene. Crocheting. Cream thread growing into a doily. Defeating Amelia's attempts to encircle her with her defeating smile.

For sixty-two years, Esene had paid little attention to her sisters-in-law. This, on the advice of her husband when she'd asked how to approach the women into whose family she had intruded. "Don't get drawn into it," he'd said. "It's the only way they know how to speak. If you say little," Albert wisely counseled in the face of their outstretched arms, the imbroglio of their embraces, the Sunday feasts, the shirts off their backs, "and act less, they'll think you agree with them. No one will argue. There'll be no one to convince. Or, if you prefer," he brushed his luxuriant black mustache with the tip of his finger, "I'll do the talking for both of us."

Which is what he did.

"She's like a silent child," his family said. "Not a thought in her head. It's probably a good thing they have no children." This was Esene's only real sadness. Not that Albert wasn't vigorous and passionate in bed. Not that Esene didn't respond, urging him. Everyone in Albert's family blamed Esene. Her family, distant by the width of a country, ceased to think about faraway grandchildren, until Esene existed for them primarily as the exotic aunt in California who mailed five-dollar bills in Christmas cards written in pencil in her large, coarse script.

For Albert (whom they had met but once) had taught her to read and write.

At first he had merely read to her every night from the evening papers, adjusting the position of his magnifying glass for the Arabic or English letters, railing against the injustices reported from around the world. Esene sat like a cat on the rug next to his chair, her head pressing against his knee.

One night he proclaimed, "Esene, I'm going to teach you to read!"

"Albert," she laughed. "Why?"

"The women in this country read."

With the same fervor that led him to stock his tiny Arabic grocery store with Coca-Cola, American cigarettes and magazines and candy, and to encourage his customers to speak English on the premises (if they could) every other Monday, he set out to teach Esene to read. She was thirty-five years old and much younger than he.

"At . . . bat . . . cat . . . This is so silly."

"Here, Esene, smoke, if it helps you relax . . ."

Shades drawn. Front door locked. To prevent discovery, because Albert wanted it to be a surprise, his surprise to unveil like a repainted statue. It was not to humiliate his sister, Amelia, who had received their mother's recipes, wordlessly, by watching and doing; who handed over to her husband without a glance all written matter; and who argued day and night with that husband over what her mother said, his sister said, what they should do, where they should go, while she expanded and puffed up until he resentfully wondered how much larger she could grow. Nor to spite Safiyah: wealthy by marriage, with her diamonds and her sheared fox wrap, whose empty head held jet stones in place of eyes and whose teeth clenched its own paws in a ring around Safiyah's elegant neck. It was certainly not to defy Albert's mother, Hasna—no, he was her favorite and he basked in her affectionate glow.

When Esene asked again, "Why, Albert?" he merely laughed and pushed her nose into a book. "Our secret," he reminded her.

Esene pronounced "tin, fin . . . bob, cob . . ." from lists of Albert's devising. Then words from a child's book that Albert searched for in the library, a book that would not cause Esene to bristle with impatience.

"You must be diligent," he instructed. "You must work every day."

"I will not miss my programs," she snapped, leaving the theme book, the pencils adrift on the couch with elaborate indifference. For one day, then two, while she expanded her radio listening to cover every available hour.

"But how will you be ready?" Albert asked. "Christmas is coming and you won't be ready. What about our plan—"

"—Your plan, Albert!"

"—to send out American Christmas cards for the first time. In your hand. Which you will write. You'll surprise them all, Esene . . . . Please."

But, for the time being, Esene said, she wanted to revive her afternoon card games with her friends, who'd wondered at her unavailability—that is, if she still had any friends, she said to him morosely; if they hadn't disappeared in the labyrinth of her many absences.

"But, Esene, you only study in the evening. You've had plenty of time for your friends."

"You don't know what I do all day," Esene sobbed. And she gathered herself to parade down the sidewalk, past the small, respectable house of Albert's mother, Safiyah's large two-story house, and Amelia's white frame cottage, nestled in a court of six equivalent structures—without a glance in their direction—to social events to which they were not invited.

"She looks different coming and going," said Safiyah.

"Less steady on her feet," Amelia observed.

"Slower."

"Drunk."

"Albert indulges her."

"Is ruled by her, you mean."

If Albert came home early, he tucked her in bed himself, tasting the lovely bourbon on her lips (which the women around the card table sipped from crystal shot glasses), slipping off her navy dress, unrolling her stockings, sliding his hands over her olive-skinned body, releasing the combs in her hair. He pulled down the shades; he loved her easily and languorously, so that before they'd finished, she was nearly asleep. Afterward, he lay on his back in their mahogany bed and pulled the covers over his face. It was the way he always slept.

As December approached, Albert increased the pace of the lessons: three- and four-syllable words in sentences, the use of the comma, the closing of a letter.

"All you need to know is enough to sign the Christmas cards," he badgered impatiently. "And write a short message." Esene adamantly refused to use a pen; they smeared and could not be erased. Albert shopped for cards they could afford, with space enough to accommodate Esene's expansive script.

As for Esene, even though she didn't love to study, even though Albert pushed and prodded her, she began to realize the power of what she was doing. She could hardly keep quiet. Words she knew floated all around her—in shop windows, on street signs, in magazines, newspapers, on packages, at church. Words she could read sat on the tip of her tongue, ready to leap off at any moment. What could she do? Deny what she knew? What was becoming automatic? Almost beyond her control? Esene's secret knowledge had begun to burn like a hot potato in her stomach; like a fox gnarling.

Albert tried to remind her: "Remember, it's our secret for now."

"Yes, yes, Albert. I know. I know."

Still, Esene stuffed magazines at the top of her shopping bag, allowing the corner fringes to peek over the edges. She asked out loud in front of Safiyah and Amelia, "Where is your Sunday paper?" Adding, after a moment's taunting silence, "For Albert."

On an evening several days before the cards were to be written and mailed, retrieved from the safety of their hiding place in the space under the kitchen sink, Esene said to old Nasef, Albert's father, who was deaf and nearly blind, "Would you like me to read you a story?" Then she turned to Albert, whose heart had made an invisible leap, and said, "Did I startle you?"

One morning soon after, the family set out to visit an ailing third cousin who'd arrived from Boston to winter in the paradise that was Los Angeles— warm, uncluttered, like the old country, healing to the joints and lungs, where the familiarity of oranges, grapes, and dates grew along the streets and in the vast spaces between buildings. Everyone disembarked from the streetcar. They shook out wrinkled skirts. The younger men placed dark hats on dark-haired heads. Dried sleep was cleaned from the corner of a child's eye. They gathered on the sidewalk to decide which way to walk: Hasna and Nasef; Albert and Esene; Safiyah and Amelia and their husbands and children.

"What street are we trying to find, for God's sake?" asked Amelia's husband.

"Hancock Street," answered Safiyah impatiently.

"Here we are then," Esene called out boldly, pointing to a street sign a few yards away.

A simple slip. A flick of the serpent's tongue, Esene's eyes opened wide, beseeching Albert.

"What did you say, Esene?" asked Amelia, slightly out of breath from the exertion of lowering herself from the platform of the streetcar.

"I said," Esene looked at her evenly, " 'Here . . . we . . . . are . . . then.' "

"What does she mean, Albert?" asked Safiyah as she joined arms with her husband.

While the children explored the sidewalk ahead of them, Albert's mother, his sisters, their husbands drew sharply toward him. His father, unaware, stood apart, left behind.

"This is the New World," Albert said softly.

"You're responsible for this?" Safiyah asked.

"The cat is out of the bag," said Esene.

The group shifted toward Esene.

"Arabic, too?" Safiyah asked.

"No. Only English."

"Can you write?"

"Yes."

Amelia burst into tears. When Albert looked at his mother, he saw a hint of surprise behind her solid deference. Albert's father, in his old man's sweater, stood holding his lightly crushed brown hat in both hands, uncaring, impassive, waiting to be urged in the right direction by a son-in-law's hands.

"How could you do this? Keep such a secret from your family?"

Albert answered, "Not a secret. A surprise."

It took some time for Albert's family to accustom itself to the sight of Esene's reading whatever came in front of her. When she was silent, they suspected she was reading and looked around the room to determine the object of her attention. After the first set of Christmas cards (Albert had chosen a Madonna and Child), Safiyah and Amelia invited Father Nicholas to Safiyah's prosperous home for coffee and cakes and steered the conversation to the great sin of pride, which caused the downfall of the favorite angel of God.

At Easter, an old woman was called in on the pretext of having lunch. Through her fingers she sifted the sand she'd brought in the broad flat brass box. "From the old country," she assured them, referring to the sand. Her eyes traveled over the ridges, which she leveled and created again according to a plan Esene didn't divine. "Beware," she finally told Esene, lifting her fortune from the sifting grains, and it was clear from the tone of her voice that it pained her to deliver the message. "The consequences of a life of following your own inclinations are not easy to control."

When the men argued American politics in Arabic and the children who went to American schools played outdoors, the women, including Esene, sat on Hasna's porch on hard-backed chairs carried from the kitchen. If Esene walked past the living room, the men's mouths snapped shut like empty purses. Even Albert's exhortations to Esene to join them did not revive their powers of speech. "They're old-fashioned," Albert would say later. "They're not the beginning and the end." Still, it bored him to sit on the porch with the women. To have to listen to Safiyah say, "You need more lemon in your tabbouleh, Esene." Or to hear Amelia add, "If I were you, I'd increase the cinnamon in the rice," as though a woman who read and had no children could expect nothing else.

The evening of the day she had read that first word out loud before Albert's family, Esene had breathed into his ear, "Oh, Albert, I didn't mean to."

"Our secret—," he began.

"What did you expect?" Esene wailed. "The words became automatic. They were swirling around in front of my eyes, in my head. It was only a matter of time before they flew out my mouth."

After dinner, Albert had walked back to his shop and rearranged everything on the shelves. He smoked. He drank a little whiskey. He sat alone while Esene, remorseful and fearful, read the evening papers. For most of one month he worked late, missing dinner at home. One night, Esene packed food and took it to the grocery.

"Give me a drink," she said, as she unwrapped the food. "You always like the taste of bourbon in my mouth."

The lights in the shop attracted an older man, a regular customer. "Something wrong?" he asked when he reached the door. "No, come in. Talk with us," Albert said in English. Esene listened this night and many of the others. When Albert decided to extend the hours of the shop into the evening, Esene joined him and the small circle of men—never more than four or five—for conversation and coffee. She began coming earlier in the afternoon, carrying their dinner so they didn't have to break away until they finally locked the door.

Albert and Esene grew old. It was his idea that Esene should learn to cook American food, and when he found a cooking class at the local adult school, and when he bought their car, he drove her every evening, reading his newspaper in the front seat while she was inside, and taking her home again when she came out.

It was her idea to get a library card.

"I need to be able to explain why I say what I say," she told Albert.

And so Esene walked stiffly up the imposing steps of the main library downtown and through the majestic double-glass doors and asked the librarian for an application. And in response to the librarian's request, on this day and this day only, Esene wrote in ink.

Albert and Esene continued to send Christmas cards each year. Albert chose them and Esene wrote them at their small kitchen table: salutations, season's greetings, expressions of love from her and Albert, and, more often than not, her opinions on the world in general or certain issues in particular, quotations from favorite articles, wise sayings, bits of advice. All in pencil in her childlike script. Esene, unfinished, yet whole; Albert, quite pleased.

Questions for Reflection and Analysis

1. What strikes you about the story as a whole? Is there a particular aspect of the story that elicits a memory or concern about teaching and learning?

2. What does the opening scene reveal about the relationships between the women in the family, between the siblings, and between the husband and wife?

3. What does Albert teach Esene, and why does he do it? What does Albert's decision to teach Esene suggest about his values?

4. Why is it so important to Albert that the lessons be kept secret? Why does his family react the way they do when they learn about the lessons?

5. What effect do the lessons have on Albert and Esene's marriage? On Esene's life experience? On Esene's sense of self?

■ *Prisoner with a* **D***ictionary*

Linh Dinh

(1963–   )

Linh Dinh was born in South Vietnam and emigrated to the United States in 1975 at the age of 12. He was educated at The University of the Arts, Philadelphia, where he studied painting. At the age of 35, he returned to Vietnam and lived there for two and a half years. He writes poetry in both English and Vietnamese. An award-winning writer, his publications include *Fake House: Stories* (2000), *All Around What Empties Out* (2003), and *Borderless Bodies* (2006).

And so a young man was thrown in prison and found in his otherwise empty cell a foreign dictionary. It was always dark in there and he couldn't even tell that it was a dictionary at first. He was not an intellectual type and had never even owned a dictionary in his life. He was far from stupid, however, but had an ironic turn of mind that could squeeze out a joke from most tragic situations. He could also be very witty around certain women. In any case, he did not know what to do with this nearly worthless book but to use it as a stool and as a pillow. Periodically he also tore out pages from it to wipe himself. Soon, however, out of sheer boredom, he decided to look at this dictionary. His eyes had adjusted to the dim light by now and he could make out all the words with relative ease in that eternal twilight. Although he was not familiar with the foreign language, and did not even know what language it was, he suddenly felt challenged to learn it. His main virtue, and the main curse of his life, was the ability to follow through on any course of action once he had set his mind to it. This book represented the last problem, the only problem, he would ever solve. The prisoner began by picking out words at random and scrutinizing their definitions. Of course, each definition was made up of words entirely unknown to him. Undeterred, he would look up all the words in the definition, which led him to even more unfathomable words. To define "man," for example, the prisoner had to look up not only "human" and "person" but also "opposable" and "thumb." To define "thumb," he had to look up not only "short" and "digit" but also "thick" and "of" and "a" and "the." To define "the," he had to look up "that" and "a" (again) and "person" (again) and "thing" and "group." Being alone in his cell night and day, without any distraction, allowed the prisoner to concentrate with such rigor that soon he could retain and cross index hundreds of definitions in his head. The dictionary had well over a thousand pages but the prisoner was determined to memorize every definition on every page. He cringed at the thought that he had once torn out pages to wipe himself. These pages now represented to him gaps in his eventual knowledge. Because they were gone forever he would never be able to know all the words in that particular language. Still, it was with an elation bordering on madness that he woke up each morning, eager to eat up more words. Like many people, he equated the acquisition of a vast vocabulary with knowledge, even with wisdom, and so he could feel his stature growing by the day, if not by the second. Although he did not know what the words meant, what they referred to in real life, he reasoned that he understood these words because he knew their definitions. And because he was living inside this language all the time, like a fetus thriving inside a womb, there were times when he felt sure he could guess at the general implications of a word, whether it was a plant or an animal, for example, or whether it indicated something positive or negative. But his guesses were always wrong, of course. Because "bladder" sounded somehow vast and nebulous to the prisoner, he thought that it must have something to do with the outdoors, most likely the weather, a gust of wind or a torrential rain or a bolt of lightning. "Father," with its forlorn, exasperated tone, made the prisoner think of something dead and putrid: a corpse or a heap of garbage. He guessed that "homicide" was a flower. He thought "July" meant "August." The prisoner was also justifiably proud of his pronunciation, which was remarkably crisp and confident, the stresses more often than not falling on the right syllables. If he were to speak on the phone, the prisoner could almost be mistaken for a native speaker, albeit one of the lower class. But if the prisoner was convinced he was gaining a new language he was also surely losing one because he had, by this time, forgotten nearly all the words of his native language. By this time he could no longer name any part of the anatomy, even the most basic, hand, nose, face, mouth, etc., and so his own body was becoming vague, impersonal, unreal. Although he was surrounded by filth, he could no longer conjure up the word "filth." The only word that came readily to his tongue, automatically, unbidden, was "prison" because that was the last thing he thought of each night, and the first thing he thought of each morning. His dreams had become entirely devoid of conversations or thoughts. Often they were just a series of images or abstract patches of colors. Sometimes they were also made up entirely of sounds, a cacophony of his own voice reciting bits of definitions. Even in his worst nightmare, he could no longer shout out "mother!" in his own language. But this loss never bothered him, he barely noticed it, because he was convinced he was remaking himself anew. As he was being squeezed out of the world, the only world he had a right to belong in, he thought he was entering a new universe. Perhaps by purging himself of his native language, the prisoner was unconsciously trying to get rid of his horrible past, because, frankly, there was not a single word of his native tongue that did not evoke, for the prisoner, some horrible experience or humiliation. Perhaps he could sense that his native tongue was the very author of his horrible life. But these are only conjectures, we do not know for sure. In any case nights and days the prisoner shouted out definitions to himself. If one were to press one's ear against the thick iron door at midnight, one would hear, for example: "an animal with a long, thin tail that commonly infests buildings." Or "a deep and tender feeling for an arch enemy." Or "a shuddering fear and disgust accompanied by much self loathing." With so many strange words and definitions accumulating, surely some profound knowledge, some revelation, was at hand? What is a revelation, after all, but the hard-earned result of an exceptional mind working at peak capacity? The prisoner was thankful to be given a chance to concentrate unmolested for such a continuous length of time. He felt himself victorious: condemned to an empty cell, he had been robbed of the world, but through a heroic act of will, he had remade the universe. He had (nearly) everything because he had (nearly) all the words of an entire language. But the truth is the prisoner had regained nothing. He only thought that way, of course, because he had to think that way. After decades of unceasing mental exertion, the only fruit of the prisoner's remarkable labor, the only word he ever acquired for sure, was "dictionary," simply because it was printed on the cover of a book he knew for sure was a dictionary. For even as he ran across the definition for "prisoner," and was memorizing it by heart, he didn't even know that he was only reading about himself.

Questions for Reflection and Analysis

1. What strikes you about the story as a whole? Is there a particular aspect of the story that elicits a memory or concern about teaching and learning?

2. How successfully does the prisoner achieve his goal of acquiring a large vocabulary in the new language? How would you character-ize the prisoner's second language acquisition on the basis of his experience with the dictionary?

3. What is the effect of the prisoner's study of the foreign dictionary on his native language? Why does it have this effect?

4. What does the story suggest about the relationship between studying and comprehending the words of a language? About how language shapes thought, or vice versa? About the connection between real life experiences and the acquisition of new vocabulary?

5. How might you interpret the title of the story on a symbolic level?

Questions for Reflection and Analysis across the Stories

These questions are designed for making thematic connections across the stories. They may also serve as a basis for creating a general or theoretical framework for understanding the process of language acquisition and the factors that promote or impede that process.

BACKGROUND FACTORS AND INFLUENCES

1. Examine the historical and political circumstances surrounding the characters' lives. How do such factors affect language learners' motivation and performance?

2. Examine the effect that a colonial system of education has on the characters' linguistic, cultural, and racial identities. On the basis of your own experiences, observations, or reading, what evidence do you see that colonial attitudes continue to affect language teaching and learning?

3. Examine how school and community attitudes toward students' first or heritage language and culture affect the characters' language and literacy acquisition. What role do you see for a student's first or heritage language and culture in the English language classroom?

4. How does the move from one country to another shape the characters' linguistic and cultural identities? How might a teacher or tutor take these factors into account in creating language lessons?

5. Examine the role families play in influencing the characters' attitudes and behavior. How might a teacher or tutor take these factors into account in creating language lessons?

6. Examine the role that age, gender, ethnicity, culture, race, religion, class, or linguistic background play in the characters' language acquisition. How might a teacher or tutor take any of these factors into account in creating language lessons?

7. How do the characters' identities outside the classroom differ from their school identities? How might an awareness of different identities shape or transform a teacher's assumptions about students' classroom behavior and performance?

THE PROCESS OF TEACHING AND LEARNING

1. What different language teaching methodologies or approaches are demonstrated in these stories? How do these different approaches affect learners' motivation or their performance? How might you revise an approach that seems to be counterproductive?

2. How are the characters' language errors addressed in different stories? Which approach to error seems to be most productive? How do you think error should be addressed in the context of teaching and learning language?

3. What role do nonverbal gestures play in facilitating communication or enabling the characters' understanding? How might teachers or tutors translate this factor into effective practice?

4. What role does silence play in the characters' acquisition of language? What might be the most effective way to address a student's silence in the classroom?

5. Note the similarities and differences between the way adults acquire language and the way children acquire language in these stories. How might teachers or tutors translate an understanding of these similarities and differences into practice?

6. Note the similarities and differences between classroom-based teaching and one-on-one tutoring in these stories. How might teachers or tutors translate an understanding of these similarities and differences into practice?

7. How are the challenges of teaching or learning English language *literacy* similar to or different from the challenges of teaching or learning *spoken* English in these stories? How might teachers or tutors translate an understanding of these similarities and differences into practice?

8. Note the similarities and differences between teaching and learning English in an English-medium country and teaching and learning English as a foreign language (for an EFL context, see "Private Lesson" by Lindsley Cameron, pp. 179–195). How might classroom or tutorial approaches be informed by an understanding of these similarities and differences?

9. Drawing on the knowledge you have gained by reading these stories, what do you think teachers or tutors could do to facilitate the process learners undergo when they transition from merely studying a language to taking ownership of the language?

10. Drawing on the knowledge you have gained by reading these stories, what factors or circumstances do you think might lead teachers or tutors to reflect on and improve their pedagogical approaches?

11. Drawing on the knowledge and understanding you have gained by reading these stories, what do you perceive to be the best ways to promote language acquisition?